DO MORE GOOD

INSPIRING LESSONS FROM EXTRAORDINARY PEOPLE

Neil Ghosh

A POST HILL PRESS BOOK
ISBN: 979-8-88845-924-9
ISBN (eBook): 979-8-88845-925-6

Do More Good:
Inspiring Lessons from Extraordinary People

Cover design by Cody Corcoran

Post Hill Press
New York • Nashville
posthillpress.com

Published in the United States of America
1 2 3 4 5 6 7 8 9 10

Advance Praise for *Do More Good*

"*Do More Good* is a playbook to do just that, offering inspiring lessons learned from global leaders from all walks of life who have looked inside themselves to identify new ways to tackle the world's most pressing challenges and take concrete steps to solve them."

—Darren Walker, President, Ford Foundation.

"*Do More Good* is an inspiring reminder that in our interdependent world, everyone has the power—and the responsibility—to make a difference in the lives of others. It couldn't come at a more important time."

—President Bill Clinton

"At a time of extreme income inequalities, burgeoning wars, polarized politics, corporate greed, spiritual anomie, and fragmented media, Ghosh provides hope and inspiration through examples of people who have made and are making a meaningful difference. It is a book to keep and to give."

—Muhammad Yunus, Nobel laureate
and founder of Grameen Bank

"Uplifting. . . .inspiring. . . .and actionable, *Do More Good* is equally relevant to the world's youth; leaders in business, politics, and the nonprofit sector; and regular citizens in this challenging time. Ghosh distills his recollections of thirty extraordinary people into the most important lessons he learned from each. Virtues of decency, empathy, hope, courage, purpose, and more come to life in these personal encounters. A must read."

—Raj Kumar, President and
Editor-in-Chief, Devex

"*Do More Good* by Neil Ghosh is thoughtful, well-written, and utterly engaging. In a world of rapid change, sound bites, social media anger, and alarmist screeds, Ghosh offers a quiet reflection. His book is a nice reminder of the humanity that binds all of us and the importance of listening. This is not just a worthwhile read. It is a restorative read, good for the soul."

—Tessie San Martin, Chief
Executive Officer, FHI 360

"This book is a recipe for a purpose-driven life. Neil Ghosh is a thought leader, and in this thoughtful and heartfelt memoir, Ghosh recounts milestones on his remarkable intellectual, professional, and spiritual journey through the intersecting worlds of business, government, and philanthropy. I found the book immensely helpful for my own personal journey."

—Dirk Elsen, former CEO, SNV
Netherlands Development Organisation

To my parents, Nilima Ghosh and Chitta Ranjan Ghosh, for their gift of empathy, and to everyone trying to make this world a better place for future generations

Life's most persistent and urgent question
is, what are you doing for others?[1]
—Dr. Martin Luther King, Jr.

TABLE OF CONTENTS

Foreword: A Message from the Dalai Lama xi
Introduction: My Inspiration—and Now Yours xiii

PART I: SIT

Chapter 1 Live with Empathy: My Parents 3
Chapter 2 Practice Compassion: The Dalai Lama 14
Chapter 3 Mentor Others: Asok Motayed 24
Chapter 4 Embrace Religious Diversity: Imam Ilyasi 33
Chapter 5 Learn from *Everyone*: Ruth Bader Ginsburg 42
Chapter 6 Look Beyond: Darren Walker 51
Chapter 7 Listen for Your Calling: Mother Teresa 62
Chapter 8 Offer Trust: Muhammad Yunus 73
Chapter 9 Think Deeply: Amartya Sen 84
Chapter 10 Respect Your "Opponents": Joe Biden 93
Chapter 11 Honor Your Principles: John McCain 102

PART II: RISE

Chapter 12 Make Your Gift Matter: José Andrés 115
Chapter 13 Serve with Humility: John Glenn 124

Chapter 14 Challenge Friends: Kevin Bacon 132
Chapter 15 Speak Out: Malala Yousafzai 139
Chapter 16 Rethink What You Know: Sal Khan................148
Chapter 17 Use Your Privilege: Angelina Jolie....................160
Chapter 18 Focus on Your Goal: Kareem Abdul-Jabbar.....171
Chapter 19 Invite Transformation: Shimon Peres 179
Chapter 20 Pave Your Own Path: Mohamed Ousri 187
Chapter 21 Improve Your Profession: Tessie San Martin....198

PART III: ACT

Chapter 22 Build Bridges: Bill Clinton..............................213
Chapter 23 Step Up: Rosa Parks.......................................224
Chapter 24 Stay True to Your Purpose: Jimmy Carter........234
Chapter 25 Make Hard Choices: Hillary Clinton..............245
Chapter 26 Engage in Public Service: Ross Perot...............256
Chapter 27 Protect Democracy: John Kufuor....................265
Chapter 28 Choose Pragmatism: Somnath Chatterjee.......275
Chapter 29 Leave a Legacy: My Son, Ryan Sohan Ghosh...288

Acknowledgments...299
Notes 303
Selected Bibliography 317
About the Author...349

FOREWORD

I am a strong believer in the power of positive role models. Every individual has a responsibility to help guide our global family in the right direction and has the potential to make a difference in society. As a Buddhist monk, I try to develop compassion myself—not just from a religious point of view, but from a humanitarian one as well. Wherever I go I have been sharing my experience with others in the hope that it will be of some benefit to them. This book, D*o More Good: Inspiring Lessons from Extraordinary People* by Neil Ghosh, contains his experiences with individuals and how they have positively impacted him. May this book provide positive inspiration to its readers.

The Dalai Lama

25 December 2024

INTRODUCTION

MY INSPIRATION—AND NOW YOURS

Live as if you were to die tomorrow. Learn as if you were to live forever.[2]
—Mahatma Gandhi

No person is an island. As we move through life, we are inevitably influenced by the people we encounter. Among the things that have made my life so fulfilling are the people I have met and built relationships with on six continents. My interactions with them have been diverse—from a simple chat with a friend about our children to a deeper conversation about youth unemployment with a minister in Morocco to a discussion of agricultural value chains with a farmer in Kenya. Such encounters have helped shape my values, how I think, and how I interact with others.

Those who influence us directly include family members, friends, teachers, employers, and colleagues. Others—public figures in business, government, sports, entertainment, or philanthropy, for example—reach us indirectly through their ideas; through the impact of their work, books, art, or music; or through our contact with the structures they have created—from roads and bridges to complex institutions of international governance and the internet. However it happens, wherever it happens, whenever it happens, we have the ability to take something from each encounter that we can use to live a happier, more fulfilling, and more socially impactful life.

From my childhood in Calcutta (now Kolkata), India, to my recent experiences as an entrepreneur, I have come in contact with many amazing individuals. I encountered them in the course of a professional journey that has included jobs in the US private sector; managerial positions with the Australian Trade Commission, SNV Netherlands Development Organisation, and an Austrian children's charity; and positions in America's defense contracting community—as well as during my travels to Asia, Australia, North America, South America, Africa, and the Middle East.

The people I have chosen to feature in this book are drawn from the realms of politics, business, philanthropy, the social sector, development economics, the nonprofit sector, sports, entertainment, and education. Many are globally recognized figures—including seven Nobel laureates—that I have met or interacted with during my career. Some are family or friends. What unites them all are the life lessons I have learned as a result of our interactions.

There are three main ways that I see we can better the world. Accordingly, I have grouped the lessons in this book into three distinct parts: **Sit, Rise, and Act**.

> ***Sit*** includes stories of my encounters with people whose impact hinges on the inner work they have done. These are people whose character—shaped by spiritual, intellectual, or societal influences—is the governing factor in their contributions to the world.
>
> ***Rise*** presents lessons I gained from individuals who—with inspiration, insight, or indignation—had either a gradual realization or a breakthrough moment that compelled them to stand up and speak out. The people in this section are united in their ability to identify new ways to make change happen.
>
> ***Act*** contains lessons from the lives of those who, by taking concrete steps, have set in motion forces that will continue to have a positive impact long after they are gone.

Each chapter consists of stories, reminiscences, reflections, conversations, and lessons learned over the past thirty years from the extraordinary people I met along the way—plus actions you can take to *do more good* in your own life, now. My parents taught my brother and me that, no matter what, we could always help someone less fortunate. Harold Kushner said it best in his foreword to *Man's Search for Meaning*, a book by Viktor Frankl: "Life is not primarily a quest for pleasure, as

Freud believed, or a quest for power, as Alfred Adler taught, but a quest for meaning. The greatest task for any person is to find meaning in his or her life."[3] The lessons in this book are personal. At the same time, it is my hope that most of them are applicable to each of us in our quest to find meaning through our actions, no matter who we are or where we live.

It is also important to note that some of the personalities featured here have published many books, including their own autobiographies. It is impossible to do justice to their life's work in fewer than 2,000 words, and that is not my goal. Instead I have focused on aspects of their lives that influenced me and impacted my life, and I consider this book an opportunity to share those lessons.

I am sure most of the individuals in this book have their flaws—certainly some of them are more controversial than others—and there is still time for even the most exemplary among them to make mistakes. But I do not seek to pass judgment. My only objective is to highlight one lesson that I learned from each. My selection is not driven by the news cycle or politics or search engine optimization. I am neither a historian, a journalist, a biographer, nor a self-help guru. My career choices, personal initiatives, perseverance, world view, and some luck combined to lead me to the "characters" in this book.

My inspiration to share the lessons I learned from these thirty extraordinary people is anchored in three core beliefs:

- Each of us can make a difference in the lives of others.
- In anyone we know, we can always find one positive attribute that we can learn from.
- Such lessons are necessary for our own happiness and for the happiness of others.

People in a position of power and fame have a tremendous opportunity to impact the lives of the less fortunate, but not everyone follows that path. I hope this book's examples of the positive impact of high-profile figures can be a wake-up call for anyone who might still be searching for meaning despite outward signs of success. Likewise, I hope my accounts of people not in a position of power or fame can inspire others like them as well. But this book is also about a lot more. It is about decency and courage, about speaking up against injustice, living a life with a clear purpose, the power of pragmatism, civility despite disagreement, keeping our eyes on the prize, innovation, and much more.

Most important, this book is about taking action. To support this process, I have included resources at the end of each chapter so readers can select from—and connect with—a wide range of organizations that are doing good work in the world. I have sought to include only the most reputable (those with ratings of at least three out of four), but I invite you to use the following online assessment tools to judge the merits of any nonprofit for yourself:

- **Charity Navigator**—Provides ratings based on financial health, accountability, and transparency.
- **GuideStar**—Offers detailed profiles on nonprofits, including financial data, mission statements, and results.
- **CharityWatch**—Rates charities based on how efficiently they use donations and their governance practices.

As with most people, my childhood and parents were the initial influences on my views of the world, and so this book begins with a chapter devoted to them. By all standards, there was never a boring moment. Not many kids could claim that their dad went to jail for his beliefs and activism. Mine did.

Likewise, my own life and career have been similarly eventful. As I traversed many sectors in my professional life—moving from India to the US not once but twice—I had some painful times. I faced job loss and discrimination based on skin color and nationality. I failed at some early business ventures and endured personal setbacks. All of this combined led to depression and a dark stage when I contemplated ending my life. As I came out of depression, I had to reevaluate myself constantly. This journey has been both exhausting and exhilarating, but through it all, I never stopped learning. Lessons from others not only sustained me but helped me thrive. Constant learning and resiliency allowed me to rebound from each setback. For every failure, I achieved something even better. I dedicate those successes to the people I met along the way.

I have written this book for the world's youth; for leaders in business, politics, and the nonprofit sector; and for regular citizens like me—not to persuade on behalf of an agenda but to promote personal growth and meaningful living. Not all the people in this book are universally recognized as role models. But I sincerely believe that the lessons I have learned provide examples of how each of us can become a better version of ourselves.

As an immigrant, a citizen, an executive, an entrepreneur, a friend, a father, and a partner, I hope these stories and lessons will inspire you as they have inspired me. But even more, I hope you will be motivated to take action; to *do more good* in this world of immense need and boundless potential.

PART I

SIT

CHAPTER 1

LIVE WITH EMPATHY: MY PARENTS

The People

My father, Chitta Ranjan Ghosh, worked for the local power supply company for nearly his entire life, earning a salary that was barely enough to cover our family expenses. My mother, Nilima Ghosh, was a homemaker.

The Lesson

When we consider helping the less fortunate, it's easy to have second thoughts that say, *I can't afford to do that.* It's easy to talk ourselves out of giving our time or anything else if we focus on the inevitable fact that others have more resources than we do. There's always someone with more. But the good news is this: Each of us has an unlimited capacity for empathy—and that's where making a better world begins. Take a moment to understand the circumstances of people in need, and before long you start to *feel* their need. And once that happens, suddenly it's not so hard to contribute something—anything—to making their lives better. So if you want to break whatever ice has kept you from doing more good, to take the first step in creating as much impact in your community as possible, do as my parents did. Make empathy a part of everything you do.

Our Connection

My parents had limited resources but unlimited empathy. As a child, I vividly remember my mother making sure my elder brother, Sandip, and I had a nutritious diet, while at times she took less for herself. Many times, my dad piled up debts to pay bills, which caused a great deal of stress in our home, yet he worked tirelessly to help the less fortunate. Even with our limited financial resources, Ma saved money in her little container for relatives who had even less than we did. She insisted that their needs were greater than ours.

I came to understand my parents' empathy most vividly when my father was arrested as an active member of the opposition CPI(M) party and the leader of a labor union. I was fourteen years old, and for me the most traumatic aspect was learning that we had to go to my school and appeal for a waiver because we could no longer afford the tuition. It was embarrassing, and I was angry—at my parents. I was afraid that my friends in school would find out about our disadvantaged financial situation. Then my mother told me that my father, as a champion of the vulnerable population, was giving voice to those who could not be heard, and I had no reason to feel ashamed. With a simple phrase, my mother transformed a moment of humiliation and resentment into a moment of pride, a moment of obligation.

How My Parents Bettered the World

I suppose my mother was the primary source of empathy. At times I felt she was churning out empathy 24/7 from some empathy machine. As an adult I have learned that it is often easier to have empathy for someone we like, someone like us, someone in distress or worse off than we are, and that it is easier to show empathy when we are feeling comfortable in our own lives. But none of this was true of my mother. For her it was empathy for all, at all times, with no exceptions, whether she was comfortable or not. She was an equal opportunity empathy distributor! It came out in the way she spoke with us and in the way she interacted with and treated all our relatives and friends, strangers, and the world around us. My mother's lessons were simple and clear: She encouraged us to understand different perspectives before rushing to judgment, and she taught us to validate the emotions of others. Empathy existed in our home long before we had a gas stove, a TV, a refrigerator, or other modern amenities.

The author's mother, Nilima Ghosh

Proof of that came in 1971, during the Bangladesh Liberation War, when East Pakistan sought independence from

West Pakistan. Refugees flooded into neighboring West Bengal, and especially into Kolkata, which lies on the border. Among the most serious immediate impacts was the severe strain on Kolkata's resources, including food, shelter, and healthcare. I remember almost every day seeing children and adults whose needs were greater than ours. Many of them would come to our house, where my mother always offered them food. In some cases it was the only food they would eat that day. At times I would wonder why more people seemed to come to our house than to other houses. After all, we lived on the third floor, so it was a lot more work to get there. I got my answer from one of these visitors—a very feeble old woman in a white sari. As she turned to go down the stairs, she smiled and said that the reason so many people came to our house was because the word had spread that my mother would never say no to anyone! Through daily examples like these, my mother taught us that no matter how unfortunate we believe our situation to be, there will always be someone even less fortunate that we can and should help. That became my moral center, my "North Star" you might say.

The author's father, Chitta Ranjan Ghosh

My father was also a great influence. He never finished college and was anxious for my brother and me to get a good education. In addition to his day job at the power supply company, he made numerous attempts at business ventures to increase the family income. He started a motorbike repair shop across the street from where we lived; he hired a woman (I remember her as *Shanti masi*) to make and package candles on the rooftop of our home; he rented a garage next door, converted it into a grocery store, and hired my unemployed cousin to run it; he bought a *paan* shop (an Indian after-dinner treat that consists of a betel leaf); he hired a friend and set up a stall to sell fireworks during the Diwali festival; and more. To the best of my knowledge, none of these ventures generated a profit, with the exception of the fireworks. As an entrepreneur, I can see the missteps he made in business.

In addition to generating profit, there was one common theme in all those ventures—creating jobs for people in the extended family or in the neighborhood. He believed in rehabilitating troubled youth, and on many occasions, young adults with alcohol or/and drug problems would join our family vacations. One such trip was to the seaside town of Puri in Odisha, along with some young adults and my paternal grandmother. We had a blast with such a diverse group of characters. Many of those youths turned their lives around, and my father was widely respected for what he did. As a young boy, I admired his passion and leadership qualities, and I yearned to follow in his footsteps.

How My Parents Made *Me* Better

The author (pointing) working with young people to address sanitation issues in the slums of Kolkata

The year after I'd been awakened to the concept of giving voice to the voiceless, and inspired by my parents' example, I started a local community organization called "Calcutta Youth Club." We were able to tap into my knowledge of the area—the people, the culture, the language, the day-to-day challenges inherent in that neighborhood—and work together with the individuals who lived there to improve our collective experience. A few years later I started a newsletter, "Sangram" ("struggle" in English), which was completely handwritten and posted in a strategic location in our neighborhood for everyone to read free of cost. In addition to bringing relevant issues to the forefront, the newsletter notified people about community events. Many literary giants of India contributed to our wall magazine, including Samaresh Basu and Shakti Chattopadhyay.

Looking back, I can detect my parents' influence in my own unusual career path, which has moved back and forth between the private sector, the public sector, and nonprofits. While I believe in the market-based economy and capitalism, my belief is tempered by empathy and the conviction that the disadvantaged should share in the benefits created by economic policies. To be sustainable, economic growth must include everyone—it must reflect and incorporate the full range of stakeholders in a given economic context. Obviously, empathy can slow the accumulation of wealth. But in the long run, I'm not sure you can have an economy without it. The very word "economy" is rooted in the Greek *oikonomia*, meaning "household management." And to the extent that society is one big household, any sensible economy would not leave anyone outside. I think I am not alone in this. Writing in *Forbes* in 2021, Mineral CEO Nathan Christensen noted that in 2020 the word "empathy" had "hit a 15-year high for searches of business content on Google," adding that "society generally and business leaders specifically have had a renewed focus on the role of empathy" and tracing the trend to national and international crises that challenged "core values, relationships and routines."[4] To me that Google data represents a global plea for guidance in troubled times, a search for an ethic we can build a household on.

The author with his parents and son in Washington, DC, in 2003

Which brings me back to my mother's kitchen. All my life I have heard from my childhood friends and relatives that my mother cooked the most delicious meals, which in India is about much more than food. It indicates a welcoming, benevolent spirit. Because of the time and care required, cooking is a real investment, and when it is shared as freely and joyfully as my mother shared it, it becomes a devotion to others. It becomes edible empathy!

Later in life, the subject came up again in very unexpected surroundings. In 1992, I met Siddhartha Shankar Ray while he was serving as Indian ambassador to the United States. Ray had held many positions in Indian politics, including Chief Minister of West Bengal, Governor of Punjab, and Union Minister of Education. I knew that he and my dad were acquainted, but beyond that I only knew that they were from opposite ends of the political spectrum, and that had had its consequences. During my meeting with Ambassador Ray he fondly remembered my dad and mentioned how he had once tried to convince my dad to change his political affiliation. I sensed a deep affection, which I found interesting, because Ray had played a major role in the imposition of the Emergency—when Indira Gandhi's Congress Party established dictatorial policies, including the policy that had triggered the incarceration of my father. I believe Ray's affection was sincere, despite the complex pressures of events I was too young to fully grasp. Growing up, I heard from different sources that many leaders of different political parties were fond of my dad, whose views they might not have shared, but whose integrity and courage were beyond dispute. Ambassador Ray then mentioned something else: He told me that he had heard a lot about my mother's cooking and hoped that one day he might join us for dinner.

Among the many gifts bestowed upon me in my lifetime, the most profound and lasting has been the gift of empathy. And for this, I thank my parents. Empathy doesn't require wealth, and it doesn't require power. All it takes is the ability to understand, acknowledge, and respond in some way to the feelings and needs of other people. If you make it a part of everything you do, you will see—every day of your life—the difference it can make.

How You Can Use Your Empathy *Now*

We often think of empathy as simply identifying with the emotions and needs of others. But to truly do more good, we can go even further by combining empathy with the action of volunteering—an easy way to put your empathy to work. But before you think, "Oh, I'm too busy" or "I don't know where to start," let me help. Volunteer work can feel like an overwhelming commitment or a project in and of itself. But the ability to transform your empathy into action doesn't have to be a daunting experience.

In fact, volunteer work comes in two forms: planned *and* spontaneous, both with great potential to have an impact on those around you. Committing to a volunteer organization is something we all know is an option for us, but sometimes we just don't know where to start. To make it easy for you, I'm sharing a few of my favorite go-to resources for planned volunteering. It will cut your time in the research phase and expand your ability to do more good more quickly.

- **VolunteerMatch**—Connects volunteers with opportunities based on location, cause, and skills. How to get involved: Search for local volunteer opportunities on their website.
- **Voices for Children**—CASA Program—Supports abused or neglected children in finding safe, permanent homes.

How to get involved: Become a Court Appointed Special Advocate (CASA) volunteer.

- **Best Buddies International**—Creates opportunities for friendship, employment, and leadership development for people with intellectual and developmental disabilities. How to get involved: Become a buddy, join a chapter, or participate in events.
- **AmeriCorps**—Brokers volunteer opportunities throughout the US. How to get involved: Apply for various service programs or find local volunteer opportunities.
- **Team Rubicon**—Unites the skills and experiences of military veterans and citizens with first responders to rapidly deploy emergency response teams. How to get involved: Volunteer for disaster response, donate, or join as a member.
- **Empathy Lab**—Develops empathy-based programs for schools and organizations. How to get involved: Participate in workshops, use their resources, or bring programs to your community.

These "empathy engines" are only a few clicks away, and—as you do more good for others—any one of them could change your life.

In addition to organized volunteering, there are many spontaneous ways to show empathy. For example, have you ever noticed that elderly person standing lost in an aisle at the beginning of an event? Going out of your way is a form of volunteering. In an instant, you can serve as an usher to help them find their seat safely and without frustration. This type of small, empathetic gesture—especially when done regularly—can become a significant way to do more good, and without planned commitment or scheduling. If you've been avoiding volunteering because of commitment or scheduling challenges, try making some of these simple actions a part of each day:

- Reach out to someone who might be feeling lonely or isolated.
- Share resources or skills with those who might benefit from them.
- Offer emotional support to friends and family going through difficult times.
- Practice patience and understanding in frustrating situations.
- Participate in community events to better understand local issues.
- Educate yourself about different cultures and experiences.
- Practice active listening in conversations, focusing on understanding others' perspectives.
- Donate to causes that support vulnerable populations.
- Challenge your own biases and preconceptions about others.
- Stand up against discrimination or injustice when you witness it.
- Engage in conversations with people from different backgrounds to broaden your perspective.

CHAPTER 2

PRACTICE COMPASSION: THE DALAI LAMA

The Person

The spiritual leader of Tibet—known as His Holiness the Dalai Lama—has played a key role in preserving and promoting Tibetan Buddhism, as well as advocating for the rights and freedom of the Tibetan people. A tireless advocate for human rights, nonviolence, and the peaceful resolution of conflicts around the world, the Dalai Lama was awarded the Nobel Peace Prize in 1989.

The Lesson

We generally think of having compassion as a matter of acting mercifully toward someone who is suffering. And yet, not only is that a limited way of defining compassion, but it also fails to recognize the power of simple kindness—whether or not the recipient is "in need"—to accumulate and make a difference in the world. We can show compassion to anyone and everyone, and that simple truth is exactly what the Dalai Lama teaches.

Our Connection

In 2011, I was excited to receive an invitation from Victor Chan, founder of the Dalai Lama Center for Peace and Education and coauthor of two books with the Dalai Lama, to attend the first Delhi Dialogue. The event brought together more than fifty thought leaders and humanitarians to engage in a three-day dialogue with His Holiness the Dalai Lama and Dr. Abdul Kalam (the eleventh president of India).

This extraordinary gathering included Pierre and Pam Omidyar, founders of eBay; Richard Moore, founder of Children in Crossfire; Ashley Judd, actress; Swanee Hunt, US Ambassador to Austria; and Jayant Sinha, later a member of the Indian Parliament, minister of finance, and minister of civil aviation. Our dialogue revolved around sharing and implementing innovative initiatives to help alleviate suffering among the very poor, especially those in the Indian subcontinent and Africa. Three issues were at the heart of our discussion: educating underprivileged children and empowering women and girls. Participants also discussed the importance of empowering rural populations (especially women and girls), resolving conflicts by nonviolent means, ensuring justice for juveniles, and creating an environment for sustainable poverty alleviation.

During the meeting, the Dalai Lama emphasized the need for all of us to show respect and compassion for low-income citizens as we undertook various development initiatives.

I cannot overstate the importance of that simple message. When we integrate our passion for development work with compassion and clear listening skills, that work is more likely to take into account the root causes of poverty and inequality. Compassion allows development professionals to address challenges in holistic and inclusive ways. It forces us to look into long-term and sustainable solutions by addressing the underlying structural issues that perpetuate poverty and inequality.

In development work, people come first. Yet we are often compelled for reasons of economics and transparency to reduce people to statistics. We know that these metrics represent a range of human situations, but it is easy to lose touch with them as we rush to gather the numbers into annual reports that drive the fundraising (which will, in turn, give us the means to implement the programs to improve those lives). Even after visiting a project designed to bring improved sanitation and better health to rural villages in Vietnam, or learning about an initiative to increase the use of clean-burning cook stoves in Andean villages, it is a struggle to remember individual stories when we later talk about "scaling up" these efforts in the corridors of our office suites in Washington, DC, or Amsterdam or Brussels. Sometimes, too, our belief in the ultimate good of the project causes us to lose contact with the actual situation on the ground 10,000 miles away. Donors like results. And investors need results. But there are no clear-cut results in development. Projects are unpredictable, subject to violent weather and bad roads and local idiosyncrasies too numerous to mention. The Dalai Lama is no development expert, yet he correctly identified the key challenge to every project's credibility and success: effectiveness ultimately depends on the trust, cooperation, and buy-in of the people we are trying to help, and our goals are only achieved if we treat those people with kindness.

On the second day of the conference, I had the opportunity to meet His Holiness. I really can't express in words the exact feeling of that moment thirteen years ago. I had a similar feeling years prior to that when I met Mother Teresa at her home in Kolkata. Like everyone who has had the honor of meeting the Dalai Lama, I was humbled by his simplicity and warmth. But there was something else: I felt his deep affection for all humanity—regardless of race, religion, skin color, gender, or national origin. And of course, one can never forget his smile.

The Dalai Lama and the author at the Delhi Dialogue

How the Dalai Lama Bettered the World

I wanted to learn more about the work of His Holiness and understand it more deeply, so I decided to read several books written by and about him. *The Wisdom of Compassion*, jointly written by the Dalai Lama and Victor Chan, is one such book. My meeting with the Dalai Lama on January 9, 2011, and the lessons from this book had a profound impact on my life and continue to influence me. I purchased one hundred copies and mailed them to colleagues and friends. Over a decade later, many still thank me for sharing it with them.

The main lesson in this book is that compassion is the key to achieving happiness, fulfillment, and inner peace. The book emphasizes the importance of developing a compassionate mindset and cultivating a genuine concern for the well-being of others, including those who may be difficult to love or forgive. Another key message by His Holiness and Victor Chan is the importance of interdependence and interconnectedness. The book beautifully articulates the transformative effects of compassion and maintains that, even if you don't act on it directly, it changes you and those around you.

When I think of the Dalai Lama, I think of how practical he is. In one interaction with Victor Chan, the Dalai Lama explained why he takes western medicine for some illnesses and Tibetan medicine for others: He believes that western medicine and Tibetan medicine each have their own unique strengths and weaknesses. He confided to Victor that he believes in Tibetan medicine's role in preventing illness but that Western medicine shines when something goes wrong or there is a serious injury.[5]

While writing about the Dalai Lama, one must not forget about his sense of humor, which is typically lighthearted and playful. He often uses it to disarm people or to make a point in a more memorable way, which he did even while discussing serious topics in our Delhi meeting. To understand his teaching in a lighthearted and accessible way, I recommend *The Dalai Lama's Cat* by David Michie. Through the eyes of His Holiness Cat (HHC), readers can gain insight into the Dalai Lama's philosophy. Throughout the book, HHC observes the Dalai Lama and his interactions with people from all walks of life, and she learns about compassion, mindfulness, and positive thinking. The book teaches readers how to cultivate these qualities in one's life. The essence of this book is the idea that inner happiness and contentment come not only from external circumstances, but from one's own mind and attitudes.

Another book—*The Dalai Lama: An Extraordinary Life*, by Alexander Norman—also focuses on the Dalai Lama's philosophy of compassion and nonviolence. The Dalai Lama believes that every human being has the potential for compassion and that it is possible to create a more peaceful world by cultivating this quality among us. His commitment to dialogue and reconciliation is legendary. Despite facing great challenges and conflict, he has consistently advocated for peaceful negotiation and dialogue as a means of resolving disputes.

The legacy of the Dalai Lama is multifaceted and far reaching, and it encompasses a range of accomplishments and contributions in the areas of spiritual leadership, human rights advocacy, interfaith dialogue, and global peace.

As I write about the message and impact of His Holiness, we are seeing a trend toward greater fundamentalism in many parts of the world. When people do not understand or respect one another's beliefs, it almost always leads to fear, mistrust, and violence. A study published in the *Journal of Applied Social Psychology* found that participants who were exposed to messages emphasizing the similarities between religious groups showed greater tolerance toward people of different religions, compared to participants who were exposed to messages emphasizing differences.[6] Similarly, a study published in the *Journal of Personality and Social Psychology* found that participants who were primed to think about the shared human experience showed greater empathy and compassion toward people of different races and nationalities.[7]

The Dalai Lama's life and teachings serve as an inspiration for people of all faiths and backgrounds who seek to make a positive difference in the world. By recognizing the commonalities between different religions and cultures, we can create a more tolerant and compassionate world.

How the Dalai Lama Made *Me* Better

In the context of my international development work, the Dalai Lama's message had an enormous influence. For me, practicing compassion means the obvious things like showing patience and having a willingness to listen. But as a person from a developing country who has worked with the poor and marginalized, I can say that in large part it means doing what you can to ensure that everyone involved in whatever you're doing is allowed to maintain their dignity, self-respect, and voice. Poverty is a condition created by a social construction that benefits some and not others. It is not a character flaw or a personal failing. But that is how it is too often perceived, and that mindset is frequently imposed on those who suffer most, to the point that many don't consider themselves worthy or capable. We talk about capacity building. Mostly this means finding technical solutions to energy or sanitation challenges, or enabling agriculture value chains[8] to work more efficiently. But the Dalai Lama helped me see the need for *inner* capacity building, the work of catalyzing kindness to help poor and marginalized people build within themselves the capacity to hope, believe, and even dream, and to see themselves as active participants in their own progress.

Inspired in part by the Dalai Lama, in 2024 I began writing a column called "Building Bridges," hosted by Patheos (The World's Homepage for All Religion), in which I post articles focused on building bridges between races, religions, and nationalities to increase understanding and stop violence throughout the world.[9]

How You Can Practice Compassion *Now*

A variety of organizations and resources are out there to help you put a compassionate mindset into action:

- **Patheos**—A web-based platform for information and dialogue about the world's religions, Patheos is dedicated to the goal of promoting mutual acceptance among people of all faiths. How to get involved: Sign up for the "Best of Patheos" newsletter or explore informative and inspiring articles on the Patheos website.
- **Greater Good Science Center**—The Center, based at the University of California, Berkeley, takes a science-based approach to well-being. How to get involved: Become a member, sign up for their free newsletter, or check out their online magazine, *Greater Good*, which includes articles on how to cultivate kindness and mindfulness in daily life.
- **The Random Acts of Kindness Foundation**—The Foundation provides free resources to promote kindness at school, home, and work. How to get involved: Visit their website to begin implementing kindness activities and accessing free educational curricula.
- **ServiceSpace**—This fully volunteer-run platform fosters gift-economy projects worldwide. How to get involved: Participate in activities like Karma Kitchen or access resources such as KindSpring that offer innovative

ways to participate in the gift economy—acts of service that transcend self-interest.

- **JustServe**—JustServe provides opportunities for practicing simple kindness through service. How to get involved: Find ways to help others in need through actionable service projects that promote kindness and compassion.
- **Charter for Compassion**—This global movement encourages cities, schools, and organizations worldwide to craft practical, actionable plans for cultivating compassion. How to get involved: Check out the Charter's events and workshops to learn practical steps for integrating compassion into daily life.
- **Kindness.org**—A research-led nonprofit that encourages acts of kindness through community projects and partnerships. How to get involved: Explore their creative and impactful ways to integrate kindness into public policies and personal practices.

When people refer to "random acts of kindness," they're usually talking about the small ways that each of us can make a difference in the lives of others. These simple actions can include sending a nice text to a friend "just because," listening actively without judgment, and letting someone go ahead of you in line. The more you make a habit of such gestures, the easier it gets to do them—and to think of other ways to brighten people's days and foster a positive environment. Kindness is contagious!

Here are a few more random acts you can try:

- Make eye contact and smile at strangers.
- Pick up litter at a local park.

- Donate gently used items to a local charity.
- Express gratitude to someone every day.
- When you spot an opportunity, simply ask, "How can I help?"
- Donate blood or register as an organ donor. These selfless acts can literally save lives.
- Compliment the unsung heroes you encounter: custodians, waitstaff, public transit workers. A kind word can brighten their day.
- Pay for the person behind you in the drive-thru or parking meter line.
- Send an entertaining card or care package to a friend going through a tough time.
- Leave uplifting notes with inspirational quotes on restroom mirrors or community message boards.
- Make a home-cooked meal for a neighbor who is ill, elderly, or a new parent.

CHAPTER 3

MENTOR OTHERS: ASOK MOTAYED

The Person

Asok Motayed is an entrepreneur who immigrated to the United States in 1971, eventually transforming a five-person engineering firm into an industry leader in the Mid-Atlantic region, employing more than 300 people across multiple states and more than ten countries overseas.

The Lesson

We usually think of mentorship as imparting wisdom or as teaching someone specific skills. Both of these can certainly be facets of a mentoring relationship. But Asok Motayed—whom I consider my most influential mentor over the decades—has shown me that mentorship is much more than instruction. It is a way of interacting with others that involves listening for what they might need, being attuned to their strengths and weaknesses, and guiding them toward their best selves. It is a way of setting an example that those around you will follow of their own accord. Each of us has the capacity to have that kind of influence—to serve as a mentor to multiple people in our lives—and we should take the opportunity to do so whenever we can.

Our Connection

Like many other immigrants to the United States, I pursued my American dream from the moment I stepped off the plane. For me, that meant earning a college degree. But in addition to my regular academic studies, I read many self-help books: *The 7 Habits of Highly Effective People* by Stephen Covey (and yes, I also read *The 8th Habit* by the same author), *Managing for Results* by Peter Drucker, *Search Inside Yourself* by Chade-Meng Tan, *Disrupt You!* by Jay Samit, *Man's Search for Meaning* by Viktor Frankel, *Destiny* by T. D. Jakes, and many others. I listened to motivational tapes by Tony Robbins and Zig Ziglar. I attended seminars, including the three-day marathon session of The Landmark Forum, and I spent almost a week in the Bahamas learning about meditation and mindfulness.

I believe these lessons helped me in my pursuit of professional success. They encouraged me to move beyond my own effectiveness and toward making a difference in the lives of others. They helped me to be a better version of myself, even though I am aware that this is a lifelong journey and I am a work in progress.

But in the course of my lessons, I learned something more important.

I realized that, along with all the books, videos, seminars, and academic lessons, we need role models—friends, family, and colleagues we can relate to, and whose experience and example we can learn from. These role models can help us internalize the information we have picked up from those other sources and guide us as we seek to apply these lessons in real life.

Finding the right mentor can mark a defining moment in our life journey. I have enjoyed many role models and mentors in my personal and professional life. Even as a young boy in India I would seek out relatives and even friends I envisioned as role models. It turned out that many of my younger cousins, friends, and neighborhood youths and adults (some of them much older than I was) came to *me* for advice and support. During my school days, my main role models were my parents and my maternal uncle Pradip Chakravarty. My childhood friend Vivek (Chaudhry) was also someone I always sought to learn from. I never let age or ideology come between my learning and growth. As a result, my mentors and mentees are both young and old, conservative and liberal. Later in life I had many more role models, including Dr. Ashim Roy, Neil Snyder, Matt Westbrook, Bill Reese, and of course Asok Motayed, who is the subject of this chapter.

The author with Gopa and Asok Motayed

In 1986, I moved from New Orleans, Louisiana, to New Carrollton, Maryland, to pursue advanced studies and better opportunities. With no academic scholarships and no savings, I needed a job quickly to pay for college and the necessities of basic survival. Luckily, I found two part-time positions—one as a waiter at an Italian restaurant and another at a pharmacy just next door. I saved money to purchase my first vehicle, a used Oldsmobile Omega (remember those?) that promptly broke down. That misfortune turned out to be a lucky break. Around that same time, I had met Asok Motayed and his wife Gopa Motayed via my childhood friend Bhaskar Roy. Somehow Asok Motayed learned that I needed a car. He decided to offer me his spare vehicle, a red Volkswagen Dasher. I was so overwhelmed by his generosity that I was reluctant to accept the offer. But I did, and it was a lifesaver. It allowed me to go to work and to continue to pursue my American dream.

How Asok Motayed Bettered the World

Asok Motayed's friendship has had a huge positive impact on my life, but I am not alone in this. Over the years, I have learned that Motayed has had a similar impact on the lives of hundreds of others. For example, many years ago, I met an engineer from Kolkata (India) at a dinner gathering hosted by my friends Dipto and Aloka Chakravarty. During a brief conversation, this engineer shared a very personal story about his journey from Kolkata to America. Having graduated from Jadavpur University, he wrote to all the Jadavpur alumni in the DC area to request help. He received only one response. Yes, you guessed it—it was Motayed.

What makes Motayed a role model? I believe it is the way he built his life with the goal of giving back to society. I think it is his professional success, his extensive knowledge of a variety of subjects, his empathy, how he deals with people regardless of their social or economic status. Most importantly, it is simply in his nature to give back without expecting any fanfare. This is what has attracted so many people to him. While most of us try hard to prove ourselves and be recognized for our good deeds, Motayed has shown that it is in the sharing of those deeds that their deeper value lies. This isn't something he talks about. He prefers to teach by example, by the motto "actions speak louder than words." We have all heard that roughly 90 percent of communication is non-verbal. Motayed may be the best example of that.

When I asked our common friends and colleagues what exactly they learned from Motayed and why they admire him, the list was long, with self-discipline and a keen work ethic at the top. But there are other qualities he has modeled that have had just as much impact on the lives of those around him: his empathy and ability to consider the perspectives of others; his positive outlook; his integrity and emphasis on doing the right thing even when it's difficult; his perseverance and resilience; and most important, his ability to positively influence others to be successful. In response to my questions, Manish Kothari, CEO of Sheladia Associates, said, "Asok has exceptional leadership and an unwavering commitment to mentorship. As a leader, Asok consistently demonstrated a profound understanding of people's strengths and areas for growth, empowering them to reach their full potential. His ability to inspire and motivate others is truly awe-inspiring. He has guided numerous individuals along their professional and personal journeys, fostering an environment of growth, learning, and success and has had a transformative impact on many lives. He gave his unwavering support during the tough period I went through, he listened without judging, advised without being supercilious, and inspired without patronizing. He has my respect, my admiration, and my gratitude, and like many others, I feel lucky to be the beneficiary of Asok da's[10] wisdom and mentorship." Over the years, I have happened to meet many successful entrepreneurs like Manish who have worked with Motayed. It's not a coincidence.

Motayed has also been a towering figure among the Bengali community in the United States. To better understand his impact, I reached out to a senior member of Sanskriti, our local Bengali organization in Maryland—a man who has known Motayed for more than forty years. In response, he made the following observations: "Asok has remained a strong guiding force for Sanskriti ever since he joined the organization in the late 1980s. His leadership, organizational skills, management style, humility, and, above all, pleasing personality that radiates both respect and compassion for all, young and old, are—to use a single word—exemplary. These qualities have earned him high regards, not only in the local community but also among the entire Bengali diaspora in the United States as well as his native city of Kolkata in India."

Not only has Motayed been a positive influence in the larger Bengali community, but he has also been an exemplar at home. He and his wife raised two daughters, Emily Motayed and Lee Mayer, both of whom are now successful entrepreneurs in their own right; both are listed in *Forbes* magazine's "30 under 30." The Motayed family is the American dream come true.

How Asok Motayed Made *Me* Better

In all the years I have known Motayed, I don't recall hearing him give specific directions on what to do or what not to do. When I was younger, I wanted easy answers to my questions, quick solutions to my problems. So Motayed's style could be frustrating. As I got a little older, I realized that there was a method to his mentoring. Instead of giving direct answers, on many occasions he asked a series of questions that enabled me to identify the real issue and come up with a course of action on my own. Rather than merely giving me fish, Motayed was teaching me how to catch them for myself.

Motayed is an avid reader, and his dedication to learning has taught me the importance of curiosity, adaptability, and embracing change. Motayed has been my go-to person for many business ideas and many life challenges. He continues to encourage me to explore and be curious. Together we launched several ventures and had our share of failures and successes, including a joint venture with a US manufacturer of safety and security devices to produce some of their products in India (unsuccessful) and a government contracting firm launched together with another friend (successful). I would say that I learned as much from the former as from the latter, largely by watching how Motayed processed the experience.

How You Can Mentor Others *Now*

One does not have to be a "person of influence" to be influential. Everyone has the potential to play the role of mentor—or mentee, for that matter. Because mentoring is not a one-way street. Even as we are being mentored, we should also find time to mentor others. In this increasingly connected and circular economy, we all will benefit from this give-and-take. This rewarding experience enables us to gain different perspectives, develop new ideas, strengthen our learning, and exercise our emotional intelligence.

As you consider ways to mentor others, you might find the following resources helpful:

- **Big Brothers Big Sisters of America**—Pairs adults (mentors) with children (mentees) to build supportive relationships that have a direct and lasting effect on the lives of young people. How to get involved: Make a donation, inquire about being matched in a mentoring friendship with a child, or attend the national Big Brothers Big Sisters conference.
- **The National Mentoring Partnership (MENTOR)**—Focuses on improving the quality and quantity of mentoring relationships for American youth. How to get involved: Become a mentor or join the Advocacy Network to help expand quality mentoring programs.
- **American Corporate Partners (ACP)**—Helps returning veterans find their next careers through one-on-one mentoring. How to get involved: Volunteer to mentor a veteran, or provide career mentorship to the spouse of an active duty service member.

I am fascinated by the idea of "paying it forward"—of sharing knowledge and expertise with the next generation. In a way, you are giving it all away for free, but you have not lost anything, because you, too, were given the same gift by your mentors. In this way, knowledge continues to accrue value over time. It is altruistic, but it is also like an investment with interest that is compounded by each generation. But unlike money, the "principal" of mentoring cannot depreciate. I think this is what so many successful people mean when they speak of the value of their accomplishments in terms that have nothing to do with money, fame, or glory. I'm thinking of people like Clayton Christensen, a professor at the Harvard Business School, who said, "The only metrics that will truly matter to my life are the individuals whom I have been able to help, one by one, to become better people."[11] And I'm thinking of John Wooden of UCLA, perhaps the greatest college basketball coach of all time, who said: "Mentoring becomes your true legacy. It is the greatest inheritance you can give to others. It is why you get up every day."[12]

Here are some daily actions you can take to pay it forward as a mentor:

- Offer to review resumes or provide career guidance through local job centers or online platforms.
- Start a peer mentoring group within your workplace to exchange skills and experiences.
- Volunteer to speak at career days at schools to inspire and guide future generations.
- Write blog posts or articles sharing your professional journey and lessons learned to guide others.
- Commit to regular check-ins with your mentees to build a stronger relationship and provide ongoing support.

CHAPTER 4

EMBRACE RELIGIOUS DIVERSITY: IMAM ILYASI

The Person

Dr. Imam Umer Ahmed Ilyasi is a prominent Islamic scholar who was also the chief imam (Muslim religious leader) of India and president of the All India Imam Organization (AIIO), leading some 500,000 imams serving an estimated 200 million Indian Muslims.[13]

The Lesson

Given how passionate people are about their religious beliefs, it is not surprising that religious differences have been one of the world's primary sources of conflict. In our increasingly diverse world, the best way we can prevent conflict is through open communication. In the realm of religion, this means engaging in interfaith dialogue. Not only does it increase our understanding of our fellow humans, but learning about other religions is interesting for its own sake. *And* it creates an environment conducive to peace. That is why, when people ask what they can do to make the world a better place, I often point them to the teachings of Dr. Ilyasi—a man for whom interfaith dialogue offers a guiding light.

Our Connection

In 2013, as part of a Global Youth Initiative (GYI) outreach to religious and spiritual leaders, I came into contact with Dr. Ilyasi. He invited me to his home in New Delhi (India), where I spent almost half a day with him. While we discussed many things during those hours together, we bonded instantly over the value of and need for interfaith dialogue.

The author with Imam Ilyasi

For a world shaken by acts of terrorist violence frequently justified by sectarian religious appeals, interfaith dialogue offers a practical means for building trust between and within faith communities.

According to "What Works? Evaluating Interfaith Dialogue Programs," a study conducted by the United States Institute of Peace, "Interfaith dialogue can unlock the power of religious traditions and provide the inspiration, guidance and validation necessary for populations to move toward non-violent means of conflict resolution." The study notes that "such dialogues have become an increasingly important tool to those who seek to end violent conflict worldwide."[14]

Ilyasi is a prominent representative of this movement. When he learned about my interest in starting a pilot project bringing together Israeli and Palestinian youth, he shared the story of his visit to Israel as part of a peace delegation of Indian Muslim leaders. The visit drew angry protests from some Indian Muslim media outlets. Ilyasi's response was clear, dignified, and steeped in deep knowledge of Islam:

"Our visit to Israel will be historic in terms of developing a dialogue between Judaism and Islam in the Indian subcontinent, where more than 40 percent of the world's Muslim population lives," Ilyasi said. "We are coming with the message of peace and goodwill from Indian Muslims who believe in the Indian tradition of resolving issues through dialogue and peaceful means."[15]

This message resonated with me, as it encapsulated the spirit animating our envisioned initiatives.

How Imam Ilyasi Bettered the World

In the decade since our meeting, I have followed Ilyasi's work with great interest and admiration as he continues to speak out against intolerance and the warping of Islamic tradition for political purposes. For example, he has focused on women's rights and encouraged the participation of women in social, educational, and religious activities. He has also spoken out against dowries and domestic violence. He has established schools and vocational training centers. And when the Taliban regime in Afghanistan barred girls from obtaining an education, he issued a fatwa (as reported by the Deccan *Chronicle*) "to make mainstream education compulsory for Muslim girls" and stressed that "all madrasas [Muslim schools] in India should lay emphasis on modern education besides religious studies."[16]

Ilyasi is aware that it may take generations for the seeds he is planting to germinate. But looking at the state of the world, he must also know that there is no alternative if the human species is to survive and flourish.

"Insaniyat (humanity) is foremost," he told the Deccan *Chronicle*. "Religion comes next."[17]

Ilyasi has shown that it is possible to be a devout follower of one's faith while also engaging with and learning from people of other faiths.

He is the epitome of the forward-looking Muslim described in the essay collection *Progressive Muslims: On Justice, Gender, and Pluralism*, edited by Omid Safi. "A progressive Muslim agenda is concerned with the ramifications of the premise that all members of humanity have this same intrinsic worth because, as the Qur'an reminds us, each of us has the breath of God breathed into our being," Safi writes. ". . . . 'Progressive,' in this usage, refers to a relentless striving toward a universal notion of justice in which no single community's prosperity, righteousness, and dignity comes at the expense of another."[18]

Ilyasi is one of many Muslim clerics to publicly condemn terrorism, and he has done so from a position of profound understanding of the many factors at work in Islamic societies. In an interview published in the Deccan *Chronicle*, he offered the following insights:

"Terrorism has become a booming global business. It has nothing to do with religious ideology. Islam does not give permission to its followers to kill even an ant. I have appealed to

Al Qaeda, Jaish-e-Mohammed and [the] Islamic State [formerly known as ISIS] to change their names immediately because they have tarnished the name of Islam and Prophet Mohammed (PBUH). These organisations are leading Muslim youth astray. Unemployment and poverty are the root causes of terrorism, and countries across the world should address these twin issues to arrest the rise of terrorism."[19]

How Imam Ilyasi Made *Me* Better

Ilyasi's focus on youth is critical, and it has confirmed my own belief that engaging young people is key to reducing violence. Westerners commonly learn of Muslim societies through media that tend to focus on leadership, with images of grizzled ayatollahs as their only reference. In fact, Muslim societies are the youngest on Earth, with a median age half that of the West. To ignore this reality is to misunderstand the forces at work in those societies, to misjudge the aspirations of hundreds of millions of people, and to miss opportunities to engage and inspire.

During our conversation, I asked Ilyasi for a message for our youth, and he said, "Amity is better than enmity, conciliation is better than confrontation, dialogue is better than war, tolerance is better than impatience, understanding is better than conflict, unity is better than division or dissidence, and sacrifice is better than demand."

This is the simple essence of interfaith dialogue, honed to a formula that anyone of any age can relate to and apply. You will notice that there is nothing overtly theological about this message. Yet it contains truths common to all faith traditions, and so it represents common ground on which to begin constructive conversations on any possible topic.

Because interfaith dialogue brings together young people from different religious backgrounds, it can help them form new friendships and even non-religious networks that they can use later to find job opportunities, create projects, receive social assistance, and push for political change. By building relationships and connections outside their own faith community, they catalyze the creation of a more inclusive society, which will lead to greater success for more people in the modern world.

By talking to other young people from different faiths, they get a deeper understanding of the diversity in their communities, and also the underlying similarities that exist between individuals who follow different religious beliefs. This creates greater acceptance and respect for one another.

At a personal level, by engaging in dialogue with people from different faiths, they end up thinking more objectively about their own beliefs and considering alternative perspectives. This often provides them with a more nuanced understanding of their own faith, which provides a spiritual grounding that can reduce their susceptibility to religious extremism or fanaticism.

Interfaith dialogue is an excellent tool for young people to develop critical thinking skills. By questioning their own assumptions and beliefs, they may become more open-minded, tolerant, accepting, and collaborative. These, too, are important qualities for success in this globalized world.

If the next generation can learn and implement these lessons, they will create a more peaceful world in which religion, instead of being a divisive force, enriches their lives and spirit.

For the skeptic, this sounds too good to be true. Does interfaith dialogue really work?

Growing up in India, I observed firsthand the positive results of the work my father did to bring people of different faiths into contact with one another. Since then, I have visited numerous communities globally and have witnessed the power of interfaith dialogue. There are no quick fixes to deeply-rooted destructive beliefs, fear, and prejudice, but in the course of my international development work in Africa, Asia, and Latin America, I have seen interfaith dialogue promote understanding and respect, foster cooperation, encourage peaceful conflict resolution, enhance peace, and strengthen democracy. The most effective ideas and solutions usually come from within the local community, and this is where interfaith dialogue is particularly valuable.

My impressions are supported by research. The United States Institute of Peace study cited above identifies the following social benefits associated with interfaith dialogue initiatives: a lower incidence of hostile graffiti, vandalism, and hate-based violence between groups; and an increase in positive references to other faith communities in media and public communications.[20]

How You Can Embrace Religious Diversity *Now*

As Dr. Ilyasi has shown, open communication among differing faith traditions is an important means of promoting understanding of our universal humanity and fostering peace in an increasingly diverse and divisive world. Through involvement with any of the following organizations and events, you too can be part of the movement to build bridges among the world's religions.

- **United States Institute of Peace (USIP)**—A nonpartisan institute founded by Congress, USIP works with local partners to prevent and resolve conflict. How to get involved: Engage with USIP's interfaith peace-building initiatives by attending their public events, utilizing their educational resources, or applying for their grants and fellowships.
- **Interfaith America**—Focused on building interfaith leadership in the US, Interfaith America offers resources and training for students, educators, and community leaders to build interfaith dialogue and cooperation. How to get involved: Donate, gain inspiration and ideas through articles in Interfaith America's online magazine.
- **United Religions Initiative (URI)**—This global network fosters local and global cooperation between people of different faiths to end religiously motivated violence and create cultures of peace, justice, and healing. How to get involved: Join URI, identify and support an action area, participate in events, or make a donation to expand URI's capacity.
- **Parliament of the World's Religions**—One of the oldest and most diverse interfaith organizations, it hosts periodic gatherings where people of all faiths can meet, share ideas, and commit to action items to address global issues. How to get involved: Join their mailing list, make a donation, or become a member.
- **Religions for Peace**—Works to transform violent conflict, promote just and harmonious societies, and advance human development. How to get involved: Apply for

an internship or employment, attend a virtual event, or contribute to the *Mindful Peace* blog.

- **King Abdullah Bin Abdulaziz International Center for Interreligious and Intercultural Dialogue (KAICIID)**—Promotes dialogue among followers of different religions and cultures around the world. How to get involved: Attend a workshop, conference, or webinar; check out KAICIID publications; or explore their e-learning and online resources.
- **Tanenbaum Center for Interreligious Understanding**—Combats religious prejudice by promoting respect for religious differences. How to get involved: Explore the Center's many online articles on ways to build respect, knowledge, community, resilience, and momentum to dispel religious prejudice.

Beyond these larger opportunities for engagement, you can also take the following simple steps to promote interfaith dialogue and understanding:

- Participate in or organize local interfaith dinners or dialogues to learn about different beliefs and practices.
- Volunteer at an interfaith shelter or community service project to work alongside people of different faiths.
- Educate yourself on different religions and share your learnings with friends to dispel myths and build understanding.
- Use social media to promote messages of peace and unity across different religious groups.
- Offer to facilitate discussions at your place of worship to explore common values shared with other faiths.

CHAPTER 5

LEARN FROM *EVERYONE*: RUTH BADER GINSBURG

The Person

Ruth Bader Ginsburg was a monumental champion of gender equality and civil rights, both as a litigator and as a Supreme Court Justice.

The Lesson

In addition to her legal achievements, Ginsburg's legacy includes the powerful example of her unwavering commitment to civility. In the face of ideological differences, she demonstrated that one can fight passionately for one's beliefs while maintaining respect for opponents. She showed that civility is not a sign of weakness but a tool for building understanding and effecting meaningful change. In these days of divisiveness and close-minded entrenchment, where true knowledge of opposing perspectives is often actively avoided, her lesson stands as both a model for behavior and a blueprint for progress.

Our Connection

I had long known about Ruth Bader Ginsburg's dedication to women's rights, as well as her love of opera. But one thing I did not know about her until late 2019 was her passion for philanthropy. And it was philanthropy that brought us together. There were several causes close to her heart. The daughter of an immigrant father, Ginsburg credited her success in life to growing up in the United States, where she had the chance to go to school and flourish. When she received a $1 million award for Philosophy and Culture from the Berggruen Institute, which called her "a constant voice for justice, equal and accessible to all,"[21] she gave the money to an array of nonprofits, including SOS Children's Villages USA, where I was CEO at the time.

Collection of the Supreme Court of the United States

Ruth Bader Ginsburg

Our entire team was deeply honored by her generosity. I decided to send her a photo book (*A Place to Dream* by photographer Jens Honoré) profiling our organization and its work globally along with a personal letter. Honestly, though I knew of her reputation for politeness, I did not expect a reply. But reply she did. Ginsburg responded with a kind note, saying she was keeping the book in the library of her chamber at the Supreme Court. I was doubly honored by her gesture, which will stay forever in my heart.

Of course, her interest in our organization should not have surprised me. In 2020, CNN reported that "Ginsburg looked to future generations for faith in a better future. In accepting the Berggruen prize, the great-grandmother said, 'One of the things that makes me an optimist is young people.'"[22] That is exactly the feeling I have every time I visit children's homes, schools, or youth centers around the world.

Ruth Bader Ginsburg died in September 2020, just seven months after sending her letter to me. I was deeply saddened by the news of her death and felt that more should be done to continue her legacy with children. After some discussion with my colleagues, I reached out to Ginsburg's daughter-in-law, Patrice Michaels, the person she credited for putting SOS Children's Villages forward for her support. Patrice and I spent hours planning several initiatives to raise awareness and funding for the vulnerable children about whom Ginsburg cared so deeply. Celine Serrao (my assistant) played a key role in facilitating things for us. Ginsburg's son, Jim Ginsburg, also joined in one such initiative called Clubhouse. These rewarding collaborations with the Ginsburg family gave me an insight into Ginsburg's core values as well as those of her immediate family. I am forever grateful for that.

How Ruth Bader Ginsburg Bettered the World

In *The Legacy of Ruth Bader Ginsburg*—a collection of essays that explores Ginsburg's life and legacy as a jurist, advocate, and cultural icon—Scott Dodson describes Ginsburg as "Diminutive yet forceful. Passionate yet rational. Strategic yet direct."[23] Given that I am not an attorney, I struggled a bit to understand some of the chapters in the book. But these essays provided me a much better understanding of the justice system in the United States and the Justice herself. The essays demonstrated why Ginsburg had such an impact in so many key areas and why she is considered a giant figure in their development. Ginsburg authored powerful majority opinions on gender equality, the rights of people with disabilities and those living with mental health conditions, and victims of environmental pollution. But she was also known for her powerful dissents, challenging majority opinions in cases ranging from voting rights to federalism. Even when she didn't author a majority opinion or dissent, her influence was felt, and Dodson reminds readers about both her direct and indirect impact in the fields of federalism, international law, criminal procedure, racial equality, abortion, congressional power, and even taxation.

Ginsburg's career highlights can be overwhelming, but I was profoundly moved not only by her eloquence, but by the great emphasis she placed on the importance of empathy. So many of her dissents challenged the Supreme Court majority to put themselves in the shoes of a single working mother, or an immigrant, or a person with a disability, and to reflect on the Constitution in light of that personal context.

Ginsburg believed that everyone has the power to make a difference in the world. Whether it's through advocacy, activism, or simply living a life that reflects your values, she believed that we all have the ability to create positive change. Tenacious and resilient in the face of adversity, she recognized that standing up for what you believe in might mean facing criticism or opposition, and so she was keen to protect those individual liberties.

Ginsburg was known for her commitment to civility and her ability to work across ideological lines to achieve consensus. It may come as a surprise that when Justice Brett Kavanaugh, a certain adversary on many issues, was nominated to the Supreme Court, Ginsburg offered to help him prepare for his confirmation hearings. And although she and Justice Antonin Scalia disagreed—often and fundamentally—they maintained a close friendship based on mutual respect and a shared love of opera. In a eulogy for Scalia, Ginsburg said, "From our years together at the D.C. Circuit, we were best buddies. We disagreed now and then, but when I wrote for the Court and received a Scalia dissent, the opinion ultimately released was notably better than my initial circulation. Justice Scalia nailed all the weak spots—the 'applesauce' and 'argle bargle'—and gave me just what I needed to strengthen the majority opinion."[24]

Ginsburg's civility was not mere politeness for its own sake. It was rooted in her love for the law as a space for truth to speak to power, hence her passion for digging deep into cases, her dedication to proper procedure, her reputation as a stickler for rules. Were the Court to lose its rigor, it would lose a lot of its legitimacy.

Civility had, for Ginsburg, a further appeal as a source of gentle persuasion. Speaking at Harvard Law School in 2015,

Ginsburg said, "Fight for the things you care about, but do it in a way that will lead others to join you."[25] While some will always be drawn to blustering bullies and even violence to achieve their ends, the search for real and lasting positive change always considers the hearts and minds of individuals. I think Ginsburg and Mahatma Gandhi would have had a lot in common.

Martha Minow, the noted legal scholar and former dean of Harvard Law School, wrote in the *Harvard Gazette*, "Justice Ginsburg also showed that it is possible to build deep and meaningful friendships with people despite severe disagreements. At this time of deep social and political divisions, there is much to learn from her life and her commitments. Above all, she changed the lives of millions as a lawyer and as a jurist by dismantling barriers to employment, education, and roles in families and society based solely on gender—and showed how law can, with persistence and vision, be a tool to bend the arc of the moral universe toward justice."[26]

How Ruth Bader Ginsburg Made *Me* Better

> "A champion of race and gender equality. A pioneering lawyer on women's equality. A civil rights hero. A feminist symbol. A major pop icon. Notorious RBG. A key justice on the nation's highest court."[27]

That is how reporter Liz Mineo described the late Ruth Bader Ginsburg in her *Harvard Gazette* column.

For me, Ginsburg was all those things and more. But what really amazed me, and served as a life lesson, was her civility—that quality of politeness that enabled her to engage in the fiercest battles on the most contentious constitutional questions while maintaining friendships with colleagues on the opposing side. It was as much her nature as it was her unique style.

During her confirmation hearings in July 1993, after becoming only the second woman ever nominated to the United States Supreme Court, Ginsburg spoke to the Senate Judiciary Committee about how she saw the court, the country, and herself. She invoked Thomas Jefferson, Alexander Hamilton, and the progress America had made in living up to the ideals embodied within the Constitution.

"America is known as a country that welcomes people to its shores," she said. "All kinds of people. The image of the Statue of Liberty with Emma Lazarus' famous poem. She lifts her lamp and welcomes people to the golden shore, where they will not experience prejudice because of the color of their skin, the religious faith that they follow."[28]

That was Ginsburg in a nutshell: impassioned, eloquent, idealistic. Her trailblazing legal career and forceful advocacy for a kinder world gave voice to many of us—and spoke directly to me, a naturalized US citizen.

I have been inspired not only by Ginsburg's ability to work alongside people with opposing views but also by her ability to learn from them. How fitting, then, for me to include her in a book about learning from others!

How You Can Learn from Everyone *Now*

Ruth Bader Ginsburg practiced civility in an extremely contentious field. As far as I can tell, that played an important role in her success. No matter what your chosen field or where your life takes you, I believe that your chance of success will increase if you stay open to friendships with people whose ideologies differ from yours. How could a greater understanding of other viewpoints *not* clarify your own thinking and lead to productive interaction?

Beyond that fundamental receptivity, you can help bring people together and promote understanding through involvement with these organizations and initiatives:

- **National Institute for Civil Discourse (NICD)**—NICD works to promote healthy and civil political debate, offering programs and resources to improve public and political discourse. How to get involved: Visit their website and explore initiatives such as CommonSense American (a bipartisan network supporting policy solutions), the Golden Rule 2020 project (advocating for respect and dignity in politics), and the Engaging Differences video series (designed to help Americans engage constructively across divides). You can sign up for programs, participate in workshops, or access educational resources through the site.
- **The Village Square**—This nonpartisan public educational forum organizes town hall-style discussions on divisive local and national issues. How to get involved: Check out their website and look for upcoming events in your area. You can attend their town hall discussions,

volunteer to help organize events, or donate to support their mission.

A few simple daily actions can make civility and open-mindedness an integral part of your life:

- Practice active listening: When someone expresses an opposing view, try to genuinely understand their perspective before responding.
- Follow news sources across the political spectrum to gain a more balanced understanding of issues.
- Participate in community forums or town halls, especially on contentious local issues, and model respectful engagement.
- Use social media mindfully. Before commenting on a controversial post, ask yourself if your response promotes understanding or division.
- Join or start a book club that intentionally selects books representing diverse viewpoints.
- Engage in "intellectual humility" exercises. Regularly challenge your own beliefs and be open to changing your mind.
- Host a "Diverse Dinner Party." Invite friends with different political views for a meal, setting ground rules for respectful discussion.
- Practice the "steel man" argument. Instead of attacking the weakest version of an opponent's argument, engage with the strongest version.
- When disagreeing, use "I" statements to express your views without attacking others. "I see it differently" instead of "You're wrong."

CHAPTER 6

LOOK BEYOND: DARREN WALKER

The Person

Darren Walker became president of the Ford Foundation—a social justice philanthropy with international influence—in 2013 and served in that role for more than a decade.

The Lesson

Many top athletes train themselves to visualize success before competition. Yet envisioning a positive outcome need not be limited to the arena of sports. If you want to improve society, there is no better way to begin than by envisioning how the world could be different. In transforming the Ford Foundation, Darren Walker did just that—picturing a world moving toward freedom from systemic injustice and inequality. By pairing his transformative vision with passion and action, Walker created a strong recipe for powerful philanthropy and social progress. If you want to learn from his example, as I've tried to do, you need three ingredients: hope—that your vision for a better society is possible; passion—that you care deeply and personally about the change you are pursuing; and action—that you take concrete steps (such as addressing underlying drivers of inequality) to achieve your goal. My key lesson from Darren Walker, then, is this: Envision a better society, care deeply, and take concrete steps toward change.

Our Connection

I joined the development sector in 2007 from the private sector without any prior training or experience in the field. Needless to say, the learning curve was steep. In particular, I struggled to reconcile what I knew and appreciated about the private sector—the ability of the free market to unleash innovation and create prosperity—and what had inspired me to move into development, namely, the need to help half of humanity move out of poverty and suffering. While I could appreciate how capitalism could feed philanthropy, at times, the two sectors seemed miles apart, or even very much at odds in their thinking, priorities, and actions.

I sought guidance and context from many sources. At one seminar, World Bank president Jim Yong Kim urged attendees to read the book *Capital in the Twenty-First Century* by the French economist Thomas Piketty. And so I did. The book is a warning about the dangers of unchecked inequality and a call to action for policymakers and society as a whole. It helped to set off a much more vigorous global debate on income inequality, and it inspired me to learn more about the various efforts SNV

Netherlands Development Organisation—my employer at the time, and for which I founded SNV USA—was undertaking to reduce poverty and address inequality through agriculture value chains, water sanitation hygiene, renewable energy, and related areas in thirty-two countries.

My work with SNV brought me in contact with the Ford Foundation and with its director, Frank F. DeGiovanni. I visited Frank many times at the Foundation's office in New York City, and we also met once in Nairobi, Kenya. SNV collaborated with the Ford Foundation on many projects in Mozambique, Zimbabwe, Ecuador, and Indonesia, mostly in agriculture value chains. Working with the Foundation was one of the most rewarding professional experiences for me due to their localized approach, their focus on building local and regional infrastructure, and their deep subject-matter expertise. One of the reasons I had decided to join SNV was its innovative market-based approach to global poverty reduction, using frameworks such as inclusive business and impact investment. The Ford Foundation was coming from the same place, and this made for a great partnership. Beyond the knowledge I was gaining, the partnership also gave me faith and hope.

It was during this time that I first encountered Darren Walker, who took over as president of the Ford Foundation in 2013. As I listened to him speak at a conference in 2014, I became very excited. Here was an innovator who was ready to shake things up in philanthropy. Importantly for me, here was someone who had found a way to bridge the gap between development and the market.

How Darren Walker Bettered the World

With Walker at the helm, the Ford Foundation has supported organizations that advocate for the protection of many of this country's most fundamental rights and freedoms—from an independent press to free speech and voting rights—as well as those that support and protect marginalized populations. It also has provided funding to organizations working to reform the education and criminal justice systems. Under his leadership, the Foundation became the first nonprofit in US history to issue a $1 billion designated social bond in US capital markets for proceeds to strengthen and stabilize nonprofit organizations in the wake of COVID-19.

I think it's fair to say that Walker has redefined the Foundation's mission to focus on addressing systemic inequality and advancing social justice. He has also emphasized the importance of measuring the impact of the Foundation's work and has encouraged the organization to adopt more rigorous evaluation methods. This is critical in an age of heightened budgetary accountability. In addition, he has pushed for the Foundation to be more strategic in its grant-making, focusing on areas where it can have the most impact.

Crucially, the Ford Foundation now focuses on addressing what it has identified as the main drivers of inequality worldwide. According to the Foundation's website, they are:

- Entrenched cultural narratives that undermine fairness, tolerance, and inclusion.
- Failure to invest in and protect vital public goods such as education and natural resources.

- Unfair rules of the economy that magnify unequal opportunity and outcomes.
- Unequal access to government decision-making and resources.
- Persistent prejudice and discrimination against women, people with disabilities, and racial, ethnic, and caste minorities.[29]

While the Ford Foundation has a history of awarding grants to individuals fighting inequality such as Martin Luther King Jr., Nelson Mandela, and James Baldwin, we can detect Walker's influence in the recognition of the complexity of inequality, and the emphasis on intersectionality in combating it.

These are themes in Walker's book *From Generosity to Justice: A New Gospel of Wealth*. In it, he argues that income inequality is a fundamental challenge facing society and that traditional philanthropy alone cannot address the systemic issues that perpetuate this inequality. Walker notes that income inequality has reached historic levels in many countries, including the United States, and that it is a barrier to social mobility and economic opportunity for many people. He argues that philanthropy has a critical role to play in addressing this issue but that it must do so in a way that addresses the root causes of inequality, rather than simply providing charity to those in need. He argues that "capitalism does not need to be a winner-take-all system," and he encourages a more inclusive form of market activity.[30]

Like many others, I see Darren Walker as a trailblazer in a new field: social justice philanthropy. He has transformed the Ford Foundation into a leader in the fight against systemic inequality, and his emphasis on impact, diversity, and inclusion has helped shape the field more broadly. Walker's contributions have been recognized by numerous organizations and institutions, including the Obama Foundation and the Carnegie Corporation of New York. Most recently, he was named 2020 Philanthropy Innovator of the Year by the *Wall Street Journal* and 2023 Foundation Leader of the Year by *Inside Philanthropy*.[31]

How Darren Walker Made *Me* Better

As I read Walker's book, its message resonated with me instantly. This was exactly the motivation of SNV leadership to launch inclusive business (aka inclusive capitalism) and impact investing initiatives. Inclusive business promotes strategies for national and multinational companies to bring local producers and providers into their production and marketing value chains, and impact investing aims to solve social and environmental challenges while generating financial profit for funding entities.

Walker's book emphasizes the need for philanthropy to move beyond traditional notions of charity and generosity toward a focus on justice and systemic change if it is to address the critical issue of income inequality. This is not an easy issue to raise in a meeting with wealthy donors. As CEO of several nongovernmental organizations (NGOs), I sometimes felt unable to speak this truth, for fear of offending or alienating those on whose support our organization depended. I admire Walker's courage to write this book, and that in turn has given *me* more courage.

It is a courage born of realizing that we have no time to lose. In a conversation with reporter Justin Worland for the "Time100 Talks" series in June 2020, Walker said, "A fundamental challenge here is that capitalism in its current form is not working for too many of us. Our privilege in this economy has been compounded, while those who don't have assets, those who are trying and striving, are feeling that they are left farther and farther behind—because they are. . . . We have seen this pulling apart of our society economically and that intersects with race and our historic realities of racial discrimination."[32]

The core challenge, then, is how to be more inclusive for our common good. From my own work, travel, and interaction with communities in Asia, Africa, the Middle East, and Latin America, I learned that inclusion is important not just for peace and harmony but also for the economic well-being of communities, no matter which part of the world we live in. The National Bureau of Economic Research has charted the role of geographic isolation, proximity, and cultural diversity on economic development from pre-industrial times to the modern era. The evidence is clear: "diversity spurs economic development, and homogeneity slows it down."[33] Other research has shown that a diversity of experiences, cultures, and attitudes can help provide a breeding ground for new ideas. How we relate to one another in our work environment and even at the local grocery store is important in facilitating our creativity.

What makes Walker's influence so profound, beyond his mastery of difficult issues and his courage to speak the truth, is his passion. This is a man who cares, a man for whom the outcome of policy is personal. I sensed this when I read an op-ed he wrote for the *Houston Chronicle* in 2016, addressing a spate of senseless killings in Louisiana, Minnesota, and Texas. He wrote,

"We have it within our power to douse the flames that threaten not one house or another, but our communities, cities and our country itself—to snuff out the embers of distrust and division that smolder beneath our discourse. Ultimately, the most effective retardant is hope—a clear-eyed hope, borne from the recognition that if we commit ourselves to realizing America's full potential, we can emerge a more unified, fair and just nation."

Those words had an impact on me, so I sent him a quick note thanking him for his courageous write up and received a reply from him. I knew then that Darren Walker was in the business of hope, and I know now that he is also a man of action and inclusion.

How You Can Look Beyond the Status Quo *Now*

The way things are isn't the way they must always be. Many large, socially responsible organizations share this conviction, and opportunities for involvement with them are many. Here are some you might consider:

- **SNV**—Committed to a "sustainable and more equitable future for all," SNV works to address the root causes of inequality by strengthening connections and capacities in and among three vital sectors—agri-food, energy, and water systems—in Africa and Asia. How to get involved: Learn about SNV's activities through their online "News and Stories" or "Knowledge Centre," or contact the organization to learn about opportunities for collaboration.
- **Global Fund for Children (GFC)**—A global non-profit, GFC invests in local organizations that advance the rights of children around the world. How to get involved: Visit their website to make a donation or

stay informed about impactful programs, initiatives, and results.

- **United Way**—United Way focuses on improving education, financial stability, and health in communities worldwide. They offer numerous volunteer opportunities and ways to donate. How to get involved: Volunteer for local programs, donate, or participate in workplace giving campaigns.
- **Amnesty International**—This global movement campaigns for human rights, addressing systemic inequality and discrimination. How to get involved: Join a local chapter, sign petitions, or participate in letter-writing campaigns.
- **Habitat for Humanity**—Habitat works to provide affordable housing to families in need, addressing one aspect of systemic inequality. How to get involved: Volunteer at local building sites, donate, or shop at their ReStore locations.
- **DonorsChoose**—This platform allows individuals to donate directly to classroom projects in public schools, reducing educational inequality. How to get involved: Browse and fund projects that resonate with you, or start a fundraising campaign.
- **The Hunger Project**—The Hunger Project works to end hunger and poverty by pioneering sustainable, grassroots, women-centered strategies. How to get involved: Become an investor (donor), volunteer, or participate in their advocacy efforts.
- **Global Citizen**—Global Citizen is a movement of engaged citizens using their collective voice to end

extreme poverty by 2030. How to get involved: Take actions on their platform, attend their events, or become an ambassador.

- **B Lab**—B Lab is a nonprofit that certifies companies meeting high standards of social and environmental performance, accountability, and transparency. They promote the idea that business can be a force for good, reflecting Walker's vision of more inclusive capitalism. How to get involved: Support B Lab by purchasing their products/services, or if you're a business owner, pursue B Corp certification.
- **Global Impact Investing Network (GIIN)**—GIIN is dedicated to increasing the scale and effectiveness of impact investing, contributing to more strategic and impactful philanthropy. How to get involved: If you're an investor, join their network. For others, educate yourself about impact investing through their resources.
- **Shared Value Initiative**—This organization helps companies find business opportunities in societal challenges. It embodies Walker's vision of aligning business interests with social progress. How to get involved: Attend their events, use their resources to implement shared value in your business, or join their community of practice.
- **Acumen**—Acumen is a nonprofit global venture fund that uses entrepreneurial approaches to solve the problems of poverty. How to get involved: Donate to their fund, take their online courses on social impact, or apply to their fellowship program if you're a social entrepreneur.

The road to change may be long, but it doesn't have to be lonely. And fortunately, the road is bordered with signposts—including the following simple actions—that can help you find your way:

- Educate yourself about social issues in your community.
- Volunteer for local organizations addressing systemic inequalities.
- Support businesses that prioritize social responsibility.
- Engage in constructive dialogues about social issues with diverse groups.
- Mentor young people from underserved communities.
- Participate in local government meetings and decision-making processes.
- Use your professional skills to assist nonprofit organizations pro bono.
- Start or join a giving circle focused on social justice issues.
- Practice conscious consumerism by supporting ethical and sustainable products.
- Share stories of positive social change to inspire others and spread hope.

CHAPTER 7

LISTEN FOR YOUR CALLING: MOTHER TERESA

The Person

Mother Teresa founded the Missionaries of Charity, which was originally dedicated to helping impoverished people in her native Kolkata. For her many decades of selfless service to others, she was awarded the Nobel Peace Prize, and after her death she was canonized as a saint.

The Lesson

Today Mother Teresa's journey is known to many millions, and her name is synonymous with unconditional love. But as a young girl she had no dreams of such notoriety. All she knew was that she had a drive to serve others, and that drive became a calling that propelled her onward. Whether or not we share

Mother Teresa's religious devotion, her lesson for me is this: we all have the capacity to listen for that voice inside us that commands our attention. You know it when you hear it, because it is a voice you cannot ignore. Sometimes our lives take detours, sometimes the voice is obscured by the noise of "just making a living"—but if it is a true calling, and you stay attuned to who you are, you will always return to it.

Our Connection

Some lessons take a lifetime to learn. Others are learned in an instant. Mother Teresa's lesson for me came in this second, instantaneous way. But its effect has lasted a lifetime.

I met Mother Teresa on a hot summer day in 1996, when I paid a visit to the Missionaries of Charity as head of the India Eastern Region office of the Australian Trade Commission. The visit was not a pilgrimage, but it was part of my very pragmatic outreach to eminent personalities in the city. I was joined by Michele Marie, my former wife, and I carried an armload of books on Kolkata's history. Mother Teresa was a petite woman who had a warm and caring smile that radiated compassion. Her deep-set, intense blue eyes were just as others had described them: piercing and filled with empathy. She wore a white sari with blue borders. The sari was symbolic of her commitment to poverty and humility. Initially our visit was

The author with Mother Teresa at the Missionaries of Charity in Kolkata

somewhat formal, almost routine. We briefly discussed the work of the Missionaries of Charity, the organization she founded, and she inquired about the work I was doing in Kolkata before autographing the books I had brought. After the three of us had taken a brief tour of the Mother House, we stood in the main corridor of the Missionaries of Charity. In that moment, the visit turned into something more than a business call. Mother Teresa took my hand and grasped it tightly. All of a sudden, I felt a unique sensation flowing through my body that even today I can't properly explain. I was completely flooded with utter joy at her love, compassion, mercy, and greatness, and completely conscious of the dignity of every human person on Earth, irrespective of race, religion and nationality.

In Hindu religion the word *darshan* is derived from the Sanskrit word *darsana*, meaning "sight," "vision," or "appearance." One performing darshan is expected to do nothing more than look at the image of a god, sacred person, or divine being. That act of looking is enough to bring spiritual fulfillment. That was the first time I felt something like darshan. Many years later, in 2011, I would undergo a similar epiphany when His Holiness the Dalai Lama held my hand. Both encounters left me feeling uplifted and somehow blessed.

How Mother Teresa Bettered the World

Born in 1910 into a prosperous Catholic family in what is now Macedonia, Agnes Gonxha Bojaxhiu—the young Mother Teresa—was influenced early in life by parents devoted to the less fortunate. As a child, she was fascinated by stories of missionaries serving in Bengal, and by the time she was twelve had decided to commit herself to her religion. Six years later she joined the Irish order Sisters of Loreto, which sent her to India, where she took her vows and became known as Mother Teresa.

As a teacher at St. Mary's High School in Kolkata in the 1940s, Mother Teresa became aware of the extreme suffering and poverty outside of the convent—and by 1948, in answer to what she described as a "call within a call"[34] from God, she resolved to work directly with the poor. With permission from the Church, she began serving ill and impoverished people on the streets of Kolkata, which led to her starting an open-air school for slum children and eventually receiving financial support and volunteer assistance to expand it.

To grasp the immensity of Mother Teresa's commitment, the scope of her vision, and the depth of her courage, it's necessary to paint a picture of Kolkata. Unfortunately, it's almost impossible for me to convey a sense of the city to someone who has never experienced it directly. Thankfully, there is YouTube, so the curious can catch glimpses of the city courtesy of travelers with GoPro cameras and cell phones. They can also find videos of Kolkata from the twentieth century and footage of Mother Teresa herself. And certainly there are photographs in illustrated history books. Of course none of these can reproduce sensations such as touch or smell. Nor can they adequately prompt a reaction in the same way the city does in real life. At a minimum, what I would wish for readers to understand is the incredible density of the place. Not just density in terms of the built environment, but also the density of lives lived there. Kolkata is a world of worlds: every square foot teems with stories, and every story is a multilayered tableau of heart and soul containing the past, present, and future of India. The mind has a hard time wrapping itself around this, and so we have statistics: a population that, after enduring the effects of rapid urbanization and famine—as well as the traumas of independence and partition—in the 1940s, rose rapidly from under 5 million in 1950 to 15.5 million in 2024.[35] These figures are helpful in a way, but they reduce all of those individual stories to identical numbers. For many people, the numbers make Kolkata easier to deal with on a psychological or emotional level. But for Mother Teresa, it was about the individual. Now imagine a soul capable of embracing all those individual stories, all that life, all those needs. That was Mother Teresa.

In 1950, Mother Teresa founded the Missionaries of Charity, a religious congregation dedicated to providing care and assistance to the poorest of the poor. She did that mostly through the same touch I experienced. She touched lepers and washed their wounds, fed the hungry, sheltered the unhoused, and sat with the dying. In so many cases, her strength was simply that she refused to look away, as so many of us do. She experienced a profound empathy for the suffering and poverty she encountered, and she believed it was her mission to alleviate it. That approach was remarkable for India, which was still dominated by the notorious caste system. The people she touched were considered "untouchables." But Mother Teresa touched everyone, giving them not only comfort but also dignity. Over her nearly seventy years of service, she developed a strong bond with the people of Kolkata, building relationships and trust with those she served and becoming deeply embedded in the community. This connection further solidified her commitment to remaining in Kolkata and continuing her work there, even as the organization expanded to more than one hundred countries.

Mother Teresa was not beyond criticism. Some faulted her relationship with supporters of less than sterling character, others criticized her for focusing on the care of individuals rather than addressing the root causes of poverty, and still others attacked her opposition to abortion, among other points of contention. I believe US Senator John McCain addressed her critics best in his book *Character Is Destiny*, one chapter of which is dedicated to Mother Teresa. McCain wrote, ". . . . I cannot help but think that the critics of Mother Teresa, who never claimed perfection for herself but was closer to it than any of us will ever reach, have at a minimum lost a sense of the possibilities in the habits of the human heart."[36]

Mother Teresa's exhausted heart finally stopped beating on Friday, September 5, 1997, at the age of eighty-seven—just a year after we had met. It was a terribly sad day for the world and for me personally. I paid my respects at St. Thomas Church in Middleton Row in Kolkata where her body lay in state. Later I attended the state funeral mass hosted by the Governor of West Bengal. Among the many dignitaries from around the world who came to honor the memory of Mother Teresa were Hillary Clinton, Bernadette Chirac, and the queens of Spain, Belgium, and Jordan. Cardinal Angelo Sodano, the Vatican secretary of state, and other church leaders led the service. In that moment I found myself wondering who could possibly fill her shoes? How was her work to go on? Who would help the poorest now?

One measure of Mother Teresa's impact lies in the recognition of her life of service. She was canonized as Saint Teresa of Calcutta in 2016. There is a beautiful chapter ("In the Footsteps of a Saint") about her path to sainthood in Kathryn Spink's *Mother Theresa: A Complete Authorized Biography*, a book I recommend to anyone who wants to learn about Mother Teresa. She was awarded the Nobel Peace Prize in 1979 and India's highest civilian honor, the Bharat Ratna (Jewel of India), in 1980. Mother Teresa became the fifth person in history to be named an honorary citizen of the United States.[37]

These honors increased the visibility of her efforts, but her real legacy abides in the ongoing work of the Missionaries of Charity. She always wanted the sisters of the order to work quietly and steadily, and by all accounts they are doing exactly doing that. As of 2023, the order had 5,750 members, serving in 760 homes in 139 countries. The Missionaries of Charity operates hospices, orphanages, soup kitchens, and homes for those suffering from HIV/AIDS, leprosy, and tuberculosis, as well as refugees and street children.[38]

I also see Mother Teresa's commitment to the poor mirrored in the biography of Pope Francis II. As Elizabeth Dias noted in an article in *Time* magazine, when Francis presided over Teresa's canonization, both served in religious orders and both were utterly devoted to the marginalized, whom they brought out of the shadows with their work. "At their cores, they share a purpose in their public service and personal spirituality: to act as a channel of God's mercy,"[39] Dias wrote. By sanctifying Mother Teresa's life, Francis essentially made her legacy the agenda of the Catholic Church and its 1.39 billion-strong global community.[40] As Dias put it, "Her mission will continue to define his papacy."[41]

How Mother Teresa Made *Me* Better

The effect on my life of meeting Mother Teresa is hard to put into words. The awareness gained that day never left me and has helped me navigate through life. For example, when I moved into the nonprofit sector to work more intentionally for the disadvantaged, I knew I was acting in tune with my life compass.

I vividly remember a conversation with a group of philanthropists in which someone asked me how I would compare Mother Teresa with other spiritual leaders I have met. I remember telling them that of all the people I have met and/or read about doing amazing and important work for humankind, Mother Teresa actually lived with the poor, and their home was her home. Although I have not resided with those I have tried to serve over the years—unfortunately, I am no saint—I have always sought to keep the people my work is trying to benefit at the forefront of my thoughts.

How You Can Listen for Your Calling *Now*

If you are reading this book, my guess is that you are more than a little curious about how you might contribute more to the world. Doing so may even be a part of your calling. And if you think of reading as an act of listening, you will know when you see an organization—perhaps one of the following—whose work resonates with your inner voice.

- **Kolkata Foundation**—Dedicated to bringing people around the world together to fight poverty in the city of Kolkata, the foundation was inspired by the groundbreaking work done by Robin Hood in New York City. How to get involved: Donate, start a fundraising campaign, or spread awareness.
- **Missionaries of Charity**—Founded by Mother Teresa, they serve the poorest of the poor in various countries.

How to get involved: Volunteer at their centers, donate supplies or money, or participate in prayer support.

- **St. Jude Children's Research Hospital**—Provides free treatment to children with cancer and other life-threatening diseases. How to get involved: Donate, volunteer, or participate in fundraising events.
- **Heifer International**—Works to end hunger and poverty by providing livestock and training to struggling communities. How to get involved: Donate animals, contribute to projects, or volunteer.
- **Water.org**—Provides access to safe water and sanitation in developing countries. How to get involved: Donate, start a fundraising campaign, or spread awareness.
- **Ronald McDonald House Charities**—Provides housing for families with hospitalized children. How to get involved: Volunteer at a local house, donate, or participate in fundraising events.
- **Meals on Wheels**—Delivers meals to seniors who are unable to purchase or prepare their own food. How to get involved: Volunteer to deliver meals, donate, or advocate for senior nutrition programs.
- **CARE International**—Fights global poverty with a special focus on empowering women and girls. How to get involved: Donate, advocate for policy changes, or participate in their Walk In Her Shoes challenge.
- **Make-A-Wish Foundation**—Grants wishes to children with critical illnesses. How to get involved: Donate, volunteer, or refer a child for a wish.
- **Kiva**—Provides microloans to entrepreneurs in developing countries. How to get involved: Lend as little as twenty-five dollars to a project of your choice.

- **Operation Smile**—Provides free surgeries to repair cleft lip, cleft palate, and other facial deformities for children around the world. How to get involved: Donate, volunteer (medical and non-medical), or join a medical mission.
- **Alzheimer's Association**—Provides support for those affected by Alzheimer's disease and advances research toward a cure. How to get involved: Volunteer, participate in fundraising walks, or donate.
- **Mercy Corps**—Provides emergency relief and supports long-term solutions to poverty, conflict, and disaster. How to get involved: Donate, fundraise, or apply for volunteer or career opportunities.

With these simple daily actions, you too can spread love and compassion:

- Practice unconditional kindness toward everyone you meet, regardless of their background or status.
- Offer a listening ear to someone in need, without judgment or interruption.
- Visit and spend time with elderly or lonely individuals in your community.
- Prepare and distribute meals to homeless individuals or families in need.
- Volunteer at a local hospice or hospital, comforting those who are ill or dying.
- Donate essential items like blankets, clothes, or toiletries to shelters.
- Offer forgiveness to those who have wronged you, and seek reconciliation.

- Advocate for the rights and dignity of marginalized groups in your community.
- Perform small acts of service for neighbors, such as shoveling snow or mowing lawns.
- Write letters of encouragement to prisoners or those in rehabilitation centers.
- Foster or adopt children in need of loving homes.
- Organize community events that bring people together and promote unity.
- Offer your professional skills pro bono to nonprofit o rganizations.
- Regularly donate blood or register as an organ donor.
- Care for abandoned or mistreated animals.
- Start a community garden to provide fresh produce for those in need.
- Teach literacy or language skills to immigrants or underprivileged individuals.
- Offer respite care for families with chronically ill members.
- Create care packages for deployed military personnel or their families.
- Volunteer at a crisis helpline, providing emotional support to those in distress.
- Organize clothing or book drives for underfunded schools or shelters.
- Offer transportation to medical appointments for those unable to drive.
- Provide companionship and assistance to individuals with disabilities.

CHAPTER 8

OFFER TRUST: MUHAMMAD YUNUS

The Person

Muhammad Yunus is the founder of Grameen Bank, which pioneered the microcredit model of lending money to the poor without requiring collateral. Yunus was awarded the Nobel Peace Prize in 2006, and in 2024 he became interim head of the Bangladeshi government.

The Lesson

It is easy to assume that the economic situation of people living in poverty is somehow their fault. What Muhammad Yunus made clear, however, is that most people in poverty want to participate and succeed. They are marginalized by economic and social forces and by insufficient education—including lack of financial literacy—but they have immense desire and potential to better themselves and contribute to their societies. By having faith in this potential, Yunus pointed the way for all of us to empower others through trust. The results can be life-changing for everyone involved.

Our Connection

I joined SNV Netherlands Development Organization (SNV) in 2007, and Yunus—who had just been awarded the Nobel Peace Prize for establishing Grameen Bank—was very much on my mind. I noticed a synergy between Grameen's philosophy and SNV's approach to alleviating poverty by empowering women. It was a very challenging but exciting time in development. It had become clear to many, including our group within SNV, that traditional strategies needed a radical rethink. SNV was taking a more entrepreneurial approach to reduce poverty. Our work was based on building local capacity and trust at the grassroots level by working hand in hand with key stakeholders in the business, government, and NGO sectors to deliver a more lasting impact. I was convinced that the poor had to be included—not as mere recipients of aid but as empowered entrepreneurs in their own right, receiving opportunity instead of alms. As I learned more about the so-called "base of the pyramid" model, the thinking of the entrepreneur and economist C. K. Prahalad (author of *The Fortune at the Bottom of the Pyramid: Eradicating Poverty Through Profits*) and Yunus (*Creating a World Without Poverty: How Social Business Can Transform Our Lives*) resonated strongly.

As with many such events in my life, it was through a combination of luck and personal outreach that I received an invitation to a luncheon to honor Yunus in Kolkata, India, in December 2007. There I met Yunus for the first time and had the privilege to experience his humility, empathy, and intelligence in person. When we spoke, I introduced the work of SNV and the role we were playing to fight poverty through building local capacity. Yunus was intrigued and wanted to learn more about our inclusive business approach. He asked me to attend a dinner event that evening, hosted by the industrialist Harshavardhan Neotia. It was another opportunity to listen to Yunus and learn about his work.

Upon returning to the US, I sent a note to SNV's CEO Dirk Elsen and global leadership, proposing that we invite Muhammad Yunus to join the SNV International Advisory Board (IAB). Agreement was swift and unanimous. That proved to be the easy part. Actually getting hold of Yunus on the phone at his home in Bangladesh took another six months, but in the end, my polite persistence paid off. When we finally spoke, I explained to Yunus why I thought his engagement with SNV's advisory board could help the work we were doing in the area of economic inclusion of the poor. I suppose I made a good case, for a formal letter was sent from SNV, and Yunus joined the IAB in February 2009.

Muhammad Yunus and the author

How Muhammad Yunus Bettered the World

The nation of Bangladesh was born on December 17, 1971, after a brief but intensely violent war of independence from Pakistan. Victory was costly. According to some estimates, three million Bangladeshis were killed, ten million had to leave the country, and up to thirty million were displaced within it. The war devastated the already weak economy of what had been East Pakistan, increasing the poverty and hardship of millions of people. Among the challenges facing the newly independent nation: reintegrating tens of millions of refugees, rebuilding destroyed infrastructure, restoring agriculture, and restarting industries. Among its most urgent needs was intellectual capital.

During the war, Muhammad Yunus held the position of assistant professor of economics at Middle Tennessee State University in the United States. He became deeply involved in advocacy work for his home country, helping to establish a citizen's committee and running the Bangladesh Information Center, which worked to raise awareness about the situation in Bangladesh and gather support for the independence movement. After the war, Yunus decided to return to Bangladesh and apply his immense talents more directly to the work of reconstruction.

He assumed a position as head of the economics department at Chittagong University, in the city of his birth. There he launched a project to study the economy of the nearby village of Jobra. He observed that if poor people had access to even small loans, it could make a huge difference in their lives. His first personal loan of twenty-seven dollars was distributed among forty-two women in the village of Jobra, and they were able to use that to support their small businesses and then repay him. It was clear to Yunus that these people were poor not because they lacked intelligence or were lazy. They were poor because the financial situation in the country did not enable them to widen their economic base. Yunus approached a local bank (Janata Bank) for a loan and was told that borrowers required collateral, which the poor by definition did not have. He saw the need for a banking system that would provide banking services to the poor, who were largely ignored by conventional banks. He also noticed that local money lenders were exploiting the poor by charging exorbitant interest rates. Without a fair source of credit, these poor villagers were trapped in a cycle of poverty and debt. He wanted to provide an alternative to these money lenders. Most importantly, Yunus noticed that financial independence had a significant impact on the status of women in a deeply patriarchal society. As in many countries of the world, hunger and poverty were more of an issue for women than for men. He believed that giving women the ability to earn an income was crucial not only in lifting families out of poverty, but also in empowering women and giving them a voice.

The Grameen Bank pilot program was born in 1976. Yunus defied conventional banking wisdom in structuring its credit program. Rather than demanding large, lump-sum payments, he instituted a daily payment program of small amounts that small borrowers could afford. How did Grameen know what the borrowers could afford? The answer was revolutionary: Trust.

First and foremost, Yunus trusts the poor. He recognizes their desire to prosper and participate, and the financial structures he built have encouraged that desire. In the Grameen system, trust plays the role performed by collateral in traditional banking. It incentivizes trustworthiness as the personal asset of the borrower. By lending to small groups of borrowers and withholding further loans to those who haven't repaid, Grameen also relies on a sort of social pressure to ensure that accounts are kept in the black. Unlike many in the banking sector, Yunus is primarily an educator—one who realizes that financial responsibility depends on financial literacy, a skill that is learned. That is why Grameen offers a range of educational opportunities, such as mandatory weekly meetings, that cultivate a culture of fiscal best practices.

Since so many borrowers were women, the concept threatened the traditional male hierarchy of banking. Established money lenders, who profited from high interest rates, saw the bank as a direct threat. There were other issues: Some 85 percent of poor women in Bangladesh could not read, and most of them were rarely free to leave home. It was a long and arduous journey, but Yunus was committed to his concept and determined that it succeed. He was so determined that he took a two-year absence from the university to officially join the project. By November of 1982, membership in the Grameen Bank had grown to 28,000. Finally, in 1983, a bank for the poor was born. As they say, the rest is history.

Today Grameen Bank stands as an unqualified success. According to the company's website, it boasts 40 zonal offices, 40 zonal audit offices, 240 area offices, and 2,568 branch offices. With over 23,690 employees, it has a presence in 94 percent of the villages in Bangladesh and serves nearly forty-five million people through 10.66 million borrower-members, 97 percent of whom are women. By November 2024, the Grameen

Bank had disbursed $39 million in loans, with a recovery rate of 96.39 percent.[42]

Reflecting on the scalability of the microcredit model, Yunus said, "The Grameen Bank is now a $2.5 billion banking enterprise in Bangladesh, while the microcredit model has spread to over fifty countries worldwide, from the US to Papua New Guinea, Norway to Nepal."[43] The US programs using the Grameen principle to address poverty-related problems are active in Arkansas, South Dakota, Oklahoma, and elsewhere.

Yunus has proven that microcredit can end poverty for many and reduce its severity for others. He has the vision of a poverty-free world by 2050, provided we create a level playing field for the poor. He believes that "in terms of human capability there is no difference between a poor person and a very privileged person. All human beings are packed with unlimited potential."[44] He argues that poverty is not created by the individual but by the system. Once the poor fall outside the system, it is very difficult to return to it, and the system actually begins to work against them.

To help the poor stay in touch with the system, he has expanded his efforts beyond microcredit. He created a cell phone company called Grameen Phone. His organization brought phones to the villages of Bangladesh and gave loans to the poor women to buy cell phones themselves, which they could then sell to make money. It became an instant success. He also created Grameen Shakti (Grameen Energy), which has popularized solar energy and biogas for home use, as well as environmentally friendly cookstoves. This is important in Bangladesh, where 70 percent of the population does not have access to electricity. The stories of Yunus's ingenuity and success are endless, and to me, they share a common thread: Trust.

Seeing potential where others see only risk, Yunus realized that social trust advances human well-being. It helps to create markets and wealth, manage corruption, and spur a robust civil society. According to Marc Epstein and Kristi Yuthas, "Trust is the basis of many aspects of microfinance operations and is a critical determinant of microfinance success."[45]

There is a lot of data on the positive impact of trust in organizations generally. According to the article "The Neuroscience of Trust" by Paul J. Zak, published in the *Harvard Business Review* in 2017, "People at high-trust companies report 74% less stress, 106% more energy at work, 50% higher productivity, 13% fewer sick days, 76% more engagement, 29% more satisfaction with their lives, [and] 40% less burnout than people at low-trust companies."

How Muhammad Yunus Made *Me* Better

Dirk Elsen and I saw SNV's International Advisory Board as a source of guidance on better ways to utilize our existing and future funding so as to make real differences in the lives of poor citizens. This is why we reached out to global thought leaders from Asia, Africa, and Latin America for knowledge, expertise, wisdom, innovation, and also for constructive criticism. In 2009, Elsen and I visited Yunus in Bangladesh for what turned out to be an important conversation. While supportive of our overall approach, Yunus raised some important questions:

- Why was SNV not using the core grant from the Dutch government to invest in specific poverty alleviation

initiatives that engaged members of the poor population, instead of hiring highly paid consultants from Europe and America?
- Would SNV be willing to compare two similar programs—one with our involvement and one without—to see if our involvement was making any difference?
- Were our workshops and trainings providing any tangible and sustainable benefits to the poor?

We responded positively about SNV's approach and the impact of our work, and also explained how SNV was transforming. For his part, Yunus shared examples of the work Grameen Bank was doing. Elsen and I felt it was a productive discussion, full of new perspectives, but we definitely left the meeting humbled, albeit more aware of the work that needed to be done. In particular, as Yunus so rightly observed, we needed to do a better job of documenting SNV's impact. For this, we needed more and better data at the ground level. Emerging technology could help, but the main thing was the will to use it and the expertise to use it well. We ultimately began to get a handle on this through our Management for Results initiative. From that time on, assessing impacts and documenting tangible results were not optional; they were integral parts of our mission to alleviate poverty.

How You Can Offer Trust *Now*

By getting involved with or otherwise supporting organizations that promote financial inclusion through microfinance or other means, you too can become part of the trust-based approach to lifting people out of poverty. As you explore ways to contribute, consider the following options:

- **Grameen Foundation**—Directly inspired by Yunus's work, the Foundation uses microfinance and technology to empower the poor, especially women. How to get involved: Visit their website to volunteer, donate, or explore job opportunities.
- **Kiva**—Enables individuals to lend small amounts to entrepreneurs worldwide, embodying the trust-based microfinance concept. How to get involved: Become a lender, volunteer as a translator, or join their internship program.
- **Accion**—Focuses on financial inclusion and innovative technologies to empower low-income individuals. How to get involved: Donate, explore career opportunities, or sign up for their newsletter.
- **BRAC**—Like Grameen Bank, BRAC originated in Bangladesh. It uses a holistic approach to development. How to get involved: Donate, volunteer, or apply for jobs and internships.
- **Opportunity International**—Provides microfinance services with a focus on savings programs. How to get involved: Donate, volunteer, or become an ambassador.
- **Women's World Banking**—Emphasizes women's financial inclusion, reflecting Yunus's focus on empowering women. How to get involved: Donate or explore career opportunities.
- **FINCA International**—Provides financial services to low-income entrepreneurs. How to get involved: Donate or apply for jobs and internships.

You can also make trust-based empowerment part of your daily life with these simple actions:

- Educate yourself about microfinance and its impact on poverty alleviation.
- Consider impact investing or socially responsible investing in your financial planning.
- Support local small businesses, especially those run by marginalized groups.
- Mentor aspiring entrepreneurs from underprivileged backgrounds.
- Advocate for financial inclusion and accessible banking services.
- Practice trust-based interactions in your personal and professional life.
- Share success stories of individuals lifted out of poverty through microcredit.
- Participate in or organize community savings groups.
- Volunteer with local organizations that provide financial literacy education.
- Engage in discussions about innovative approaches to poverty reduction.

CHAPTER 9

THINK DEEPLY: AMARTYA SEN

The Person

Amartya Sen is an economic theorist, teacher, and author who has had enormous influence in shaping the way people measure and address poverty. He received the Nobel Memorial Prize in Economic Sciences in 1998.

The Lesson

Throughout most of the past century, a person's income was the sole determinant of whether they were impoverished. Your income either put you below the poverty line or above it. By thinking deeply about poverty and human development, Amartya Sen came to understand that poverty is not merely a lack of income, but the inability of individuals to pursue their goals and live fulfilling lives. That insight—and the "capability approach" that grew out of it—has transformed how policymakers and organizations around the world approach poverty reduction. Most of us are not public intellectuals, yet there is a lesson here for everyone. By examining the world holistically, thinking deeply, and considering all aspects of a problem, we can help to create and implement more effective ways of improving the human condition.

Our Connection

Growing up in India, especially as a Bengali, I had heard of Dr. Amartya Sen. I knew that the Indian poet and writer (and Nobel laureate) Rabindranath Tagore had suggested the name "Amartya," which means "immortal," to Sen's parents, who belonged to the Bengali upper caste known as Baidya. However, I did not realize the impact of Sen's work in the field of economic theory until I launched the US office of SNV Netherlands Development Organization in Washington, DC, in 2007. In fact, I must admit that it was my Dutch colleagues who made me aware of Sen's extensive work on famine and inequality. I was rather amazed to learn about Sen's popularity globally—even Queen Máxima of the Netherlands had expressed an interest in meeting him.

That was almost ten years after Sen was awarded the 1998 Nobel Memorial Prize for his contributions to welfare economics and social choice theory and for his interest in the problems of the poorest members of society. Over the next few years, I raced to bring myself up to speed on the work of this thinker. But I always felt like the characters in *Alice in Wonderland*, running faster but never catching up. The reason was that Sen never stopped thinking, writing, teaching, accomplishing, and influencing. By the time I had learned about one achievement or accolade, he had piled on two more!

In December 2013, I was visiting my parents in Kolkata with my son, Ryan. One morning, I happened to read in the newspaper that Sen was visiting the city and would be appearing at the iconic Netaji Bhawan to discuss his book *An Uncertain Glory: India and Its Contradictions.* I immediately decided to attend and brought Ryan along for what I expected to be a memorable occasion. As expected, the modest space of this historic home was crowded with people eager to hear Sen speak. He did not disappoint. Sen examined the progress and challenges faced by India in various areas, including education, healthcare, gender inequality, poverty, and political participation. As he does in the book, Sen provided a critical analysis of India's development and offered insights into the country's potential for achieving more inclusive and sustainable growth.

After Sen's address, we made our way through the crowd, and I was able to have a brief conversation with him about SNV's work in poverty alleviation and good governance. My journey to know this amazing man more personally began that evening.

The author and Amartya Sen in Harvard Square

Soon after, Dirk Elsen, SNV's global CEO, and I devised a plan to ask Sen to join the SNV Global Advisory Board. We reached out to his office, and they agreed to allocate some time for a brief meeting between his teaching commitments at

Harvard University. We traveled to Cambridge, Massachusetts, the Boston enclave where this fabled university is located, and patiently waited outside his classroom. When Sen had concluded his class, we accompanied him to the cafeteria. He listened carefully about the work SNV was doing in more than thirty countries with smallholder farmers and was particularly interested in our initiatives in the area of women's empowerment. He was sufficiently impressed to agree to join the SNV Global Advisory Board on the spot, albeit with two caveats: that we send him regular updates on SNV's work and that we not demand too much of his time. Of course, we agreed instantly.

As the founder and executive director of SNV USA, part of my duties involved managing the relationship with SNV's Global Advisory Board members. As promised, I kept Sen abreast of key developments and sought guidance when needed.

Ever since the initial encounter at Harvard, I had wanted to meet with Sen again in person. I felt that there was so much more that SNV—and I—could learn from him and his work. Finally an opportunity arose. In April 2015, we met for lunch near his home in Harvard Square. The discussion that afternoon was wide-ranging—from SNV's work on global poverty alleviation and my work with the younger generation to combat violence, to his books, his engagement with Nalanda University, and his views on various political parties in India. He wanted to know more about me, and given his own work with the poor, he was intrigued to learn of my father's social activism work in West Bengal and the fact that it had landed my dad in jail during the Emergency period (1975–77).

It was one of the most stimulating and rewarding conversations I have had in my entire life! One memorable moment during that lunch came when I asked Sen when the world could expect his memoir. His response reflected his unique life journey, as he explained that the memoir needed to capture his life not only in the US but also in India, Bangladesh, and the UK—and that would take time. Six years later, in 2021, Sen's memoir, *Home in the World: A Memoir*, finally appeared. I bought it immediately and devoured it. The book is extremely thought provoking, touching on subjects as varied as Sen's childhood (in Dhaka, Myanmar, and Santiniketan), the rivers of Bengal, Bengali society, the Second World War and its impact on the world, and Sen's thoughts on liberty and freedom.

Interestingly for a memoir, the book does not really conclude. For all of its breadth, it is like a river that flows on, with no end in sight. Because for Sen, there is no retirement.

How Amartya Sen Bettered the World

One of Sen's contributions is the concept of "capability approach," which argues that poverty is not simply the lack of income or resources, but the inability of individuals to pursue their own goals and live a fulfilling life. He argues that poverty can be reduced by expanding the capabilities of individuals to live a life they value and have reason to value. This idea has had a significant impact on how policymakers and international organizations approach poverty reduction. Sen has also been a strong advocate for social and economic policies that address the root causes of poverty, such as education, health care, and economic opportunities, as well as emphasizing the importance of empowering individuals through education and training. Sen has made significant contributions to social choice theory, which explores how collective decisions are made in societies.

He has influenced countless individuals through his teaching positions at a number of prestigious universities, including Harvard, Cambridge, and Oxford.

Edward Luce of the *Financial Times* captured Sen perfectly in a review of his memoir. "Sen is more than an economist, a moral philosopher or even an academic. He is a life-long campaigner, through scholarship and activism, via friendships and the occasional enemy, for a more noble idea of home—and therefore of the world."[46]

How Amartya Sen Made *Me* Better

During an interview with Sen in 2021, Christina Pazzanese of *The Harvard Gazette* asked him why he remained so busy twenty-three years after receiving his Nobel Memorial Prize. Sen replied, "People have given up hope that I might retire. But I like working, I must say. I've been very lucky. I've never done, when I think about it, work that I was not interested in. That is a very good reason to go on."[47]

Even now, at the age of ninety-one—an age at which many if not most public intellectuals have long since yielded the stage to those younger than themselves—Sen remains a professor at Harvard, using his platform to raise awareness about issues related to poverty, inequality, and social justice. He is credited as one of the founders of modern social choice theory, which explores how collective decisions are made in societies, and his contributions have had a significant impact on the fields of economics, social welfare, and political philosophy. His work continues to influence scholars and policy makers around the world.

I am most fortunate to have stayed in touch with Sen over the years. I remain drawn to him for his moral clarity, his compassion, his belief in a secular India, and his lifetime of work to empower vulnerable communities. He continues to inspire me not just for his ideas, his intellect, and the impact he has had globally, but also for his passion and relentless desire to improve the lives of others, even at an age when most people have long since retired.

After reading Sen's memoir, it is clear to me that my own retirement may have to wait much longer than I had originally planned. So much still needs to be done, and there is no real reason why I should not be among those who are doing it.

How You Can Think Deeply *Now*

Worldwide poverty has been an intractable problem for so long that many organizations have been created to address it in innovative ways. As you consider which of the following to support or get involved with, you might gain insights that lead you toward new paths of research and advocacy.

- **The Pratichi Trust**—Founded by Sen to work on education, health, and gender equality in India and Bangladesh. How to get involved: Donate to support their projects or explore volunteer opportunities.
- **United Nations Development Programme (UNDP)**—Incorporates Sen's capability approach in its Human Development Index. How to get involved: Explore volunteer opportunities, internships, or job openings.
- **Human Development and Capability Association (HDCA)**—Promotes research and networking in the

field of human development and capability approach. How to get involved: Become a member, attend conferences, or contribute to their journal.

- **Abdul Latif Jameel Poverty Action Lab (J-PAL)**—Conducts rigorous evaluations of poverty alleviation programs, in line with Sen's emphasis on evidence-based policy. How to get involved: Apply for research positions, attend their courses, or use their resources.
- **Innovations for Poverty Action (IPA)**—This nonprofit research and policy organization discovers and promotes effective solutions to global poverty problems through evidence-based approaches to development. How to get involved: Explore job openings, internships, or volunteer opportunities. You can also donate to support their research, attend their events, or use their research findings to inform your own work or advocacy efforts.
- **RESULTS Educational Fund**—This grassroots advocacy organization works to create the public and political will to end poverty. How to get involved: Join a local RESULTS group, become an advocate, participate in their campaigns, attend their national conference, or donate to support their work. They also offer fellowship programs for young leaders.

In keeping with Sen's emphasis on expanding human capabilities and freedoms, here are some actions you can take to contribute directly:

- Educate yourself about multidimensional poverty and share this knowledge with others.

- Support local educational initiatives, such as tutoring programs or adult literacy classes.
- Advocate for improved access to healthcare in your community.
- Promote gender equality in your personal and professional life.
- Engage in discussions about social and economic policies that affect vulnerable populations.
- Support businesses that prioritize fair labor practices and worker empowerment.
- Volunteer with organizations that provide skill-building opportunities for disadvantaged individuals.
- Encourage critical thinking and open dialogue in your social circles.
- Stay informed about global development issues and share reliable information with others.
- Practice and promote inclusive decision-making in your workplace or community groups.
- Support initiatives that provide access to information and technology in underserved areas.
- Participate in or organize community forums on local development issues.
- Encourage political participation and voting rights awareness.
- Mentor someone from a disadvantaged background in your field of expertise.
- Promote cultural activities that celebrate diversity and foster understanding.

CHAPTER 10

RESPECT YOUR "OPPONENTS": JOE BIDEN

The Person

After representing Delaware for thirty-six years in the US Senate, Joe Biden served as vice president under Barack Obama before becoming the forty-sixth president of the United States.

The Lesson

In these politically polarized times, it is easy to cast scorn upon—or even demonize—those who hold opposing views. But if we stop for a minute, if we remember that people on the "other side" are also citizens with a right to their beliefs and opinions—citizens who might even be members of our own family—and that a working democracy depends on mutual respect among its citizens as well as its leaders, then we create a better environment for productive discourse and informed decisions. Joe Biden, with his commitment to decency, honesty, and empathy in both his personal life and his politics, exemplifies this mindset.

Our Connection

Many years ago, a brief encounter with Senator Joe Biden engraved forever in my heart the importance of friendship and decency in politics.

In 2002, I attended a social gathering in Washington, DC, at which two senior senators were present: John McCain of Arizona, a Republican, and Joe Biden of Delaware, a Democrat. I spoke briefly and cordially with each. My conversation with Senator McCain focused on service-disabled veterans and the steps we could take as a nation to honor their sacrifices by creating more opportunities for them. During my conversation with Senator Biden, I asked, "Am I shaking the hand of the next president of the United States?" His response took me by surprise. He smiled and gestured affectionately toward McCain. "No," he said. "That's him."

Joe Biden and the author in 2002

Even as a complete outsider, I could sense the deep and abiding respect between these men from different ends of the political spectrum. They were political rivals, yes, but also friends and fellow statesmen engaged in the effort of maintaining and strengthening democracy.

Encyclopedia Britannica defines decency as "polite, moral, and honest behavior and attitudes that show respect for other people."[48] The emphasis here is on behavior, how one actually acts in the world. As such, decency is essential to a functioning democracy as it fosters mutual respect and trust between citizens and their leaders.

Biden doesn't just understand this, he lives it. As Walter Shapiro, award-winning journalist and lecturer in political science at Yale University, wrote in an opinion piece in *Roll Call*, "During the more than four decades, dating back to the Nixon administration, that Biden has been in public life, there have been more charismatic political leaders and wiser policymakers. But it is hard to think of anyone who, in basic human terms, has been more decent than Joe Biden."[49]

As a fundamental attitude, decency encompasses the ability to walk a mile in the shoes of someone else, to practice empathy in all things. Throughout his career, Biden has demonstrated a deep understanding of the struggles that many Americans face, working tirelessly to address issues such as healthcare, civil rights, and economic inequality. He has been praised for his ability to connect with people from all walks of life and for his willingness to listen to different perspectives. Like the people he serves, he has weathered personal tragedy and professional setbacks, only to bounce back and renew the fight for what he believes in.

This quality is evident in moments that transcend politics, those moments of great hardship—such as a natural disaster or a school shooting—when the nation looks to the President as the "consoler in chief." This, and not ideology, is Biden's true calling. When tornadoes devastated towns in western Kentucky—a deeply "red" part of the country—Biden's compassion, sincerity, and support won the trust and respect of people who had seen him only as a political enemy. He promised federal assistance and showed true empathy for the plight of the traumatized residents.

How Joe Biden Bettered the World

One must understand the immense personal losses endured by Biden to appreciate how he made the world better. It is ironic that, although he was among the youngest US senators ever, he was perhaps the most deeply shaped by loss and grief. In 1972, he lost his wife and baby daughter in a car accident. To be with his sons—both critically injured in the accident—he began commuting from Wilmington to Washington every day, a routine he maintained for decades out of devotion to his family. Then, in 2015, one of his surviving sons passed away from a rare brain cancer. These devastating events didn't just affect Biden personally. They also influenced major decisions in his political career, from his priorities in the Senate to his decision not to run for president in 2016.

Over the years, I have heard and read numerous stories about Biden. Almost every story highlights his working-class background, his Catholic values, his mother's principles of social justice, and his father's mantra to keep getting up after being knocked down as the forces that have made him the relatable, authentic, empathetic—and also resilient—person he is.

Scholars, historians, and economists will ultimately be the judges of how President Biden improved the world. It is common for every president to get credit for things initiated by someone else and get blamed for things caused by a different administration. Biden's supporters will point to many domestic accomplishments, including the COVID-19 response, the American Rescue Plan, the $1.2 trillion infrastructure investment bill, job creation, social justice and equity, and others. On the international front, they will point to bringing the US back into the Paris Agreement; strengthening alliances with NATO and other international partners; reaffirming the US commitment to global security; emphasizing diplomacy and multilateralism in addressing global challenges, including nuclear proliferation and regional conflicts; and proposing comprehensive immigration reform to address the status of undocumented immigrants and improve the immigration system. They would also cite increased aid to support foreign development projects, disaster relief, and poverty reduction in developing countries. Biden made history by picking California senator Kamala Harris—who would go on to become the first woman of color to be nominated for president by a major political party—as his running mate. He also appointed the first Black woman to the Supreme Court, Justice Ketanji Brown Jackson. In each of these actions, President Biden has aimed to create a more just, prosperous, and secure world—domestically and internationally.

Biden's critics on the right and left will have different views on many of his accomplishments. His presidency was hampered by low approval ratings, mostly resulting from concerns about high consumer prices, comparatively lenient border policies, the chaotic withdrawal of US forces from Afghanistan, and his inability to achieve peace in Gaza.

Such a contradictory legacy is inevitable, I think. It is easy to sit on the sidelines and criticize. But to really accomplish something, it is necessary to wade into the fray, to find common ground with opponents, to take responsibility for making tough but necessary decisions. Policy is not made by purists, but by pragmatists, like Biden, who are driven to produce results that make a difference in the lives of people. By this token, Biden may suffer more than other presidents in the eyes of posterity precisely *because* he has accomplished so much.

How Joe Biden Made *Me* Better

My interaction with then-Senator Biden and Senator John McCain brought back numerous memories from my childhood. Many of my father's close friends belonged to the opposition party that put him in prison for his political views, yet these friends respected my father and admired his courage and tenacity. That kind of mutual respect was on display between Biden and McCain.

As Biden demonstrates, politics is collaborative, and to get things done, you have to work with others—many of whom will not share your views. To find the votes you need, you may only get 10 percent of your dream, but that's better than nothing, and it's the beginning of a conversation that can grow over time and eventually bring you closer to 20 or 30 percent—or more. In the meantime, you have established a foundation of decency and respect with your opponents, a modicum of trust that can help you expand the conversation in other directions, with beneficial results for all.

One of my good friends is a former US Marine, a devout Christian, and a good and honest man. We disagree on many political and social issues, but what binds us together is our twenty-plus years of friendship, genuine respect for each other and our respective families, and love for our country.

Throughout his career, Biden demonstrated a deep understanding of many Americans' struggles, working tirelessly to address healthcare, civil rights, immigration, the environment, national security, economic inequality, and many more areas of concern. In my travels throughout the world, including rural America, I also try to connect with and understand the individuals I meet. I have found that there are always commonalities and that sometimes they may surprise you.

How You Can Respect Your "Opponents" *Now*

In an election, we commonly refer to those on either side of the ballot as opponents, but as citizens, we're not really opponents at all; we're people with opposing political views. Once we think of it this way, we're already cultivating respect for one another.

The following organizations and initiatives can help you take Biden's example of decency to the next level:

- **Bipartisan Policy Center**—Promotes bipartisanship to address key challenges facing the nation. How to get involved: Attend events, use their resources, or support their initiatives.
- **Braver Angels (formerly Better Angels)**—Brings together Red and Blue Americans to depolarize America. How to get involved: Join a workshop, become a moderator, or start a local alliance.

- **Future Caucus (The Millennial Action Project)**—Works to activate young policymakers to bridge the partisan divide. How to get involved: Join their network, attend events, or support their programs.
- **Committee for a Responsible Federal Budget**—Educates the public on issues with significant fiscal policy impact. How to get involved: Use their resources, attend their events, or support their work.
- **The Village Square**—Organizes community conversations on divisive issues. How to get involved: Attend local events or start a chapter in your area.
- **The American Exchange Project**—Connects high school students from different political and cultural backgrounds. How to get involved: Apply as a student or support the program.
- **The Aspen Institute's Citizenship and American Identity Program**—Addresses how Americans can find common ground. How to get involved: Attend their events or use their resources.

There are a number of simple actions you can take on your own to promote civil discourse and foster mutual respect:

- Actively listen to people with different political views without interrupting or arguing.
- Share articles from reputable sources across the political spectrum on social media.
- Engage in respectful political discussions with friends and family who have different views.
- Attend local town hall meetings and ask thoughtful questions to politicians from all parties.

- Practice empathy by trying to understand the motivations behind opposing viewpoints.
- Volunteer for organizations that promote bipartisanship or civil discourse.
- Avoid using derogatory language or name-calling when discussing political opponents.
- Participate in community events that bring together people from diverse backgrounds.
- Challenge your own assumptions and biases about political issues and candidates.
- Use social media to promote civil discourse rather than partisan attacks.
- Support politicians and initiatives that prioritize bipartisanship and compromise.
- Practice finding common ground in personal and professional disagreements.
- Educate yourself on the complexities of political issues from multiple perspectives.

CHAPTER 11

HONOR YOUR PRINCIPLES: JOHN MCCAIN

The Person

John McCain (1936–2018) was a US Navy pilot, prisoner of war, and US Senator known for placing his principles above party politics.

The Lesson

Nearly everyone can think of a time in adolescence when they put the desire for popularity ahead of their allegiance to a true friend. You might still regret such behavior in your own life. As an adult—and especially for a leader—similar forces play out, yet the stakes are even higher. What was once devotion to a friend is now a matter of adherence to one's principles. Principles and the courage to put them into action are supremely important in a democracy because they enable individuals to stand up for their beliefs, regardless of class or affiliation, even in the face of opposition or adversity. Courageous leaders are willing to take bold steps to address critical issues, even at the risk of their political careers. There is no better example of this for me than Senator John McCain.

Our Connection

In 2002, I attended a social gathering in Washington, DC, at which McCain was present. We spoke briefly and cordially, but meaningfully. Our conversation focused on veterans, especially service-disabled veterans, and on the steps our government should take to honor their sacrifices by creating more opportunities for them. McCain listened intently and mentioned several initiatives he had in mind to support veterans. This wasn't just chitchat. I had the impression of his full attention, his expertise, his concern. Here was an elected representative actually problem-solving with a constituent. In later years I learned that McCain had introduced the Clay Hunt Suicide Prevention for American Veterans Act (2015) to increase access to mental health support for veterans. It has become law. McCain also co-sponsored an amendment to the National Defense Authorization Act of 2016 to cover the travel costs for families of troops killed in

John McCain

overseas missions. The amendment was adopted by the Senate by unanimous consent. My encounter with McCain left me with an indelible impression of his sincerity. American politics is full of big, bold words; John McCain filled those words with actual substance.

How John McCain Bettered the World

John McCain was a decorated pilot who spent more than five years as a prisoner of war during the Vietnam conflict. Despite being subjected to torture, he refused to be released before other prisoners who had been held longer, demonstrating his commitment to the military code of conduct and his personal sense of honor.

The experience of captivity had a profound impact on him and informed his approach to public service. As a senator from Arizona from 1987 until his death in 2018, McCain was a strong advocate for human rights and was known for his opposition to torture and other forms of inhumane treatment of captured enemy combatants.

In the Senate, the courage that enabled him to survive captivity expressed itself in political independence. He was willing to break with his own party when he felt it was the just thing to do. In 2017, for example, when the entire Republican caucus lined up to repeal important provisions of the Affordable Care Act, McCain cast the deciding vote to uphold them, preserving access to healthcare for millions of Americans.

His principled independence was legendary. In 2008, he was the Republican candidate for president, pitted against Barack Obama, a largely unknown young senator from Illinois whose African-American ethnicity was a problem for some voters. At one of McCain's town hall events in Minnesota, a woman in the audience suggested that Obama was an "Arab," which for certain segments of the electorate was—and, sadly, remains—code for "terrorist." Without blinking, McCain responded, respectfully but firmly, "No, ma'am. He's a decent family man [and] citizen that I just happen to have disagreements with on fundamental issues and that's what this campaign's all about."[50] Despite receiving boos from his audience, McCain stood his ground.

Even today, that response stands out for me as a sign of honor. He could so easily have pandered to prejudice for votes, and then maybe retracted it, the damage having been done, but as always, he took the high road. He may not have said what some wanted to hear, but he was widely praised for his decency and courage.

At a town hall meeting in Ohio during the campaign, McCain told his audience—many of whom had lost their jobs due to outsourcing and free trade agreements—the level truth rather than promising them the impossible. "I know that's small comfort to you, but I can't look you in the eye and tell you that those steel mills are coming back," he said, explaining that, if elected, he intended to increase opportunities for job training in the new economy. And with his characteristically relatable sense of humor, he reminded them that, like his once-ailing campaign, "sometimes you get a second chance."[51]

McCain has been emblematic of another kind of courage: the courage to consider other viewpoints, to stay open to compromise and conciliation, to trust in the good faith of one's adversaries based on a common set of values and traditions. This enabled him to co-author the Bipartisan Campaign Reform Act with Senator Russ Feingold (D-WI), which banned so-called "soft money" contributions to political parties, usually from corporations and large organizations, in order to encourage small donations of "hard money" for individual candidates, widely seen as a democratizing piece of legislation.

This approach made McCain a champion of American moderates. He was a vocal critic of extremism and bigotry in all its forms. He publicly repudiated hate speech and intolerance and was known for his opposition to far-right groups and individuals.

What was his secret? In his book, *Character is Destiny*, McCain uses Shakespeare's enduring guidance—"to thine own self be true"—to illustrate the importance of integrity for today's world. This book is a reflection of the value McCain placed on character. In one particularly powerful chapter, he wrote, "It is your character, and your character alone, that will make your life happy or unhappy. That is all that really passes for destiny. And you choose it. No one else can give it to you or deny it to you. No rival can steal it from you. And no friend can give it to you. Others can encourage you to make the right choices or discourage you. But you choose."[52]

John McCain bettered the world by setting examples. It may have been hard to pin down his ideology, but the way he lived his life, treated others, conducted himself in affairs of state, made difficult decisions, represented his state and country—all of these were instantly understandable and influential.

Jonathan Allen of NBC News shared the following observation regarding John McCain's lasting impact on American politics: "McCain's legacy will be about a trait, more than any individual cause, that was both larger than himself and is in perilously short supply in American politics right now: honor.

In the hours after McCain's death. . . .it was a word that showed up repeatedly in statements from Republicans and Democrats, a group so politically diverse it included former Vice President Joe Biden, a Democrat who was on the ticket when Barack Obama defeated McCain for the presidency in 2008, and Sen. Ted Cruz, a Texas Republican who is among the most conservative members of Congress."[53]

Perhaps the most telling testament to McCain's impact can be seen in the many individuals and organizations working to carry on his legacy of political independence, courage, honor, and service:

- The McCain Institute for International Leadership was founded in 2012 by the late senator and Arizona State University (ASU). The Institute focuses on a number of different areas, including human rights, national security, democracy, and global development. It conducts research, provides leadership training and education, and works with partners around the world to develop innovative solutions to complex global problems. Currently McCain's widow Cindy, the McCain family, and the senator's trusted friends continue to advance his mission through the Institute.
- The IRI's (The International Republican Institute) McCain Fellowship for Freedom (MFF) brings together young leaders from around the world to continue the legacy of IRI's twenty-five-year Chairman Senator John McCain of fostering a new generation of democratic leaders on every continent.
- Congress created the Cyberspace Solarium Commission (CSC) in the John S. McCain National Defense

> Authorization Act for Fiscal Year 2019 to "develop a consensus on a strategic approach to defending the United States in cyberspace against cyber attacks of significant consequences."[54]

* In dedicating a library in Arizona in honor of his longtime friend John McCain, President Joe Biden remarked, "John is one of those patriots who, when they die, their voices are never silent. They still speak to us. They tug at both our hearts and our conscience."[55]

How John McCain Made *Me* Better

John McCain is a shining example of courage and honesty that is especially important to me, given my own story. From the moment I arrived in the United States from India as a young man, I have cherished and admired those qualities in so-called "ordinary" Americans, from the Carolinas to the Midwest to the Pacific Northwest, in small towns and big cities alike. Certainly, among these diverse multitudes one can find less charitable individuals and groups, and extremism is on the rise here as well as in other countries. But I've found that for every zealot espousing a closed-minded ideology, there are tens of thousands of Americans—Republicans, Democrats, and independents—whose open minds and open hearts provide a critical mass of kindness and understanding. After almost four decades of residing in the US and participating in American life, I have come to see that all that kindness and understanding rests on a foundation of courage and decency. Taken together, these qualities not only make an open society possible, they also fuel our economic and social progress, and are vital to our national security, and our global leadership. They might seem intangible, but they become concrete in policies and actions that affect real lives. In the post-9/11 world, the United States adopted a new "ends justifies the means" approach to fighting terrorism, adopting waterboarding and other methods of torture in order to gain information from captives. McCain saw clearly that this was the surest way to lose the fight. While he was a military man, he recognized that a nation's true strength lies not in the volume of its weaponry, but in its dedication to its stated values.

At a meeting with President George W. Bush and Senator John Warner (R-VA) at the White House in December 2005, McCain expressed this viewpoint eloquently. "The United States is not like the terrorists. . . . What we are is a nation that upholds values and standards of behavior and treatment of all people, no matter how evil or bad they are," McCain said, adding that rejecting torture "will help us enormously in winning the war for the hearts and minds of people throughout the world in the war on terror."[56]

As an immigrant to America, I was won over by the highest ideals that this nation attempts to embody. John McCain—and his legacy of honor and goodwill—likewise holds a special place in both my heart and my mind.

How You Can Honor Your Principles *Now*

Among the principles that John McCain held dear were democracy, human rights, bipartisan cooperation and problem solving, courageous leadership and public service, support for veterans, and opposition to torture. Regardless of your particular principles and priorities, his example points the way toward maintaining them in the face of opposition. The following organizations have missions that intersect with some of McCain's priorities and can give you ideas for how they—or others like them—might align with and amplify your own.

- **The McCain Institute**—Advances character-driven leadership based on security, economic opportunity, freedom, and human dignity. How to get involved: Attend events, apply for programs, or support their initiatives.
- **International Republican Institute (IRI) McCain Fellowship for Freedom**—Fosters a new generation of democratic leaders worldwide. How to get involved: Apply for the fellowship or support their programs.
- **Human Rights Watch**—Founded in 1978, this organization investigates and reports on human rights abuses around the world. How to get involved: Make an emergency gift to support people in places of crisis and conflict, keep up with the latest human rights issues and news, or learn how to take action to counter injustice.
- **Center for Victims of Torture**—Works to heal the wounds of torture on individuals, their families, and their communities. How to get involved: Donate, volunteer, or advocate for their cause.
- **Amnesty International**—Campaigns for human rights worldwide. How to get involved: Join a local group, sign petitions, or donate.
- **International Rescue Committee (IRC)**—Responds to humanitarian crises and helps people whose lives are shattered by conflict and disaster to survive, recover, and gain control of their future. How to get involved: Volunteer, donate, or advocate for their cause.

- **Anti-Defamation League (ADL)**—Fights antisemitism and all forms of hate, works to defend democratic ideals and protect civil rights for all. How to get involved: Report incidents, participate in their programs, or donate.
- **Freedom House**—Works to defend human rights and promote democratic change, with a focus on political rights and civil liberties. How to get involved: Use their resources, support their advocacy efforts, or donate.
- **Veterans of Foreign Wars (VFW)**—Advocates for veterans' rights and provides support services to veterans and their families. How to get involved: Join if eligible, volunteer, or donate to their programs.

Beyond involvement with these or other organizations, there are plenty of ways that you can cultivate the personal courage and integrity to honor your principles:

- Stand up for your beliefs, even when it's unpopular or difficult.
- Engage in respectful dialogue with those who hold different views.
- Educate yourself on important issues from diverse, reliable sources.
- Speak out against discrimination or injustice when you witness it.
- Support political candidates based on their principles rather than party affiliation.
- Volunteer for organizations that align with your values.
- Encourage open and honest discussions about difficult topics.

- Practice active listening and empathy in conversations with others.
- Challenge your own assumptions and biases regularly.
- Participate in local government or community organizations.
- Write to your representatives about issues that matter to you.
- Mentor others in ethical leadership and decision-making.
- Share stories of principled leaders to inspire others.
- Practice moral courage in your daily life by making ethical choices, even when they're difficult.

PART II
RISE

CHAPTER 12

MAKE YOUR GIFT MATTER: JOSÉ ANDRÉS

The Person

José Andrés is a renowned Spanish-American chef, restaurateur, and humanitarian, best known for popularizing the concept of tapas (small plates) in the United States.

The Lesson

Everyone possesses unique skills and talents. These gifts are valuable—whether it's cooking, teaching, inventing, managing, caring for patients, organizing, or any other ability. When our talents are directed toward helping others and addressing societal challenges, they can serve a purpose beyond personal success. And they can have a ripple effect, encouraging more people to contribute their own talents for the greater good. Andrés's example has inspired many chefs and others throughout the world to engage in philanthropy and social causes. With a little creative thinking—and awareness of the needs in our communities—each of us can find ways to make our gifts matter even more than they already do.

Our Connection

Globally, two million people die each year from illnesses associated with harmful and inefficient cooking and heating practices. As someone who developed asthma at a young age from inhaling the smoke from our family stove—which burned cow dung and coal—I was especially excited to learn about the Global Alliance for Clean Cookstoves (GACC), now known as the Clean Cooking Alliance (CCA), through which I would eventually meet Chef José Andrés. Launched in 2010, CCA is a public-private partnership hosted by the United Nations Foundation. Its stated purpose is to save lives, improve livelihoods, empower women, and protect the environment by creating a thriving global market for clean and efficient household cooking solutions.

As CEO of SNV USA, and in consultation with SNV leadership in the Netherlands, I decided to join this important alliance. By providing alternatives to cooking methods like the ones I grew up with, CCA seeks to reduce the incidence of pneumonia, lung cancer, bronchitis, and cardiovascular disease, especially in women and children—and to help reduce emissions of carbon dioxide, methane, and black carbon, all of which contribute to climate change.

The Alliance was launched to get millions of households to adopt clean cookstoves and fuels by 2020. Its work has been instrumental in increasing awareness about the benefits of clean cooking solutions and improving the lives of millions of people worldwide. As of 2023, more than 1.5 billion people have gained access to clean cooking since CCA's founding in 2010.[57]

After joining CCA as culinary ambassador in 2011, Andrés worked with US Secretary of State Hillary Clinton, Global Ambassador Julia Roberts, and the Alliance's many partners (including SNV) to raise awareness about this issue. In 2012, Andrés and I participated in a panel discussion that focused on the need for clean cookstoves in developing countries.

The author (second from left) and José Andrés (fifth from left) among other panelists at a Global Alliance for Clean Cookstoves discussion

Although this was the first time I met him, I already knew a bit about Andrés and the impact he could have. In 1993, before I left for India, my office was in a rundown building at 627 E Street NW, in Washington, DC. There was a nightclub (the Insect Club) on the ground floor, directly below our office. The neighborhood was part of the Penn Quarter, an area strong on vacant lots, underused buildings, and crime, and weak on dining and entertainment options. When I returned to the area five years later, I could hardly recognize the now-bustling commercial quarter. Across from our old office stood Jaleo, a trendy restaurant opened by José Andrés. Along with other pioneering establishments, Jaleo helped to attract more restaurants, shops, and cultural institutions to the area, contributing to the revitalization and growth of the Penn Quarter into one of DC's most dynamic neighborhoods.

How José Andrés Bettered the World

Born in Mieres, Spain, in 1969, Andrés emigrated to the United States in the early 1990s with fifty dollars in his pocket. Despite his limited resources, he pursued his passion for cooking and worked his way up in the culinary world. His story is an inspiring example of determination, hard work, and the pursuit of dreams. It is also a model of social entrepreneurship.

In 2010, in the wake of a devastating earthquake in Haiti, Andrés founded World Central Kitchen (WCK). As described by *Leaders Magazine*, this nonprofit organization provides "fresh meals in response to crises, while working to build resilient food systems with locally-led solutions. . . . By partnering with organizations on the ground and activating a network of local restaurants, food trucks, and emergency kitchens, WCK serves comforting meals to survivors of disasters quickly and effectively. To support regional economies, WCK prioritizes purchasing local ingredients to cook with or distribute directly to families in need."[58]

Jose Andrés explains the WCK approach this way: "We don't just deliver raw ingredients and expect people to fend for themselves. And we don't just dump free food into a disaster zone: we source and hire locally wherever we can, to jump-start economic recovery through food. After a disaster, food is the fastest way to rebuild our sense of community. We can put people back to work preparing it, and we can put lives back together by fighting hunger."[59]

WCK has served over 400 million meals[60] in crisis zones around the world, including Puerto Rico, Lebanon, Australia, Texas, Louisiana, and Gaza. More recently, WCK has built up a Food Producer Network to help create resilience ahead of the next disaster. It trains aspiring chefs in skills and safety to build their careers and the food economy, and it advocates for more hunger relief and better nutrition. And it launched a $1 billion climate disaster fund to support communities impacted by the climate crisis.

"Food relief is not just a meal that keeps hunger away," Andrés said in an interview with *Leaders Magazine*. "It's a plate of hope. It tells you in your darkest hour that someone, somewhere, cares about you."[61]

The efforts of Andrés and the World Central Kitchen go well beyond feeding the hungry. They have also built school kitchens, distributed clean cookstoves, provided culinary training, and formed social enterprise ventures—such as a fish processing plant—that empower people and strengthen economies through skill-building and jobs.

Widely recognized for both his culinary and his humanitarian work, Andrés has been honored by the James Beard Foundation, which named him Best Chef of the Mid-Atlantic Region in 2003, as well as Humanitarian of the Year in 2018; *Time* magazine, which included him on the list of the World's 100 Most Influential People in 2012 and 2018; and President

Barack Obama, who awarded Andrés the National Humanities Medal in 2015.

How José Andrés Made *Me* Better

Andrés's work illustrates the power of using your gifts—and the skills acquired in developing them—to help others. Not only have his humanitarian efforts expanded his reach and influence, but they have also helped to meet the world's needs in ways he could have hardly imagined when he first built his career as a chef.

In my years of serving nonprofit organizations in leadership roles, I refined my organizational skills as I faced the daily challenges of bringing people together to meet difficult goals. At the time, I didn't think of these skills as a gift—or even an aptitude. Yet in the light of Andrés's example, I later realized they were both.

Beginning in 2018, I became immersed in efforts to protect vulnerable children around the world. My experience as CEO of SOS Children's Villages USA gave me valuable knowledge of the sector committed to housing children in need. After moving on from that role, I asked myself what someone like José Andrés would do in my position. How could I combine my organizational skills with my knowledge of helping children and apply them to do more good in the world? That was when I became involved in the Ousri Family Foundation's projects in India and Morocco, which seek to fund local organizations that can get kids off the streets and into a home, give them access to a proper education, and provide a healthy environment in which to grow.

Sometimes all it takes to unlock new doors is knowing what has been possible for others.

How You Can Make Your Gift Matter *Now*

José Andrés's story teaches us that our gifts can find uses that exceed the expected. To someone dining at a restaurant, a meal is often seen as a combination of convenience and entertainment. But to someone in need, a meal can provide comfort and hope—in addition to vital sustenance. Most of us are not world-renowned chefs, but we can all do something to combat world hunger. While you're considering ways to make your own gift matter, here are some food-related organizations that you can support:

- **World Central Kitchen (WCK)**—Provides fresh meals in response to crises while building resilient food systems. How to get involved: Volunteer, donate, or participate in their chef training programs.
- **Clean Cooking Alliance (CCA)**—Works to create a thriving global market for clean cooking solutions. How to get involved: Support their initiatives, spread awareness, or contribute to research efforts.
- **James Beard Foundation**—Celebrates, nurtures, and honors chefs and other leaders making America's food culture more delicious, diverse, and sustainable. How to get involved: Attend events, apply for scholarships, or donate.
- **Feeding America**—Nationwide network of food banks that feeds more than forty million people in the US

through food pantries, soup kitchens, shelters, and other community-based agencies. How to get involved: Volunteer, donate, or advocate.

- **The Hunger Project**—Works to end hunger and poverty by pioneering sustainable, grassroots, women-centered strategies. How to get involved: Donate, fundraise, or become an activist.
- **Action Against Hunger**—Leads the global fight against hunger, saving the lives of malnourished children and ensuring families can access clean water, food, and training. How to get involved: Donate, fundraise, or apply for job opportunities.
- **Slow Food**—A global, grassroots organization that prevents the disappearance of local food cultures and traditions. How to get involved: Join a local chapter, participate in events, or support their campaigns.

You can also take steps as an individual to improve the food system for all:

- Support local food initiatives and farmers' markets.
- Reduce food waste in your daily life.
- Learn about food insecurity in your area and ways to address it.
- Practice conscious consumption by choosing ethically sourced products.
- Organize or participate in community meals or food drives.
- Share meals with neighbors, especially those who might be in need.

- Advocate for policies that address hunger and food insecurity.
- Learn about sustainable cooking practices and implement them at home.
- Use social media to raise awareness about food-related issues.
- Participate in or organize fundraisers for food-related causes.
- Encourage your workplace or school to engage in food-related charitable activities.

CHAPTER 13

SERVE WITH HUMILITY: JOHN GLENN

The Person

In 1962, John Glenn became the first American astronaut to orbit the Earth. He later served his country as a US senator from Ohio.

The Lesson

When we accomplish something, we usually feel good about ourselves. But does that make us better than other people? Mostly, it means that we are more fortunate. To serve others most fully, it helps to remember that—given different initial conditions—they might be serving you instead. When you realize that everything on this planet is contingent, with this knowledge comes a humility that can make it easier to do good. We may not have the perspective that John Glenn gained from outer space, but to better serve others, we all can remain humble about our accomplishments.

Our Connection

I spent my entire childhood until twenty-one (when I left India for the United States) in a rented apartment in a three-story building in Kolkata, India. There was no playground in the nearby vicinity, so often I climbed up to the rooftop where I found space to hide, play, read comics, and watch the sky.

I vividly remember calling—more like screaming, actually—to summon the entire family to see rainbows from our rooftop. It was an overwhelming experience, filling me with the first stirrings of awe and wonder. Even now whenever I see rainbows, I am transported back to those childhood days and feel a deep appreciation for the beauty of the natural world and a sense of humility in the face of its majesty.

Not too far from our home was the Birla Industrial and Technological Museum, where I went numerous times to watch science shows, including one about astronomy. Much later, my parents took the family to the Birla Planetarium for a very special show. It was a fascinating journey through the cosmos, an amazing representation of the Milky Way, star clusters, and nebulae spanning more than 10,000 years of star positioning with absolute astronomical accuracy. I found it completely breathtaking.

Like many of us who grew up during the "space age," I was immersed in the drama of exploration and was driven to learn as much as I could. It was a strange feeling to discover that faraway countries like the United States and Soviet Union were sending actual men into space and even to the moon. I wondered, how was it possible? Who are these brave people traveling to outer space and back? I was seven years old when Neil Armstrong took one small step for man, one giant leap for mankind. Much later in my life I learned that John Glenn had been the first American to orbit the earth—a milestone he achieved in 1962, the year I was born.

Many years later, I found myself seated next to John Glenn and his wife Annie at a conference in New York City. I must admit, for a moment I was that little awestruck boy on the rooftop again. But by then, I knew a bit more about John Glenn—enough to appreciate his journey as that of a true American hero, and a humble one.

John Glenn and the author

How John Glenn Bettered the World

At age twenty, John Glenn earned a private pilot's license. Two years later—with the US in the midst of the Second World War—he had completed advanced training in the Marine Corps and was flying fighter jets in the Marshall Islands. By war's end, he had flown fifty-seven combat missions, and he went on to fly even more missions in Korea.[62]

After the Korean War, Glenn volunteered for the dangerous job of test pilot, during which he became the first pilot to complete a supersonic transcontinental flight. Glenn was one of the first seven astronauts chosen to participate in NASA's Mercury program, whose goal was to put a man in orbit and return him safely to Earth. He was older and less educated than his fellow candidates, but his dedication, attention to detail, and courage won him the opportunity—on February 20, 1962—to become the first American to orbit the Earth. His circumnavigation of the planet made him an instant national hero and showed the world that the US was a serious contender in the space race with the Soviet Union. Considered too old to join subsequent space missions, including the 1969 moon landing, Glenn retired from duty. In 1974, after several failed candidacies, he was elected to the Senate, where he served until 1999.

Glenn was destined to return to space. His mission of almost nine days on the space shuttle orbiter Discovery—launched Oct. 29, 1998, when he was seventy-seven—made him the oldest human to venture into space. On Discovery he participated in a series of tests on the aging process. The aging population had been a focus of his work as a US senator, and here he was, once more putting himself at risk to push the boundaries of the human experience, acting this time as test pilot for the human body.

His participation came about because, three years before, while reading a book on space physiology and medicine, Glenn came across a list of fifty-two physical changes routinely experienced in space by orbiting astronauts, such as osteoporosis and cardiovascular issues. Those tested had been very fit men who ranged in age from their early thirties to their fifties, yet who had developed conditions typical of elderly people. When Glenn checked, he learned that there were no plans to send an older person into orbit to advance our knowledge in this area.

"I wondered why the science had to wait," he wrote in *John Glenn: A Memoir*. "Shuttle flights were going up regularly. Why couldn't room be made on one of them for some experiments on senior citizens? And then I began to think, 'Why not me?'"[63]

How John Glenn Made *Me* Better

Like my first encounters with many of the personalities featured in this book, meeting Glenn triggered—or perhaps I should say *launched*—both instant inspiration and gratitude. Inspiration, as I knew about John Glenn's values of perseverance, courage, and dedication. Gratitude, because I could never imagine meeting, let alone sitting next to, this American hero.

And yet, the strongest lasting impression was of his humility. He was a bona fide superstar, yet he was constantly wondering what more he could do to serve others.

John Glenn's memoir is a rich and detailed account of his life and career. In it he recounts the exhilaration of the launch into orbit, the challenges he faced in space, and the sense of pride and accomplishment he felt upon returning to Earth. Reading his book, I felt that Glenn was equally excited about public service. He represented his home state of Ohio in the US Senate for twenty-five years. In his memoir he describes his experiences as a senator, including working on issues such as nuclear disarmament, environmental protection, and health care reform. He emphasized the importance of working across party lines to get things done.

His 1962 orbit of Earth, which almost ended in disaster, demonstrated his skill and resolve. First, the automatic control system failed, but Glenn was able to take manual control. "The malfunction just forced me to prove very rapidly what had been planned over a longer period of time," Glenn said.[64] Then telemetry showed that the spacecraft's heat shield had come loose, which meant reentry into the Earth's atmosphere could result in the capsule's incineration. Glenn and the NASA team at Mission Control in Houston, Texas, tackled the problem by leaving the retrorocket pack in place to stabilize the heat shield—which worked, except that as he was flying in from orbit, Glenn saw big chunks of flaming debris falling with him. Was the rocket pack breaking up (bad) or was it the heat shield (very, very bad)? "Fortunately," he said during an interview, "it was the rocket pack—or I wouldn't be answering these questions."[65]

John Glenn was a man of great determination who never gave up on his dreams and who was willing to take risks to achieve his goals. He faced many setbacks and challenges throughout his life, both as a pilot and politician, but he continued to work hard and push ahead. His perseverance ultimately led him to achieve his goals.

With all his accomplishments, he was also known for his down-to-earth nature and humble demeanor—exactly how I remember him from our chance meeting in New York. Throughout his life he emphasized the importance of staying grounded—ironic, indeed, for a man famous for flying into outer space—and he believed that true success was not just about individual achievements, but about having a positive impact on others. Glenn's humility was evident in both his personal and professional life. He was known for his integrity, kindness, and willingness to help others, and he remained dedicated to public service long after he hung up his space suit.

In his book, John Glenn tells a story we must hear. His narrative of steadfastness, devotion, courage, and honor is both a great adventure tale and a source of powerful inspiration for an age that needs these values more than ever.

In an interview with the *Cincinnati Enquirer* in 2002, Glenn said, "If I can inspire young people to dedicate themselves to the good of mankind, I've accomplished something."[66] He certainly inspired me—and at the same time taught me to remain humble about whatever I might accomplish.

How You Can Serve with Humility *Now*

These organizations all offer opportunities for selfless service:

- **Rotary International**—A global network of 1.2 million people committed to taking action for lasting change, Rotary International offers service projects that often promote humility and selflessness. How to get involved: Join a Rotary Club or Rotary Action Group or become part of a Rotary Fellowship.
- **Doctors Without Borders**—This international medical humanitarian organization helps people worldwide where the need is greatest, delivering emergency medical aid to people affected by conflict, epidemics, disasters, or exclusion from healthcare. The volunteers and staff exhibit humility through their dedication to serving others under challenging conditions. How to get involved: Volunteer if you have medical skills, attend an event, donate to support their mission, or raise awareness about their work and global health issues.
- **The Salvation Army**—Known for its charitable efforts, the Salvation Army provides a wide range of community programs that foster humility by helping those in need without discrimination. How to get

involved: Volunteer at local Salvation Army centers, donate goods or funds, or participate in their holiday giving programs.

By disposing you to think of others, humility can actually elevate your deeds. You can begin cultivating humility right now with any of these simple actions:

- Volunteer at local shelters, food banks, or other community service organizations.
- Practice active listening in your daily interactions, valuing others' opinions and learning from their perspectives.
- Engage in self-reflection to recognize and appreciate the contributions of others to your own success and well-being.
- Offer your skills and knowledge in a mentorship capacity, focusing on the mentee's growth rather than personal recognition.
- Show gratitude daily, acknowledging the acts of kindness and support you receive from others.

CHAPTER 14

CHALLENGE FRIENDS: KEVIN BACON

The Person

Kevin Bacon is an actor, musician, and philanthropist who has been featured in over sixty movies and appeared with so many other actors that a game has been named after him: "Six Degrees of Kevin Bacon." (This pun refers to the stage play and film *Six Degrees of Separation*, which makes the point that each of us is, at most, only six points of contact away from any other person on Earth.)

The Lesson

We usually associate "peer pressure" with its negative connotations: young people pressuring their peers, either directly or indirectly, to engage in risky behavior. But peer pressure can also be applied to achieve positive ends. Sharing information about causes we support can make our friends aware of how they, too, can do more good. With social media networks at our fingertips, many of us have the ability to influence hundreds—or even thousands—of people. And those people, in turn, have the potential to increase that influence exponentially.

Our Connection

In 2007, when Bacon wanted to leverage his brand to give back, he embraced the "Six Degrees" concept in his typical good-natured way: He founded an organization called SixDegrees.Org. During my tenure as CEO of SOS Children's Villages USA, one of our board members introduced me to Stacy Huston, executive director of SixDegrees.Org. From her I learned much more about the thrust of the organization's mission—connecting people and organizations to causes they care about and encouraging them to act. (Very much the idea of this book, in fact—especially the last section of each chapter.) I was very much interested in forming a partnership between SOS and SixDegrees.Org to raise funds for the vulnerable children and youth that SOS serves.

Kevin Bacon

At that time, SixDegrees.Org had developed a revolutionary web-based platform called 6Tag, a messaging app for launching socially driven campaigns to raise financial support, volunteerism, awareness, and anything else a charity might need to fulfill its mission. Inspired by the wildly successful ALS Ice

Bucket Challenge, 6Tag gives users the opportunity to challenge their friends and family to produce thirty-second videos, create awareness, and raise funds for a great cause.

In December 2018, we issued a joint press release announcing that Kevin Bacon's SixDegrees.Org was partnering with SOS Children's Villages USA to support vulnerable children and youth in the United States through the #HomecomingChallenge. Sadly, the initiative did not reach its fundraising goal, but true to its nature, the connection mattered. The association with Bacon increased awareness of the work that SOS was doing (and still does) globally to ensure that all children have a loving home and the opportunity to reach their potential. Kevin Bacon, Kyra Sedgwick, Jesse Metcalfe, Beverley Mitchell, and other celebrity influencers participated in this #Homecoming Challenge and declared that every child deserves a place to call home. That's important.

How Kevin Bacon Bettered the World

In a recent podcast ("Ask Kevin (Almost) Anything—Total Eclipse, Earth Day, and the Game that Started it All"), Bacon shared the story about the birth of SixDegrees.Org, now a public 501c3. He had heard about the game—invented in 1994 by three Albright College students—from several friends, and then Howard Stern had discussed it on his radio show and other celebrities had mentioned it. Bacon hoped the game would go away. When it didn't, he embraced the concept and came up with the idea of challenging his friends to do something good in areas they cared about. SixDegrees.Org was born out of a strong desire to create a lasting positive impact. Over the years, the organization has grown from a celebrity experiment into a valuable and rewarding global project, operating independently with a board of directors that Bacon chairs.

Kevin Bacon turned a lighthearted game into a game-changing charitable movement, reaffirming the desire for and power of global connection. SixDegrees.Org has supported various causes in the areas of education, health, the environment, and social justice, and has partnered with many nonprofit organizations to raise millions for various charitable causes.

With support from the general public, companies, and foundations, SixDegrees.Org focuses on connecting people to resources, sharing stories, and amplifying causes to positively impact communities. Through connections—the currency of celebrity culture—the organization drives awareness of and engagement in important issues. Key accomplishments of SixDegrees.Org include the following:

- **Youth Empowerment**—Creating safe community spaces for young people.
- **Equality and Justice**—Transforming equality into equity.
- **Sustainability**—Supporting conservation, renewable resources, and responsible stewardship.
- **Emergent Issues**—Addressing future crises collaboratively with local leaders and residents.

In a *Forbes* magazine interview, Bacon was asked, "How would you like to be remembered?" He replied, "I just want to do what I can do here and now and not think so much about what's going to happen when I'm gone."[67] That's Kevin Bacon.

How Kevin Bacon Made *Me* Better

Bacon's goal of practical empathy is simple, and I think we can all relate to it. In an interview with *Virgin Pulse* ("Kevin Bacon's Guide to Empathy: Unveiling the Infinite Power of Connection"), he was asked to share an instance where empathy impacted a decision or action he had made in his professional or personal life. Bacon replied, "I was once working with an elderly actor who was really struggling. We had a long day in front of us, and I was getting frustrated. The director quietly asked me to start messing up. I did, and the other actor came alive."[68]

While writing about Kevin Bacon, I feel obliged to mention his wife, Kyra Sedgwick, an Emmy and Golden Globe-winning actress, producer, and director. I never met her, but I feel we have a lot in common. On a recent SixDegrees.Org podcast, Bacon asked his wife to name the source of her empathy. Sedgwick revealed that injustices around the world had filled her with despair, made her angry, and spurred her to action. She emphasized that change does not have to be anything big. It's often the small and incremental actions that all of us can do that will make a difference.[69]

Their stories resonated with me. Growing up in Kolkata, I felt a similar anger and frustration, until I found my own way to take action, to change those things that had bothered me.

Their remarks on the power of small gestures triggered another memory. It was Easter Sunday, 2016. I was at my neighborhood CVS drug store when I observed a woman in her late sixties or early seventies picking up trash that someone had tossed to the curb. I decided to acknowledge her. "People like you make this world a better place," I told her. She was overwhelmed with emotion at my simple gesture. "You just made my Easter," she said, laughing and crying at the same time. "You made my Easter as well," I replied.

At the time, I was aware of a change in the frequency of the world, you might say. As if this connection of two strangers, born out of goodwill and generosity of spirit, had somehow helped to tip the scales in favor of compassion and understanding. It wasn't part of a strategic master plan, but something simple and spontaneous. Multiply such moments by four or five per day, by eight or nine billion people, and you begin to see the world-changing potential of what started as a game.

How You Can Challenge Friends *Now*

Outside of your personal network of friends and followers, you can get involved with any of these organizations, which have large and established networks:

- **SixDegrees.Org**—Founded by Kevin Bacon to connect people and support various causes. How to get involved: *Donate directly to SixDegrees.Org or engage with the organization across its social platforms.*
- **GlobalGiving**—A global crowdfunding platform for grassroots charitable projects. How to get involved: Donate to projects, start a fundraiser, or list your nonprofit project.

Not ready to connect with a large organization? Connect with your friend groups, workplaces, and communities! Not only is it easy to leverage your connections to create positive change, but it can also be both fun and rewarding. Here are some ways to get started:

- Share information about causes you care about on social media.
- Introduce friends with shared interests to collaborate on projects.
- Organize a small fundraiser within your social circle.
- Volunteer with a local organization and bring a friend.
- Start a giving circle with friends or colleagues.
- Use your professional skills to help a nonprofit pro bono.
- Participate in or organize charity walks/runs with your network.
- Share volunteer opportunities with your social and professional circles.
- Host a discussion group about social issues in your community.
- Use your birthday or special occasions to fundraise for a cause.
- Connect nonprofits you support with potential donors or volunteers.
- Engage your workplace in corporate social responsibility initiatives.
- Use platforms like LinkedIn to share content about social causes.
- Organize a "give back" day with your friends or family.
- Challenge friends to match your donations to causes you care about.

CHAPTER 15

SPEAK OUT: MALALA YOUSAFZAI

The Person

Malala Yousafzai is a Pakistani woman who became a world figure when, as a young girl, she stood up to—and spoke out against—the oppressions of the Taliban. Her courage in supporting every child's right to an education led to her receiving the Nobel Peace Prize in 2014.

The Lesson

When did you last feel stifled or overpowered by forces in the world? Chances are, you're feeling pressure—*oppression* of some kind—even now. When we succumb to such forces, they silence us, shut us down. And with each of us who shuts down, it becomes more difficult for others to resist, to keep from shutting down, too. Eventually, when any of those powerful forces finds itself completely unchecked, an entire society suffers. As

Malala taught me by example, we must not allow ourselves to be silenced, no matter the cost.

Our Connection

During my professional journey, I have been extremely fortunate to meet many amazing human beings who are doing amazing things. And with many I have had meaningful interactions. But in 2013 when I met Malala, I found myself speechless. Her aura was simply overwhelming. Ten years later, while watching the 2023 Academy Awards on TV, I was excited to see Malala Yousafzai on the fabled red carpet. The Pakistani activist known around the world by her first name was attending as executive producer of *Stranger at the Gate*, a documentary short film that had already won numerous awards and was now in the running for an Oscar. Her appearance stirred memories that I feel honored to share with you.

Malala Yousafzai and the author

I met Malala during a Clinton Global Initiative meeting in New York City—and while it was a fleeting social encounter, it left a lasting impression on me. I had never met a sixteen-year-old with such determination, focus, and courage.

This was in the middle of a remarkable period in her life. Just one year earlier, in October 2012, Malala had been shot in the head by a Taliban gunman for speaking out against that group's restrictions on female education. Two years later, she received the Nobel Peace Prize—at age seventeen, the youngest recipient ever. But these dates mark neither the beginning nor the end of her amazing journey, from which I have gained, and continue to gain, so much inspiration.

How Malala Bettered the World

Malala was born and raised in the Swat Valley of Pakistan. It was a home birth, because her parents could not afford the hospital. They named her after Malalai of Maiwand, a Pashtun folk hero from southern Afghanistan who had led a rebellion against the British. The name proved to be both accurate and ironic. Malala's father was an educator and education activist who had started his own school. Growing up in this environment, and attending her father's school, Malala also became passionate about education. Then, in 2007, the Pakistani Taliban moved into the Swat Valley. With an ideology compelling the strict subjugation of women, they quickly acted to shut down girls' schools, including that of her father.

In 2009, when she was just eleven, Malala seized her first opportunity to speak out. She began to write an anonymous blog about life under the Taliban for the BBC's Urdu website. Her father later told a BBC journalist, "Malala's voice was the most powerful voice in Swat because the biggest victim of the Taliban was girls' schools and girls' education and few people talked about it. When she used to speak about education, everybody gave it importance."[70]

Eventually the Pakistani armed forces were able to expel the Taliban from the Swat Valley, but the threat to Malala remained, and she was at even graver risk after her identity was revealed. Well aware of the danger, she continued to speak out. When a gunman boarded her school bus and threatened to shoot everyone unless the girl known as Malala stepped forward, she did so, knowing that her life was about to end.

If her Pashtun fighting spirit gave her the courage to step forward, it was ironically the British who came to her rescue after she was shot. She was airlifted to the UK, where she underwent lifesaving surgery. She awoke ten days later, an international icon.

Malala and her family remained in the UK, where she continued her education, ultimately earning a degree in philosophy, politics, and economics from Oxford University. In the aforementioned BBC article, Malala noted, "For my brothers it was easy to think about the future. They can be anything they want. But for me it was hard, and for that reason I wanted to become educated and empower myself with knowledge."[71]

Despite the brutal attack on her life, Malala has continued to speak out about the importance of education for all children, especially girls. She also established the Malala Fund, with a focus on breaking down barriers to girls' education.

As I write this, nearly 119 million girls around the world are unable to attend school.[72] Girls in different countries, regions, and cultures face different barriers to accessing education. In perhaps the most heartbreaking example, the Taliban regime in Afghanistan now forbids all girls over the age of twelve to attend school.[73] I have visited schools where children are attending but learning is not adequate.

Through its Education Champion Network, Malala Fund provides funding, capacity development, and connections to education advocates and activists who are working to change policies and practices that keep girls from going to school. I especially admire the organization's localized approach, which supports highly effective individuals who have already demonstrated the ability to advance girls' education in their communities. These Education Champions know how powerful their voices can be.

Education is the path to self-determination. On the power of self-determination Malala and the Taliban would agree—the former because she prizes it, the latter because they fear it.

According to UNICEF, the benefits of girls' education are many. "Girls who complete a secondary school education earn more, marry later and raise children who are healthier and better nourished. Educated girls are less likely to face discrimination. They are safer and better protected from exploitation and abuse. They invest more in their communities. And they contribute more to the economy and to society."[74]

Malala's influence has transcended borders and inspired a generation of young women to fight for their rights and create a better world for themselves and future generations. Her story has raised awareness about the barriers that young women face in accessing education, particularly in regions where education for girls is not a priority. Her activism has inspired many young women to become advocates for social change in their own communities. By speaking out against gender discrimination and promoting equal opportunities for all, she has inspired a new generation of activists to challenge traditional gender roles and stereotypes.

As a symbol of resilience, determination, and courage, Malala serves as a role model for people all over the world. Her story demonstrates that even the youngest individuals can make a difference when they stand up for what they believe.

How Malala Made *Me* Better

Why did I find it so hard to speak up when I met Malala? Most likely, I was humbled by the mere presence of someone both so young and so accomplished. But her life story has prompted me to reflect on speaking up, and out. It is not always an easy thing. There are so many inhibitions—fear, shame, self-doubt. There is cynicism, which tells us that our voice probably doesn't matter. There is the voice of pragmatism, which might tell us that this is not the time or place to speak up, lest we offend, or suffer consequences we might not be willing to afford. Most of us find it uncomfortable to speak out even when we see or hear things that in our heart we know are wrong. Malala was always empowered, since she was never trained to believe otherwise. She never doubted herself or her worth. She never accepted a subordinate role because of her age, gender, ethnicity, or social status. Instead, her education freed her mind to aspire to a better world for herself, her family, and eventually all humanity. I think about what it must have been like on the bus that day, staring into the muzzle of a gun. It took courage to speak up on that day, to be a vehicle for truth. To be silent would have been merely a different kind of death. Instead, she changed the world.

And she also changed *me*. Ever since I met her, I have felt that silence is not an option. As a result, I have made it a practice to write and post articles on LinkedIn and other social media channels whenever I encounter an issue in the world that compels me to speak out. Even writing this book—which, to one degree or another, has been motivated by everyone included in it—is a response to her influence. When change is needed, to communicate is to advocate, and that is something each of us can do.

How You Can Make Your Voice Heard *Now*

It was October 2012 when the Taliban tried to take away Malala's voice. It was through her blog that she broadcast herself to as many people as possible, and it proved effective enough to threaten a brutal oppressor. Today, the landscape has changed completely. It's more difficult than it has ever been to stand out, online, in a crowd of voices. But there are also more choices where you can point your voice. These organizations, platforms, and apps will help you get started:

- **Malala Fund**—Founded by Malala to continue her work in girls' education, the Fund provides education and opportunities for girls worldwide. How to get involved: Donate, fundraise, or become an advocate.
- **PEN America**—Defends and celebrates free expression through the advancement of literature and human rights. How to get involved: Become a member, attend events, or participate in campaigns.
- **5 Calls**—App that facilitates contacting elected representatives in Congress about important issues. How to get involved: Download the app and make calls.
- **Broadway Advocacy Coalition**—Brings together artists and policy experts to enact social change. How to get involved: Attend events, participate in programs, or donate.

- **Americans for the Arts**—Supports arts and culture as a path to creating vibrant communities and contributing to social change. How to get involved: Use their "Arts Impact Explorer" primer, join as a member, or participate in their initiatives.

Don't allow yourself to be silenced. To raise your voice for change, practice any of the following actions:

- Share your opinions on social media platforms responsibly and thoughtfully.
- Write letters to local newspapers or online publications about issues you care about.
- Attend local town hall meetings or community forums and voice your concerns.
- Support and amplify marginalized voices in your community.
- Educate yourself on current events and social issues.
- Have respectful discussions with those who hold different views.
- Sign petitions for causes you believe in.
- Volunteer for organizations that align with your values.
- Use art, music, or writing to express your views on social issues.
- Stand up against bullying or discrimination when you witness it.
- Encourage others, especially young people, to share their thoughts and opinions.
- Practice active listening to understand different perspectives.
- Participate in peaceful protests or demonstrations for causes you support.

- Use your professional skills to contribute to causes you care about.
- Share stories of people who have spoken out and made a difference.

CHAPTER 16

RETHINK WHAT YOU KNOW: SAL KHAN

The Person

By creating Khan Academy—a revolutionary online platform that provides free, high-quality education to millions—Sal Khan challenged traditional educational models and promoted equality worldwide.

The Lesson

We all tend to accept the status quo, the way things happen to be, as the way they must stay. In reality, of course, everything is subject to change—and most things can be changed for the better. By leveraging technology and emphasizing personal, mastery-based learning,[75] Sal Khan added a major innovation to the world's educational landscape. And while most of us won't make an impact on that scale, I believe that everyone can benefit if we each make a habit of examining and reevaluating the ideas and practices that we take for granted. You never know where a small shift in thinking might lead.

Our Connection

I got to know Salman (Sal) Khan the same way that Bill Gates did: by watching his educational videos with my child.

Another way of looking at it: Sal Khan made it possible for my son Ryan to enjoy the same education as the children of one of the wealthiest persons on Earth.

The author with Sal Khan at the Global Philanthropic Forum in San Francisco

I had an opportunity to meet Khan in 2013 in San Francisco at the Global Philanthropic Forum. He was introduced at the forum by moderator Jane Wales (president and CEO, World Affairs Council) as "an extraordinary social entrepreneur who has absolutely revolutionized education."[76] At that conference, Khan told the audience why we need to move away from traditional and outdated teaching models. New technologies have afforded us great opportunities to more effectively teach our kids—and we need to make full use of them.

It was refreshing to see Sal Khan at this event, on "my" turf in the development/philanthropy sector. In my limited exposure, I had not seen many organizations in philanthropy championing online education for all, the pillar of Khan's philosophy. In my youth, I had worked with vulnerable populations in Kolkata, India, so I understood the value of universal education in addressing poverty and many other challenges that vulnerable populations face. Naturally, during my tenure at SNV USA, I was very excited to receive our first major funding, from the Bill & Melinda Gates Foundation, to support a school meals program in Kenya, Mali, and Ghana. But this almost qualified as an outlier.

How Sal Khan Bettered the World

Inclusive education is the core principle of Khan's brainchild, Khan Academy. The Academy makes high-quality educational content accessible to millions of people around the world via simple, easy-to-follow animated videos on YouTube. Its online platform offers a vast library of lessons, practice exercises, and assessments in subjects ranging from math, biology, chemistry, physics, and computer programming to history, art history, finance, and economics. Each video is a digestible chunk, approximately ten minutes long, and especially produced for viewing on the computer. Khan Academy reaches an average of more than seventeen million learners from kindergarteners to adults each month.[77]

And it's all free.

Khan Academy videos have been translated into multiple languages, making education accessible to non-English speakers as well. This accessibility has been particularly beneficial for students in underserved communities—particularly in developing countries—and for those with limited access to traditional educational resources.

Khan's individualized outreach doesn't stop there. The Academy offers personalized learning by allowing students to learn at their own pace and revisit concepts as needed. Despite the video format, learning is tailored to each student's strengths, needs, and interests—including enabling student voice and choice in what, how, when, and where they learn—to provide flexibility and support that enables mastery at each level. FSG (a mission-driven consulting firm) conducted a study of a statewide pilot of Khan Academy in Idaho with 173 teachers and 10,500 students during the 2013–14 school year. Their study found that students who completed 60 percent or more of their grade-level math through Khan Academy experienced 1.8 times their expected growth on the mathematics portion of the NWEA MAP Growth Assessment, a widely used test.[78]

Khan argues that our education system is inefficient and full of inequalities and there is a huge mismatch between what students need to know and what they are taught in school. I found Khan's model of equitable access to quality education for all absolutely thrilling for the same reason Khan did.[79] "Who knows where genius will crop up?" Khan asked. "There may be a young girl in an African village with the potential to find a cancer cure."[80] The idea gave me goose bumps.

There have been numerous success stories of Khan Academy students who have benefited from the platform's resources and support. The most memorable one for Khan was one email he received via YouTube, early on, before Khan Academy had officially been born. A student who was frustrated with the traditional mode of teaching wrote to tell Khan that his very informal videos had changed his life. As a hedge-fund manager, Khan was not used to getting this kind of letter. But he soon became familiar with examples (like the ones below) of students whose learning journeys had been transformed by his methods:

- Ambarish Raj, a student from Bihar, India, used Khan Academy to prepare for the entrance exams for the prestigious Indian Institutes of Technology (IITs). Despite coming from a modest background and lacking access to quality coaching, he achieved an outstanding score on the IIT entrance exam and secured admission to IIT Delhi.
- Moises Vazquez, a student from Los Angeles, California, used Khan Academy to improve his math skills. He went from struggling with math and having doubts about his future to becoming proficient in the subject. Moises eventually earned a scholarship to the University of Southern California, where he pursued a degree in mechanical engineering.
- Nhi Ngo, a Vietnamese student living in Finland, used Khan Academy to supplement her learning in mathematics. She found Khan Academy's instructional videos and practice exercises helpful in understanding mathematical concepts and improving her problem-solving skills. Nhi later became a mathematics teacher and continued to use Khan Academy's resources to support her students' learning.[81]

How Sal Khan Made *Me* Better

Similar to how I've felt about all the individuals featured in this book, I wanted to learn more about what triggered Khan to start his Academy and how he came up with the revolutionary idea to change the way we think of education.

To gain insight on his journey, I read his book, *The One World School House*. I learned about his family background, which placed a high value on education. I learned about his parents—his father from Bangladesh and his mother from Bengal—who raised him in Metairie, near New Orleans, Louisiana. His own education did not directly prepare him to develop a pedagogical theory and set of best classroom practices. But it did lead him to degrees in mathematics, electrical engineering, and computer science from MIT—all of which helped him become a disruptive innovator, the mindset from which the Academy would spring.[82] Khan touches on many important topics, such as how education happens, active vs. passive learning, what our tests really test, the future of transcripts, the future of credentials, whether creativity can be taught, and thought-provoking facts about how we learn. Among the many takeaways for me, two stood out: Khan's emphasis on mastery-based learning, where students are given the time and support needed to master a concept before moving on, thus ensuring a solid foundation and preventing knowledge gaps from building up over time; and his advocacy of personalized learning experiences that cater to each student's individual needs, pace, and learning style. He believes that technology can play a crucial role in facilitating personalized instruction and providing tailored resources and feedback.[83]

To illustrate these approaches, Khan recalls how his first student, his cousin Nadia, transformed her grades. Looking back at my own life trajectory, I could relate to the importance of mastery-based learning. Throughout my school life I felt I needed more time to grasp certain math concepts and seldom had the courage to speak up. It made me feel inadequate and at times utterly sad. As an adult, I have tried various coping mechanisms to counter those deficiencies and focused on strengthening other skills I have.

As I learned more about Khan's accomplishments, I became convinced that rethinking education can address many of the challenges that we face today, both at home and in the wider world. Social entrepreneurs like Sal Khan are providing the vision and the tools free of cost to empower individuals, foster critical thinking, and promote positive societal changes. There are numerous ways in which education can make a difference. It opens up opportunities for employment, entrepreneurship, and economic growth, leading to improved living conditions. It can raise awareness about hygiene, nutrition, disease prevention, and reproductive health, leading to healthier lifestyles and reduced mortality rates. Education is instrumental in achieving gender equality. Education fosters understanding, empathy, and respect for diversity. By promoting inclusive values and teaching about different cultures, religions, and perspectives, education can help reduce prejudice, discrimination, and conflicts, promoting peaceful coexistence. Education plays a crucial role in raising awareness about environmental challenges and promoting sustainable practices. It can equip individuals with the knowledge to address climate change and to practice conservation, resource management, and sustainable development. Last but not least, education equips citizens with critical thinking skills, enabling them to participate actively in democratic processes, make informed decisions, and hold governments accountable. It cultivates a culture of civic engagement, human rights awareness, and social responsibility.

The importance of rethinking education became even more clear to me during the pandemic, while I was CEO of SOS Children's Villages USA.

Early on in the pandemic, I started to worry that the concerns of children and youth—who, even in the best of times, often go unaddressed—might fade into invisibility as the world focused its attention elsewhere. Despite the important role that school closures played in protecting more vulnerable parents and grandparents, children's education was put at risk. Unable to access their traditional classrooms, students quickly fell behind in their academic attainment.

According to a Brookings Institute study of 5.4 million US students in grades 3–8, "the cumulative impact of the COVID-19 pandemic on students' academic achievement has been large."[84]

The decline was rapid, but not evenly distributed. According to Brookings: ". . . . test-score gaps between students in low-poverty and high-poverty elementary schools grew by approximately 20% in math (corresponding to 0.20 SDs) and 15% in reading (0.13 SDs), primarily during the 2020–21 school year. Further, achievement tended to drop more between fall 2020 and 2021 than between fall 2019 and 2020 (both overall and differentially by school poverty), indicating that disruptions to learning have continued to negatively impact students well past the initial hits following the spring 2020 school closures."[85]

Meanwhile, as doctors and nurses struggled to cope with the impacts of the coronavirus, scientists raced to develop a vaccine that would stop the virus in its tracks and prevent further harm to people's health and livelihoods. Their efforts were a striking testament to the power of education: In this moment of crisis, our collective well-being depended almost solely on the ability of our most highly educated immunologists to outsmart the virus.

I was struck by the central role played by education in this global public health emergency while speaking with children and youth at SOS Children's Villages in Florida and in Debre Tabor and Debre Markos, in Ethiopia. In Florida, I spoke with Maria, an articulate and ambitious fourteen-year-old. She had learned quite a lot about COVID-19 in school and worried about its impact on her community. She was participating in her school's distance-learning efforts. In Ethiopia, I spoke with sixteen-year-old Amhara, who had dreams of being a doctor, and eighteen-year-old Fassil, who was determined not to let blindness deter him from pursuing his dream of becoming a lawyer. Although the kids I spoke with lived in markedly different societies, the threat posed by the coronavirus and its impact on their education was something they all had in common.

For all of its destructive tragedy, the coronavirus pandemic was also a "teachable moment" for humanity. It revealed what was working and what wasn't, in just about every field of human endeavor. School and college closures gave a huge boost to online and hybrid models, including Khan's. But they also revealed the limitations of these models, prompting another spurt of innovation and creativity to appeal to students whose learning habits have changed.

Khan's model, and others like it, are attracting attention not merely because they are more effective at meeting students "where they live," but also because they can address these kinds of social and economic issues. Peter Laugharn, formerly executive director of the Firelight Foundation and now CEO of the Conrad Hilton Foundation, described Khan's model in his blog at the *Alliance* magazine as a "blended learning" that "combines online delivery and human instruction, paced according to the needs of individual learners." Laugharn adds that "the implications of this approach for schooling systems in the global South and its push toward quality education for all are only just being grasped." In the same blog, Laugharn rightly points out that Khan Academy has all the elements of social entrepreneurship—"a person armed with an idea, a prototype that expands to a surprising scale, and an unexpected improvement in [solving] a previously intractable problem."[86]

As I reflect further on Khan's book, *The One World School House*, his journey from a hedge fund job (yes, he has an MBA from Harvard) to setting up Khan Academy has been inspirational. He vividly recounts securing his first $100,000 startup funding from philanthropist Ann Doerr and his first meeting with Bill Gates. But for me, the real heart of the book is Khan's vision of an inclusive and affordable education system that would establish education as a fundamental human right, and that would level the playing field of learning both within communities and across national and socioeconomic boundaries. That vision—and the inspiration it offers—has remained with me as a reminder of the kind of change that creative thinking can make possible.

How You Can Rethink What You Know *Now*

Once you commit yourself to creative thinking, you'll find it becomes easier to make the leap from the usual to the possible. If you make lifelong education part of your journey—either as a student, as a teacher, or as a supporter of educational initiatives—you'll find it becomes easier still. And helping others grow and reevaluate their knowledge is a great way to catalyze new ideas. To get started, connect with any of the following organizations and resources:

- **Khan Academy**—Provides free online education in various subjects. How to get involved: Use the platform to learn, volunteer as a translator, or donate to support their mission.
- **Code.org**—Promotes computer science education and coding skills. How to get involved: Learn to code, volunteer as a teacher, or organize an Hour of Code event.
- **DonorsChoose**—Connects donors with teachers needing resources for classroom projects. How to get involved: Donate to projects, create a fundraising page, or if you're a teacher, submit a project.
- **Teach For America**—Places talented individuals in high-need schools. How to get involved: Apply to become a corps member, donate, or partner with them as an employer.
- **Coursera**—Offers online courses, certificates, and degrees from universities and companies. How to get involved: Take courses, become an instructor, or partner as an institution.

- **Creative Commons**—Provides free, easy-to-use copyright licenses for creative and academic works. How to get involved: Use CC licenses for your work, donate, or volunteer in various capacities.

With these tips for creative living and thinking, you can prepare to make a difference right away:

- Practice mindfulness meditation to enhance creative thinking.
- Keep a daily journal to explore and develop ideas.
- Engage in regular brainstorming sessions, alone or with others.
- Try new experiences and learn new skills regularly.
- Embrace failure as a learning opportunity.
- Set aside dedicated time for creative pursuits.
- Collaborate with people from diverse backgrounds.
- Regularly challenge your assumptions and beliefs.
- Engage in creative exercises like free writing or sketching.
- Create a stimulating environment that inspires creativity.
- Attend workshops or seminars on innovation and creativity.
- Use online platforms like Skillshare or MasterClass to learn from creative professionals.

CHAPTER 17

USE YOUR PRIVILEGE: ANGELINA JOLIE

The Person

The mother of six children, Angelina Jolie is an Oscar-winning Hollywood actor and humanitarian who has been involved in various charitable causes and philanthropic work throughout her career.

The Lesson

It is said that you are never too limited to do good. Nor are you too well placed. As the daughter of Hollywood icons and a public figure through her own illustrious acting career, Angelina Jolie has consistently leveraged her global profile to advocate for compassion and justice. And even though her fame has made it possible for her to make a difference on a larger scale than most of us could achieve, there is a lesson here for us all: if you have a deep desire to improve the world, you can—and should—use whatever privilege you have to make it happen.

Our Connection

By the time I joined SOS Children's Villages in 2018, Jolie had already been a long-time supporter of the organization. I learned that in 2001, Jolie visited an SOS Children's Village in Cambodia while filming the movie *Lara Croft: Tomb Raider*. The following year, she adopted her son Maddox from Cambodia. I also came to know about Chenda Run and Komarey—two girls from our SOS Children's Village in Cambodia who participated in the film *First They Killed My Father*, which Jolie directed. The film provides a personal and intimate account of the Khmer Rouge regime and its devastating impact on the lives of millions of Cambodians. It tells the powerful and harrowing true story of Loung Ung's (author and human rights activist) experiences as a child during the time the Khmer Rouge ruled Cambodia.

Soon after I joined SOS Children's Villages as USA CEO, I decided to reach out to Jolie with the hope of reengaging her in our work. As is so often the case in the world of celebrities, time and attention are limited, and the demands for them are overwhelming. It is often necessary to work with intermediaries who are no less accomplished in their own careers, and who are often very well placed to make a difference in areas of interest to the celebrities. In this case, my colleagues provided a contact: a personal friend of Jolie's in London. I made an effort to contact her office, and after several tries, along with a good deal of patience and persistence, I went to London to meet this contact. During my tenure with SOS, I met with Jolie's contact twice in London and communicated with her extensively about

SOS's work, exploring numerous possible avenues of extended collaboration. After several years of conversations, we finally arranged a face-to-face meeting with Jolie and the leadership of SOS Children's Villages in Austria, something I am very proud of.

Jolie made several visits to SOS villages in different parts of the world to see the conditions for herself, and she has my utmost respect for that. Jolie also sponsored several children. Once I received a note from her office requesting to sponsor a particular girl in Ethiopia, which was especially pleasing to me, as I was also sponsoring a girl in one of our villages in Ethiopia. On one occasion, Jolie leveraged her network to allow SOS's work to be featured in *People* magazine and included SOS in her brand affiliation with Christian Louboutin for a unique marketing campaign that raised funds for the organization.

During my tenure, Jolie's friend in London shared with me many articles that Jolie published in various magazines, while I would occasionally share my own writings with her. On one occasion, knowing Jolie's strong compassion for the plight of refugees, I shared my *Stanford Social Innovation Review* (SSIR) article ("Supporting Children Who Lack Parental Care from All Sides") with Jolie via this friend. I also knew that Jolie was co-writing a book for children, which has recently been published as *Know Your Rights and Claim Them: A Guide for Youth*.

Jolie has continued to support the work of SOS Children's Villages and other organizations striving to improve the lives of children around the world. She has also contributed financially to SOS Children's Villages over the years and has advocated for greater attention and resources to be directed toward the needs of vulnerable children. Her support for the organization has helped raise awareness of the importance of providing stable, nurturing care for children who have experienced trauma or loss.

How Angelina Jolie Bettered the World

Jolie's role as goodwill ambassador for the Office of the United Nations High Commissioner for Refugees (UNHCR)—which she had held since 2001—expanded when she was appointed a special envoy in 2012. In that role, Jolie brought much-needed attention to many major crises that resulted in mass population displacements. She has traveled to numerous countries to raise awareness about the plight of refugees and advocate for their rights and well-being.

While war often forces people to flee their countries, it also creates conditions in which people can become victims of sexual violence. Along with former UK Foreign Secretary Lord William Hague of Richmond, Jolie started the Preventing Sexual Violence in Conflict Initiative on behalf of such victims. This initiative aims to raise awareness of sexual violence in conflict zones and to support prevention and response efforts. It is now supported by 156 countries.

Jolie has also been a strong advocate for education, particularly for girls in developing countries. She co-founded the Education Partnership for Children of Conflict, which helps fund education programs for children affected by conflict.[87]

Beyond these efforts on behalf of children, Jolie also uses her celebrity to help protect endangered species, to combat HIV/AIDS, and to promote access to healthcare in developing countries.

Jolie told *Vogue* in 2020, "I see all people as equal. I see the abuse and suffering and I cannot stand by. Around the world, people are fleeing gas attacks, rape, female genital mutilation, beatings, persecution, murder. They do not flee to improve their lives. They flee because they cannot survive otherwise. What I really want is to see an end to what forces people out of their homelands. I want to see prevention when we can, protection when needed and accountability when crimes are committed."[88]

Jolie is a classic example of a celebrity who has used her platform to raise awareness of important issues and advocate for the most vulnerable. She is an inspiration to all of us.

How Angelina Jolie Made *Me* Better

For a long time, I considered the life and work of Angelina Jolie—who was raised in the comfort of Hollywood with far more privilege than I ever had—to be far from applicable to my own. Growing up in a two-bedroom apartment in Kolkata, India, and coming to the US with very few resources and even fewer connections, I seldom thought of myself as privileged. Yet by the time I was in contact with Jolie's office through my leadership role at SOS Children's Villages, gaining increased exposure to her work, I came to feel differently. My experience as the head of nonprofits had given me a privileged vantage point from which to build a network of connections, and I began to understand that this could be leveraged just as Jolie had leveraged her celebrity.

One way I am now trying to serve is by acting as an advisor to social organizations, bringing my network into play to help them achieve their goals. In the process, I have learned this: there is nothing so gratifying as putting privilege to use.

How You Can Use Your Privilege *Now*

In our increasingly unequal world of extreme privilege and extreme want, of the overexposed and the invisible, it often seems that only those directly affected by poverty or injustice make the effort to change the world for the better. The assumption seems to be that it is "their" problem, so it is "their" fight. Yet they are not well positioned to make a difference. So, it is always inspiring to me when individuals who enjoy great privilege give of themselves to empower others.

Of course, privilege itself is relative. You don't have to be a celebrity to have access to more resources than someone living in poverty. And the rest of us can always add our support to causes that celebrities have embraced and made more visible. The following list can help you get started:

- **Preventing Sexual Violence in Conflict Initiative**—Co-founded by Angelina Jolie and William Hague to combat sexual violence in conflict zones. How to get involved: Sign their petitions, organize awareness events in your community, or participate in the social media campaigns to spread awareness.
- **Elton John AIDS Foundation**—Founded by musician Elton John to support HIV/AIDS prevention and care. How to get involved: Participate in their fundraising events, become a peer educator for HIV prevention, or join their advocacy efforts for policy change.
- **Clara Lionel Foundation**—Founded by singer Rihanna to fund groundbreaking education and emergency response programs around the world. How to get involved: Participate in their online education

initiatives, volunteer for their emergency response teams, or organize local fundraising events.

- **Leonardo DiCaprio Foundation (now part of Earth Alliance)**—Founded by actor Leonardo DiCaprio to protect wildlife and ecosystems. How to get involved: Participate in their conservation volunteer programs, join their climate action campaigns, or organize local environmental clean-up events.
- **Charlize Theron Africa Outreach Project**—Founded by actress Charlize Theron to support African youth in the fight against HIV/AIDS. How to get involved: Become a youth ambassador for HIV/AIDS awareness, participate in their health education programs, or organize screening events for their documentaries.
- **The Tony Robbins Foundation**—Founded by motivational speaker Tony Robbins to empower individuals and organizations to make a difference in their communities. How to get involved: Participate in their leadership development programs, volunteer for their food drive initiatives, or become a mentor in their youth programs.
- **Whitaker Peace & Development Initiative (WPDI)**—Founded by actor Forest Whitaker to promote peace, reconciliation, and social development in communities impacted by conflict and violence, with a focus on youth in Africa. How to get involved: Volunteer for their youth programs, participate in their online peace education courses, or organize awareness events in your community.

- **LeBron James Family Foundation**—Founded by NBA star LeBron James to support education and family well-being. How to get involved: Mentor students in their educational programs, volunteer at their community events, or participate in their family support initiatives.
- **Clooney Foundation for Justice**—Founded by actor George Clooney and human rights lawyer Amal Clooney to advance justice in courtrooms and communities around the world. How to get involved: Participate in their TrialWatch program to monitor trials, join their legal advocacy efforts, or help translate legal documents for their international cases.
- **Shawn Carter Foundation**—Founded by rapper Jay-Z to help individuals facing socioeconomic hardships further their education. How to get involved: Become a mentor for scholarship recipients, volunteer at their college prep workshops, or assist with their professional development programs.
- **Novak Djokovic Foundation**—Founded by tennis champion Novak Djokovic to support early childhood education. How to get involved: Volunteer as an early childhood educator, participate in their parenting workshops, or assist in organizing their sports-based youth development programs.
- **Eva Longoria Foundation**—Founded by actress Eva Longoria to help Latinas build better futures through education and entrepreneurship. How to get involved: Mentor young Latina entrepreneurs,

volunteer as a STEM tutor, or help organize their career development workshops.

- **Oprah Winfrey Leadership Academy for Girls**—Founded by media mogul Oprah Winfrey to provide educational and leadership opportunities for girls in South Africa. How to get involved: Volunteer as a virtual mentor, participate in their leadership workshops, or help organize career fairs for the students.
- **The Happy Hippie Foundation**—Founded by singer Miley Cyrus to fight injustice facing homeless youth, LGBTQ youth, and other vulnerable populations. How to get involved: Volunteer at LGBTQ youth shelters, participate in their art therapy programs, or help organize awareness events for homeless youth.
- **Batonga Foundation**—Founded by five-time Grammy Award winner Angélique Kidjo to promote gender equality and female empowerment. How to get involved: Donate to ensure every African girl and young woman can unleash her full potential.
- **Born This Way Foundation**—Co-founded by singer Lady Gaga to support the wellness of young people. How to get involved: Become a peer-to-peer mental health supporter, participate in their kindness campaigns, or help organize their youth mental health workshops.
- **Roger Federer Foundation**—Founded by tennis great Roger Federer to enable children to access quality education. How to get involved: Volunteer as a teacher in their educational programs, assist in organizing their sports and education camps, or help with their early childhood development initiatives.

- **Barefoot Foundation**—Founded by singer Shakira to promote universal education and early childhood development. How to get involved: Volunteer as a teacher in their schools, assist in their nutrition programs, or help organize their arts and music education initiatives.
- **The Michael J. Fox Foundation for Parkinson's Research**—Founded by actor Michael J. Fox to find a cure for Parkinson's disease. How to get involved: Participate in their clinical trials, become a research advocate, or help organize community fundraising events for Parkinson's research.
- **Dolly Parton's Imagination Library**—Founded by singer Dolly Parton to gift free books to children from birth to age five. How to get involved: Become a local program champion, volunteer at book distribution events, or help organize community reading sessions for children.

Privilege comes with a responsibility to help others. Even small actions such as these can contribute to meaningful change:

- Educate yourself about global issues and share that knowledge with others.
- Use your social media platforms to raise awareness about important causes.
- Volunteer your skills or time to local community organizations.
- Donate to reputable charities that align with your values.
- Mentor someone from a less privileged background.
- Advocate for inclusive policies at your workplace or school.

- Support businesses owned by marginalized groups.
- Use your network to connect people in need with resources or opportunities.
- Speak up against discrimination or injustice when you witness it.
- Practice conscious consumerism by supporting ethical and sustainable brands.
- Participate in or organize fundraising events for causes you care about.
- Share your platform (if you have one) with voices from marginalized communities.
- Use your voting rights to support policies that help the underprivileged.
- Offer pro bono professional services to nonprofit organizations.
- Encourage your workplace to implement socially responsible practices.

CHAPTER 18

FOCUS ON YOUR GOAL: KAREEM ABDUL-JABBAR

The Person

Kareem Abdul-Jabbar—basketball icon, social activist, scholar, historian, author, actor, and recipient of the 2016 Presidential Medal of Freedom—is a multifaceted figure whose contributions to the sport of basketball and to American society have had a lasting impact.

The Lesson

It's practically guaranteed: along the road to accomplishing anything, you're going to have setbacks. Distractions, illness, unexpected turns of events—or, for some, the negative impacts of systemic social injustice. Any one of these can derail us if we let them. But if you persevere in the face of adversity, if you "keep your eyes on the prize" and focus on the long game, you can overcome whatever stands between you and your goal.

Our Connection

I met Kareem Abdul-Jabbar at a reception in Beverly Hills, California, sometime in 1987-88, when he was at the height of his dominance on the basketball court as the center for the Los Angeles Lakers. That was thirty-some years ago now, but the encounter left a lasting impression. It was an overwhelming experience for a young student—only recently arrived in the US—to meet this towering legend. In the years that followed, I reveled in his success in sports but also took note of his impact in the area of social justice. As I've become more involved in the social sector over the past seventeen years, my admiration for Abdul-Jabbar has grown exponentially.

The author with Kareem Abdul-Jabbar

How Kareem Abdul-Jabbar Bettered the World

When I informally surveyed them, almost all of my friends knew about Abdul-Jabbar's achievements on the basketball court—three NCAA collegiate championships at UCLA, six NBA championships, six NBA Most Valuable Player awards, selected nineteen times as an NBA All-Star, and a place in the basketball Hall of Fame. Many knew about his appearance in the 1980 comedy *Airplane*, but only a few had read any of his books or knew that he had twice received the Columnist of the Year award from the Los Angeles Press Club's National Arts and Entertainment Journalism Awards. Most of them knew very little about his tireless and outspoken activism in the areas of race, religion, social justice, and civil rights.

Among his many contributions:

- Abdul-Jabbar has been a vocal advocate for Muslim Americans and has spoken out against discrimination and prejudice.
- He has criticized the movie industry for its lack of diversity in casting, writing, and production.
- He has spoken out against systemic racism and emphasized the need for reform and accountability in law enforcement.
- He has been involved in civil rights advocacy since his student days in the late 1960s and early 1970s, participating in protests and demonstrations at a time when many believed athletes should "shut up and play ball."

I admired his skills as a player, but I gradually came to admire him more as a thinker and leader.

Abdul-Jabbar once said, "I can do more than shoot a ball through a hoop. My greatest asset is my mind."[89] Based on everything I have read about him, his actions speak louder than his words. Kareem is the founder of the Skyhook Foundation, whose mission is to "'Give kids a shot that can't be blocked' by bringing educational STEAM opportunities to underserved communities."[90] The foundation's flagship program immerses children from diverse urban neighborhoods in a hands-on outdoor learning experience. With a focus on activities that blend science, technology, and nature, the program is designed to inspire young people toward a love of learning and a mindset that makes education a priority. As studies have shown, nothing has a greater impact on socioeconomic mobility. In my experience—growing up in Kolkata, India, and later working with educational initiatives in Africa, Asia, the Middle East, North Africa, and Latin America for SNV USA, Global Fund for Children, SOS Children's Villages USA, and now the Ousri Family Foundation—this has been crystal clear to me all my life.

Abdul-Jabbar has written seventeen books. Most of them explore the often-overlooked history of African Americans. My personal favorite is *Black Profiles in Courage*, which Abdul-Jabbar cowrote with Alan Steinberg. The book offers a comprehensive and inspiring look at the lives of twenty notable African Americans who demonstrated courage and resilience in the face of adversity, and it has had a significant impact as a work of historical and cultural scholarship. The profiles include well-known figures such as Frederick Douglass, Jackie Robinson, and Martin Luther King Jr., as well as lesser-known figures like Claudette Colvin, who refused to give up her seat on a Montgomery, Alabama, bus months before Rosa Parks more famously did the same.[91] This book made the *New York Times* best-seller list, but for Abdul-Jabbar, that accolade was not as important as its impact. In a 2012 interview with Alison Beard that appeared in the *Harvard Business Review*, Abdul-Jabbar explained, "The best reward was teachers in inner cities telling me the book made it possible for them to figure out their black-history lesson plans."[92]

How Kareem Abdul-Jabbar Made *Me* Better

Along with my enduring admiration for Abdul-Jabbar, I have seen him as a constant source of inspiration over the years. His book *Black Profiles in Courage* even helped inspire the book you now hold in your hands.

In *Giant Steps*, another of his books, Abdul-Jabbar describes his early struggles with racism and discrimination, as well as his spiritual awakening and conversion to Islam. The book recounts his journey toward self-discovery and growth, and emphasizes the importance of hard work, dedication, and discipline in achieving success both on and off the court. Abdul-Jabbar shares insights on the importance of practice, the need for mental and physical discipline, and the value of teamwork and cooperation.

In the same *Harvard Business Review* interview mentioned above, Abdul-Jabbar was asked how he dealt with occasional racism during his college and pro basketball career. "If you let it distract you, you're playing into their hands," he replied. "Their whole purpose is to distract you and prevent you from succeeding. And for me, success was the goal. My success and the success of other black Americans was exactly what would silence people who indulged in racism. So, it was 'Keep your eyes on the prize.' That was one of the messages of the civil rights movement, and I tried to do it."[93]

The book, and the interview, took me back to my own days as a student in Kolkata, leading demonstrations and protests on behalf of the city's marginalized population. We demonstrators were beaten by police, who saw in our cry for justice only the threat of disorder and who reacted with violence designed to break our spirit and our will to demand change. Through those early experiences, I came to recognize that the only way to keep going is to stay focused on your ultimate goal, be it a championship or social progress.

Abdul-Jabbar's story—and his success—has been a constant reminder of this lesson.

How You Can Focus on Your Goal *Now*

I will forever cherish meeting such an iconic figure as Kareem Abdul-Jabbar so soon after moving to the United States as a wide-eyed student from India, and later following his journey. My hope is that his story, and those of others in this book, will help sustain you in *your* journey toward change, both in yourself and in the world. If your goal includes working to lift up underserved communities, empower marginalized groups, or achieve racial justice, you might find these resources useful:

- **Skyhook Foundation**—Founded by Abdul-Jabbar to bring STEAM education to underserved communities. How to get involved: Volunteer, donate, or partner with the foundation for educational initiatives.
- **Equal Justice Initiative**—Works to end mass incarceration and excessive punishment in the US. How to get involved: Donate, volunteer, or use their educational resources.
- **Asian Americans Advancing Justice**—Fights for civil rights and empowers Asian Americans to create a more just America for all. How to get involved: Volunteer, donate, or report hate incidents.
- **UnidosUS**—Advocates for Latinos in the areas of civic engagement, civil rights, education, the workforce,

and more. How to get involved: Become an advocate, donate, or join their email list for updates.

Societal change doesn't happen overnight, so it's important to cultivate practices that can keep you motivated over the long term. These can help:

- Engage in continuous learning about social issues and history.
- Practice resilience in the face of setbacks or discrimination.
- Use your skills or platform, however small, to advocate for positive change.
- Challenge your own biases and assumptions regularly.
- Support and uplift voices from marginalized communities.
- Set long-term goals for personal growth and societal change.
- Incorporate physical and mental discipline into your daily routine.
- Practice active listening when engaging with others about social issues.
- Encourage teamwork and cooperation in your personal and professional life.
- Share educational resources about social justice with your network.
- Reflect on your own privilege and how you can use it to effect change.
- Support athletes and public figures who use their platform for activism.
- Engage in respectful dialogue with those who hold different views.

- Celebrate the achievements and contributions of diverse individuals in your field.
- Stay focused on your ultimate goals, even in the midst of adversity.

CHAPTER 19

INVITE TRANSFORMATION: SHIMON PERES

The Person

In the course of his seventy-year political career—much of which he devoted to building Israel's military capacity—Shimon Peres served as both prime minister and president of Israel. He won the Nobel Peace Prize in 1994 for his efforts to promote peace between Israel and Palestine and spent the last two decades of his life as an advocate for peace.

The Lesson

As children, most of us pass through predictable developmental phases: dependence on and allegiance to our parents, rebellion, consolidation of our identities and values, and reconciliation as we reach adulthood. Once we mature, however, such internal changes become less common. Yet, as Shimon Peres showed—and as psychologists will attest—our capacity for transformation as adults remains limitless. Both our views and our actions can change. With experience, dialogue, and open minds, we can transform both ourselves and the way we approach the world.

Our Connection

From an early age, I observed my father working as a community leader to resolve conflict and build bridges. I have tried to follow in his footsteps.

When I founded Global Youth Initiative (GYI), my vision was rooted in that philosophy. The goal of GYI was to facilitate collaborations across racial and religious boundaries, encourage dialogue between youth and decision makers, and ultimately inspire a new generation to embark on careers of compassionate service to humanity. In formulating this vision, I was thinking of young people around the world—especially children in areas that seem forever locked in cycles of violence. Not surprisingly, Israeli and Palestinian children and youth came to mind.

Imagine growing up in a world without hope. Children and youth in regions of conflict like the Palestinian territories don't have to imagine it. They live it.

And yet there is always one avenue of hope: Peace.

I admired Peres's efforts to build peace, and his role as Israeli foreign minister, in conducting the secret negotiations with the Palestinians in Oslo, Norway, beginning in 1993. His work there led to the signing of the Oslo Accords and laid the foundation for a possible future resolution to one of the world's most intractable conflicts. He showed that, by committing absolutely to the goal of peace, it was possible to see that the so-called obstacles were dead ends.

So, after founding GYI, I reached out to the office of President Peres (as well as to President Bill Clinton, the Dalai Lama, Indian Muslim leader Umer Ahmed Ilyasi, and many others), seeking his comments about this initiative. In January, 2013, I received a note that said, "I think peace should be pursued not only among governments but among people." A year later, I had the honor and great privilege of briefly meeting Peres during a Clinton Global Initiative conference in New York. He was ninety-one in 2014, and his charisma was still impressive.

Shimon Peres and the author in New York City in 2014

How Shimon Peres Bettered the World

It is a matter of record that Peres served as an aide to Israel's first prime minister, David Ben Gurion, when he was only twenty-three, on his way to becoming the country's prime minister, president, foreign minister, and head of several other ministries. Some may also know that he immigrated to Palestine from Poland in 1934 and grew up partly in a kibbutz, where he was schooled in both military training and practical socialism. But many do not know that his grandfather and the rest of his family who remained in the town of Wiszniew perished in the Holocaust. It was not surprising that he made his reputation as "Mr. Security," the man identified with building the Israeli Defense Forces and who, as defense minister, greenlighted military operations such as the 1976 raid at Entebbe, Uganda, which freed Israeli citizens held hostage by terrorists.

What was surprising was his transformation from his country's most prominent "hawk" to its most prominent "dove." I have read dozens of articles to understand it. The more I read, the more I have come to admire the courage behind his evolution into a master of negotiation and an architect of peace.

In a sense, it was logical. Having helped to secure Israel's existence, he could not help but turn his attention to its future. For Peres, a future of constant war was unthinkable and unacceptable. His vision was more positive. In an article published by Santa Clara University's Markkula Center for Applied Ethics, Peres wrote, "As for our region, the Middle East, Israel's role is to contribute to the region's great and sustained revival. It will be a Middle East without wars, without fronts, without enemies, without ballistic missiles, and without nuclear warheads."[94]

That kind of a future required more than tanks and fighter jets. It required negotiation, sacrifice, trust. And so Peres became as strong an advocate for peace negotiations with Israel's Arab neighbors as he had been a leader of armed forces against them. Not surprisingly, he faced virulent and implacable opposition. For one thing, Israel's history with Arab states was one of mutual mistrust. Israel owes its existence to a United Nations resolution, and its right to exist has repeatedly been questioned both verbally and militarily. Distrust of its Arab neighbors is widespread in politics and society, especially on the right. The unresolved political status of Palestinians who find themselves living in territories under Israeli control has been a source of tension and violence for decades. Meanwhile, the geopolitical importance of the Middle East has invited the interest and involvement of regional powers and superpowers pursuing their own interests.

Over the decades, Peres built coalitions outside of the traditional alignments. He became close friends with West German Chancellor Willy Brandt and Swedish Prime Minister Olof Palme, two leaders forging a middle ground between the superpowers of East and West. As vice president of Socialist International—a commitment to socialist practices had been a constant since his youth—he entered into a dialogue with Palestinian leaders on a possible two-state arrangement. His evolution was not without conflict. He fought hawks in his own Labor Party to support the peace treaty between Egypt and Israel, which required Israel to forfeit settlements and military bases in the Sinai Peninsula.

In the autumn of 1994, he shared the Peace Prize with his own prime minister Yitzhak Rabin and the Palestinian leader Yasser Arafat for their efforts to create peace in the Middle East. It was his "finest hour" as a peacemaker, though he would continue to advocate on behalf of the process. For example, despite their differences, Peres paired with rightist Benjamin Netanyahu in 2007 to serve as president of Israel, while Netanyahu served as prime minister. Israeli heads of state are not directly involved in political decision-making, but Peres, a Nobel Peace laureate, used the presidency as a platform to advocate for peace with the Palestinians, taking a more conciliatory stance than Netanyahu.

Even after leaving politics at an advanced age, Peres remained committed to promoting peace and reconciliation in the Middle East. In 1996, he founded the Peres Center for Peace and Innovation. Today the organization he founded "develops and implements impactful and meaningful programs with a focus on promoting a prosperous Israel, nurturing and highlighting innovation, and paving the way for shared-living between all of Israel's citizens and lasting peace between Israel and its neighbors."[95]

How Shimon Peres Made *Me* Better

In his final work, *No Room for Small Dreams*, in 2017, Peres reviews Israeli history from the perspective—and with the insights—of one who has both witnessed and influenced it. He reveals the courage it took to make difficult decisions under pressure as well as to seek painful but potentially rewarding compromises. This is a book written from the trenches of the real world by a man who remained committed to his high ideals, even though he was dealing with very practical, non-idealistic matters in the very messy context of politics. There is a lesson for the younger generation here, and that is the need for negotiation, with oneself as well as with others. That lesson has not been lost on me.

Peres had a vision and a clear message, and he was an experienced and gifted leader. I will always remember how President Clinton described Peres in his eulogy: "Wise champion of our common humanity. . . . He started his life as Israel's brightest student, became its best teacher and ended up its biggest dreamer. . . . He lived 93 years in a state of constant wonder over the unbelievable potential of all the rest of us to rise above our wounds, our resentments, our fears to make the most of today and claim the promise of tomorrow."[96] The life lived by

Shimon Peres gives me hope that transformation is possible for all of us.

How You Can Invite Transformation *Now*

It sounds simple, but we do have the ability to wage peace instead of war. It takes just as much courage as war—probably more, because sticking up for peace often means opposing your allies as well as your adversaries. In the end, though, there is no other way for humanity to survive.

Here are some organizational "weapons" you can use to transform the world toward peace:

- **Peres Center for Peace and Innovation**—Founded in 1996 by Shimon Peres, this organization develops programs promoting peace and innovation within Israel and with its neighbors. How to get involved: Volunteer, donate, or participate in their programs.
- **Seeds of Peace**—Brings together young leaders from conflict regions to build relationships and skills. How to get involved: Apply for their programs, volunteer, or donate.
- **Search for Common Ground**—Works to transform how the world deals with conflict. How to get involved: Volunteer, donate, or use their conflict resolution resources.
- **United States Institute of Peace**—Promotes international conflict resolution and prevention. How to get involved: Attend their events, use their educational resources, or apply for grants.

- **Alliance for Peacebuilding**—Network of organizations working to end violent conflict and build sustainable peace. How to get involved: Become a member, attend their annual conference, or support their initiatives.

The following simple tips can help you remain open to self-transformation:

- Practice mindfulness meditation to increase self-awareness.
- Keep a reflective journal to track personal growth and changes.
- Seek out diverse perspectives through reading, travel, or conversations.
- Regularly challenge your own assumptions and beliefs.
- Set personal growth goals and review them periodically.
- Engage in lifelong learning through courses, workshops, or online platforms.
- Practice empathy by putting yourself in others' shoes.
- Embrace failure as a learning opportunity.
- Develop a growth mindset, believing in your ability to change and improve.
- Seek feedback from others and be open to constructive criticism.
- Engage in volunteer work or community service to broaden your perspective.
- Try new experiences that push you out of your comfort zone.
- Practice forgiveness, both for others and yourself.
- Engage in regular self-reflection and self-assessment.

CHAPTER 20

PAVE YOUR OWN PATH: MOHAMED OUSRI

The Person

Born into a Muslim family in Morocco in 1959, Mohamed Ousri is a self-made, entrepreneurial businessman who became successful in real estate in the US and has since dedicated himself to finding homes for vulnerable children.

The Lesson

Most of us have a tendency to become discouraged or give up if we feel disconnected from the centers of power in our fields. In the Washington, DC, area—where I have spent most of my career—you are said to be either inside or outside the Beltway (the freeway that encircles the city). If you want to drive change, it's better to be inside. But I have also met "outsiders," such as my friend Mohamed Ousri, who manage to have an enormous impact. They and their stories serve as an example that you don't always need to be well connected to change the world. If you have passion, persistence, and the vision to pave your own path, you can work wonders.

Our Connection

Sometime in 2005, Ousri the successful businessman visited Marrakech, Morocco, as he frequently did. While walking to his hotel, he caught sight of two young girls sleeping under a car in the parking lot. He estimated their ages to be eight and eleven. He immediately moved them to a safe place. These were not the first children to sleep on the street in Marrakech, nor were they the first he had passed in his life. But this particular time—I call this his "moment of obligation"—Ousri realized that he couldn't be a mere spectator to suffering, that he had to play a role in finding a solution. And so the man who had made his living building infrastructure for insiders dedicated himself to finding homes for the ultimate outsiders: vulnerable children.

Since he was not "connected," Ousri went about things in his own way. He researched organizations working to save vulnerable children, and he started to sponsor those that he found to be effective and trustworthy. One of the organizations that benefited from his donations was SOS Children's Villages, where I worked. This is how we met and where we formed an instant connection.

I had my first deep glimpse of Ousri's true character when we traveled together by road in Morocco in 2019, visiting multiple locations of SOS Children's Villages. Obviously Ousri was no ordinary donor. He didn't just mail in a check—he came on site visits. He wanted to see if money was being well spent, but more than that, he wanted to make sure that children were actually benefiting from the programs we were running. He didn't just speak with local project leadership but also met with children and youth, listened to their stories, and looked deeply into their faces. It was during this trip that I got to know a person from a humble background who worked very hard and built a diversified business portfolio but never forgot his roots. I saw a man who believed that every human being has the potential to grow if they have the right tools. I got to know a committed husband and a father of two beautiful children, Sammy and Sarah. Our connection was rooted in basic human values. His love and dedication for his family, his love for the country of his birth and for his adopted country, the United States—and most important, his idea of giving back—touched me deeply.

The author and Mohamed Ousri at the Dar Tifl orphanage soccer field in Marrakech

How Mohamed Ousri Bettered the World

Ousri's support of vulnerable children extends beyond Morocco. While he has never visited India, he decided a few years ago to fund the construction of several children's homes (not affiliated with SOS Children's Villages) throughout the country, which, he has told me, now provide shelter to close to 250 vulnerable children and youth. During my recent trip to India, I visited one of those homes. Ousri has taken a deliberate and conscious approach to using his foundation to support children from all religions and faiths. This deliberate approach resonated with me given the increasing polarization among religions and also the increasing nationalistic tendencies globally. Ousri says, "It does not matter if these homes are run by Christian or Hindu or Muslim or Jewish organizations. All children must have a safe home, love, and a good education."

In time I have come to appreciate the ethical foundations of Ousri's worldview. He is open-minded and embraces diverse perspectives and beliefs, including those related to religion. That involves a willingness to consider and understand ideas that may differ from his own worldview. This open-minded attitude goes hand in hand with freedom of thought, conscience, and religion, as well as the right to practice one's religion without discrimination or persecution. He recognizes and respects the fundamental human rights of all individuals, regardless of their religious beliefs, which is crucial for fostering tolerance.

I asked Ousri what forces had shaped his outlook. Without any hesitation he said it was his education and exposure to diverse beliefs, alongside his family environment. He explained how education played a vital role in his understanding the facts about other religions, and not the propaganda and myths that so often cloud our perceptions of others. He continued to explain how learning about different religions—their beliefs and practices, as well as their historical and cultural contexts—helped him develop a broader understanding of and appreciation for religious diversity. Education supported his critical thinking and helped him hone the skills required to challenge stereotypes or misconceptions about other religions. He explained that it had also helped to have a diverse group of friends (not just acquaintances) like me, someone who happens to have been born into a Hindu family, and also his other friends from other religions. This exposure to different religious communities, engaging in interfaith dialogues, and experiencing different religious ceremonies or rituals all helped shape his inclusive approach to humanity.

Ousri believes that education and exposure, although very important, are not enough to create a more compassionate society. Parents have a huge responsibility. He credits his parents for his outlook toward other religions and the world at large. Both his mother and father always put others' interests before their own. This foundation shaped Ousri's outlook and added altruism to his ambition. This upbringing also shaped his belief and his thirst for knowledge of other people, cultures, and religions. The more he learned, the more he embraced interfaith dialogue. Ousri is following in his parents' footsteps. In 2018, he took his teenage son and daughter to the Philippines to meet Father Matthieu Dauchez, founder and director of ANAK-Tnk, an organization Ousri supports. He wanted his children to experience true selfless compassion in action. ANAK-Tnk was founded to support Manila's most unfortunate children—those living in extreme poverty in the city's streets, slums, and even landfills. Ousri and his children learned a lot more about these children and their life journey from Father Dauchez. One particular child—a four-year-old found hiding from predators in a treetop—had made a lasting impact on Ousri's life, leading him to support Dauchez's work.

I am excited about the grassroots initiatives by Ousri in India, the Philippines, and Morocco, as they will enable dialogue and cooperation and understanding among diverse religious and national communities. The example set by people like Mohamed Ousri should encourage leaders and policy makers all over the world to look at vulnerable children and youth not as Hindu children, Christian children, Muslim children, or Jewish children but as our children. The hope is that conversation can lead to collaboration in efforts to help, where the problems are too big for one organization or faith community to solve on its own.

How Mohamed Ousri Made *Me* Better

During my time in the nonprofit sector, I worked with government agencies from multiple countries, multinational corporations, foundations, and individual donors to address important issues. What I most enjoyed was learning about individual donors—their life stories, their giving philosophy, and how they were impacting local communities. Individual donors gave $327 billion in 2021, or two-thirds of all charitable dollars in 2021.[97] For me it is a great source of learning and inspiration to read not just about Warren Buffett, Bill Gates, Melinda Gates, Pierre Omidyar, Pamela Kerr, and MacKenzie Scott but also to get to know individuals like Mohamed Ousri. His name may not be as well known, but his efforts share a common source of compassion, gratitude, and obligation.

On my return flight from a recent trip to India, I had time to reflect on Ousri's work and to wonder about the conditions that had spawned his views and led to his activism. Fortunately, within a few months (April, 2023), I had another opportunity to travel with Ousri to Morocco, as a friend and advisor to his foundation. This time we met the leadership of Atlas Kinder Foundation and its first children's home, Dar Bouidar, located about 20 miles south of Marrakech. Founded by Hansjorg Huber, a Swiss national, Dar Bouidar is considered a model for the construction of other children's villages. In addition to the houses, which represent the family home for the Atlas Kinder, who live here with their foster moms, there is a school, a kindergarten, a nursery, two doctors' offices, a therapy center, and an "integration house" for children with disabilities. An amphitheater, a mosque, and a farm have also been built in Dar Bouidar.

This visit gave me another opportunity to observe Ousri and glean insights into his thought processes and into the influences on his thinking and his world view. We visited Dar Tifl Marrakech, another local residential home where Ousri had supported the construction of a brand-new soccer field. He and I spent the afternoon with the children and their teachers. The dedication of these teachers, who work with the children day in and day out, continues to amaze me. We identified the basketball court at Dar Tifl Marrakech that will need renovation. I could see that there was still plenty to do in Marrakech, and I sensed that we would both be returning soon to build more homes in Morocco. I made a personal commitment to him to dedicate some of my time to building more homes for vulnerable children, wherever they may be.

How You Can Pave Your Own Path *Now*

Ousri's example shows that you don't need to be an "insider" or have traditional access to power to create significant positive change. With passion, persistence, and vision, individuals can have a profound impact on society. Your particular path might ultimately lead you to support a cause specific to your interests, but if you don't know where to begin, helping vulnerable populations like children in need is an excellent place to start. The following organizations are always looking for passionate individuals to help them accomplish their important work:

- **SOS Children's Villages**—An international organization that provides alternative care for children who have lost parental care. Ousri supported their work in Morocco. How to get involved: Sponsor a child, volunteer at local villages, or donate to support their programs.
- **The Ousri Family Foundation**—Founded by Mohamed Ousri, the organization brings together top aid organizations in a coordinated way to help children in India and Africa and around the world. How to get involved: The Ousri Family Foundation may not take donations but consolidates the power of those who want to help into something useful. If you are interested in collaboration, please connect with the foundation via its website or connect with the author at www.neilghosh.org.
- **The Calcutta Social Project**—This organization works to unleash the true potential of underprivileged women and children living in the slums of Kolkata through human development services focused on education, shelter, and nutrition. How to get involved: Donate to their programs and volunteer if you are in Kolkata, India.
- **UNICEF (United Nations Children's Fund)**—A global organization working in over 190 countries to

protect children's rights and provide humanitarian aid. How to get involved: Donate, volunteer, become a UNICEF USA supporter, or participate in their various campaigns and programs.

- **Antyodoy Anath Ashram**—Since 1995, they have run an orphanage for abandoned and destitute children in Paushi, a remote village in the Purba Medinipur district of the West Bengal state in India. How to get involved: Donate to their programs and volunteer if you are in Kolkata, India.
- **Save the Children**—An international non-governmental organization that promotes children's rights and provides relief and support to children in developing countries. How to get involved: Sponsor a child, donate, volunteer, or participate in their advocacy efforts.
- **Boys & Girls Clubs of America**—A national organization providing after-school programs for young people. How to get involved: Volunteer at a local club, donate, or become a mentor.
- **World Vision**—A global humanitarian organization tackling the causes of poverty and injustice. How to get involved: Sponsor a child, donate to specific causes, or participate in their youth ambassador program.
- **ANAK-Tnk**—Founded by Father Matthieu Dauchez, this organization supports street children in Manila, Philippines. How to get involved: Donate to their programs, volunteer if in Manila, or organize fundraising events in your community.
- **Children's Defense Fund**—A nonprofit child advocacy organization that works to ensure a level playing field for

all children in the United States. How to get involved: Join their local chapters, participate in their training programs, or support their policy advocacy efforts.

- **Global Fund for Children**—Finds, funds, and strengthens innovative community-based organizations that empower vulnerable children and youth. How to get involved: Donate, spread awareness, or explore partnership opportunities if you're part of a grassroots organization.
- **Child Mind Institute**—A national nonprofit dedicated to transforming the lives of children and families struggling with mental health and learning disorders. How to get involved: Donate, participate in their events, or use and share their educational resources.

Any of the following practices can help you identify your own path toward doing more good:

- Identify a cause you're passionate about in your local community.
- Start small by volunteering or donating to local organizations.
- Educate yourself about social issues and share knowledge with others.
- Use your professional skills to offer pro bono services to nonprofits.
- Organize fundraising events for causes you care about.
- Mentor a child or young adult from an underprivileged background.
- Create awareness campaigns on social media for important issues.

- Collaborate with like-minded individuals to start grassroots initiatives.
- Practice and promote religious and cultural tolerance in your daily life.
- Engage in conversations with people from diverse backgrounds.
- Support ethical and socially responsible businesses.
- Encourage your workplace to engage in corporate social responsibility.
- Travel responsibly and support local communities when you do.
- Teach your children or young people in your life about giving back.
- Look for unconventional ways to use your talents for social good.

CHAPTER 21

IMPROVE YOUR PROFESSION: TESSIE SAN MARTIN

The Person

Along with her role as CEO of a global nonprofit organization working in more than sixty countries to advance equity, health, and well-being, Tessie San Martin has been a tireless advocate for transparency and accountability among nonprofit organizations providing aid to developing countries.

The Lesson

Nearly all of us have to work for a living. We can approach our professions as simply a means to an end—paying the rent or mortgage and putting food on the table—or we can invest something of ourselves in making improvements that change our professions for the better. During my years in the nonprofit sector, Tessie San Martin showed me how to do the latter. While her focus on governance might not apply to all sectors or professions, each of us can take a hard look at the weak points in our working worlds and find ways to improve them. All we have to do is care enough.

Our Connection

I joined the nonprofit sector (also known as the "third sector") after spending the early parts of my career in both the public and private sectors. Fourteen years later, I returned to the private sector, but I remain involved in philanthropy and impact investing as an advisor to several nonprofit organizations.

Spending time in these different worlds has given me the opportunity to compare and contrast the ways in which they function. I have always believed that organizations, regardless of which sector they operate in, should be accountable to the same basic code of ethics and standards of professional behavior. The means of ensuring that accountability is known as *governance.* While my experience working with nonprofit organizations has been overwhelmingly positive, I have observed challenges in that area. Over time, and by comparing my own experiences and listening to those of colleagues, I have come to see these challenges as widespread in the sector, perhaps even commonplace. So much so, in fact, that nonprofit governance is a field of research in its own right, with expert practitioners who provide insight and guidance. Among my colleagues, Tessie San Martin has provided an abundance of both.

San Martin and I first met during my tenure as CEO of SNV USA (an affiliate of SNV Netherlands Development Organization). Over the years I have consulted with her on multiple occasions. She and I worked closely together after I accepted the CEO role of SOS Children's Villages USA, as her organization at the time, Plan USA, had a similar governance structure.

Tessie San Martin

I could always relate to her, not only because we shared similar values and passion, but also because of her engaging personality and empathy. Whenever I reached out, she was welcoming and available, even joining my board meeting at SOS Children's Villages USA as a guest speaker. Like many in the third sector, she has dedicated her career to creating a better and more just world for people everywhere, and I have drawn much inspiration from her emphasis on good governance over the years.

How Tessie San Martin Bettered the World

Prior to joining FHI 360, Tessie San Martin was CEO and president of Plan International USA, group vice president at Abt Associates, director for the Operations Group of the World Bank's Multilateral Investment Guarantee Agency, and a partner at PriceWaterhouseCoopers (PwC). San Martin's diverse professional journey has given her a comprehensive perspective—one that she has put to use as a forceful advocate for good governance and aid effectiveness, serving as co-chair of the Modernizing Foreign Assistance Network (MFAN) and a board member of both Friends of Publish What You Fund, which supports greater aid transparency, and InterAction, which convenes United States–based nongovernmental organizations working to eliminate extreme poverty and strengthen human rights and citizen participation.

Among San Martin's many contributions to her profession has been the ability to articulate the main obstacles to—and possible solutions for—achieving better governance in the nonprofit world. Key points include the following:

- Nonprofits are not "owned" by anyone, so it is not clear who is asking the big questions: Is this entity really making a difference overall? Is it financially healthy? Is it ethically run?
- Nonprofits are not subject to the same discipline that commercial entities face in the market, where profit and loss are reliable measures of success. Feedback from beneficiaries might help, but asymmetries of information exist between providers and recipients of products and services. These asymmetries get even more pronounced when the recipients of support are marginalized and their voices/opinions are discounted.
- Metrics to evaluate the bottom-line health, effectiveness, or impact of nonprofits are not well developed, and where they exist, they are poorly understood. The accounting for nonprofits is less well understood by the public than accounting in the private sector. Charity rating agencies tend to focus on "overheads" (which are

> easily manipulated and not really comparable across entities) and top-line growth. Metrics around impact are hard to come by and not sophisticated. So nonprofits produce their own so-called "vanity metrics" to document their impact for donors and membership, but is anyone really looking under the hood and evaluating the rigor of those metrics?

So what is to be done?

In the absence of external regulation, San Martin believes that reform must come from within, by creating strong boards that are well prepared, outfitted with the right set of skills, engaged at every meeting, able to exercise independent judgment, and armed with explicit norms and mandates that empower them to hold CEOs and management accountable to overarching principles of good governance.

I have come to realize that many volunteer board members do not have the time, experience, or skills necessary to manage a good CEO. So many times, instead of the members managing the CEO, the CEO is tasked with the responsibility of managing the board. It is a huge waste of time and effort.

San Martin and I agree that a good board can do great work and a dysfunctional board can do great damage. I have seen both. Boards are often susceptible to nepotism and personal interest and politics, which can hurt the nonprofit. Sometimes too much emphasis is placed on congeniality and consensus, creating a culture in which board members are afraid to bring "unpleasant" ideas to the table and speak up against other board members. Instead of being the place where necessary and difficult conversations take place, too many boards operate by the rule, "See no evil, hear no evil, speak no evil." It is important to ensure that boards are diverse, representative, and possess the necessary skills and expertise to oversee the organization effectively. A few helpful practices recommended by San Martin:

- Choose the board chair wisely. This is a person who needs to not just be committed to the organization and its mission but willing and able to bring hard-nosed business judgment to conversations with the CEO. Charities are businesses, after all. And leadership must insist on clear metrics to judge performance and be willing to ensure there is accountability to deliver its expectations.
- Ensure that the board and the chair are regularly evaluating their own performance.
- Set term limits for the board chair and board members to maintain board discipline and work against the tendency to be overly collegial.
- Establish a robust board candidate pipeline for identifying, vetting, and considering members.
- Establish a strong board leadership pipeline, and set clear roles for chair, vice chair, treasurer, and other leadership roles.
- Build strong committees.
- Regularly review and update board bylaws to adapt to changing conditions and evolving organizational needs.
- Support the CEO's vision (not the board's vision) and provide the CEO with expert advice.

San Martin has been a vocal champion of these messages and has worked relentlessly to increase awareness while also implementing policies at her own organizations. Not surprisingly, she is highly regarded in the NGO sector for the "tough love" she provides.

How Tessie San Martin Made *Me* Better

San Martin's push toward better governance was important for me as I was getting my feet wet in the third sector. At times, the norms of leadership and organizational behavior I witnessed didn't always make sense, and I began to doubt my own managerial abilities. Conversations with San Martin about governance confirmed my observations and my disappointment. But they also showed me how to become part of the solution, and this renewed my dedication to the missions of my organizations and helped restore my overall sense of purpose.

To give you a sense of San Martin's impact on my thinking about governance, I would like to share some lessons I gleaned from her and others over the years.

But first, what is the third sector, and why is governance an issue?

The third sector was born as an extension of the public (or government) and the private (for profit) sectors. It is an umbrella term for a group of voluntarily organized, private, nonprofit, and self-governing entities. Examples of third-sector organizations include charities, foundations, nongovernmental organizations (NGOs), international nongovernment organizations (INGOs), community groups, and cooperatives. The third sector plays a crucial role in addressing various social issues, such as poverty, education, healthcare, environmental conservation, civil rights, threats to democracy, vulnerable populations, and community development. Third-sector organizations rely on donations, grants, and other forms of funding (public and private) to support their activities. The most recent addition to this sector are social enterprises—hybrid entities with both economic and social bottom lines.

Because the third sector includes varying organizational forms with distinct development histories and conditions, few studies have successfully investigated the third sector globally with a special focus on governance. It is important to note that there are hybrid organizations incorporating features of two or even three sectors. The third sector claims legitimacy from not being corrupted by special interests, as is alleged at times of government, or by the profit motive, which drives business. Third-sector organizations also claim legitimacy from the virtue of their causes.

But the virtue of the ends does not absolve us from the need to scrutinize the means; it's natural to ask if we have all the elements of proper governance in this sector. What are the accountability structures? How do they differ from those in government or the private sector? What does that tell us about the role of governance and what qualities are required of leadership?

I will admit that this chapter is not a rigorous analysis of the subject, and its focus is not policy. Rather, I am sharing some observations and learnings from San Martin and others I have met on the important issue of governance in the nonprofit sector.

Governance is critical in the third sector not only because of its broad and idealistic mission, but also because of its immense social and economic impact on the lives of hundreds of millions of people. Most Americans may not be aware of the size of that impact. A 2022 review of the health of the sector reports that "nonprofits contributed $1.4 trillion to the nation's economy during the first quarter of 2022, with growth in the gross value added by nonprofits exceeding the overall Gross Domestic Product (GDP) by 1%."[98]

That kind of money compels us to ask how it is being spent. The answer is: We could do better.

In his book *Banker to the Poor*, the Nobel Prize-winning social entrepreneur and microfinance pioneer Muhammad Yunus argues that foreign aid has become a kind of charity for the powerful, leaving poor people to become poorer. He shared the results of a study conducted by a research institution in Bangladesh that concluded that, "of the more than $30 billion in foreign donor assistance received in the last twenty-six years, 75 per cent never actually reached Bangladesh in the form of cash", but instead was spent on equipment, commodities, and consultants in and from the donor countries themselves.[99]

The problem may not be limited to a few bad apples. In his provocative book *Winners Take All: The Elite Charade of Changing the World, New York Times* journalist Anand Giridharadas argues that many development initiatives fail to address systemic problems—and can even reinforce inequalities—because the very entities working to solve the problems are deeply invested in the systems that create them in the first place. The book urges us to examine the power dynamics of aid more closely, question the influence of elites, and take a more inclusive approach to systemic change beyond philanthropy and corporate social responsibility.[100] To summarize his thrust on governance, Giridharadas starts one of his chapters with a quote from Upton Sinclair: "It is difficult to get a man to understand something when his salary depends on his not understanding it."[101]

While we must listen to these important voices and rethink our approaches when and where we are able, it is equally important to remember that there are thousands of dedicated professionals doing incredible work in the third sector every day and night, saving lives, reducing poverty, educating the next generation, protecting vulnerable children, fighting for justice, protecting our environment. I was fortunate to observe some incredible work by colleagues at SNV Netherlands Development Organization, Global Fund for Children, SOS Children's Villages, and many others with whom we partnered.

I believe that the INGO community and the third sector are at a crossroads. The sector has played a critical role in addressing a range of social issues and can be credited with contributing to progress toward many significant human development goals. However, authoritarian rule, polarizing populist politics, and unregulated markets have provided a fertile breeding ground for disinformation about the impact and role of this sector. Any loss of credibility for one organization can undermine the credibility of the entire sector and reverse decades of success. To remain effective, legitimate, and relevant in the future, the third sector must embrace organizational change and invest in new capabilities—with better governance primary among them.

How You Can Improve Your Profession *Now*

If your profession falls outside of the nonprofit sector, this discussion of good governance might not seem—at first—relevant to you personally. But by sharing San Martin's role in improving her field, I wanted to show by example how everyone can learn to think critically about issues and processes in their own spheres of employment.

For those in the nonprofit sector, the following organizations and resources provide concrete avenues for enhancing accountability, transparency, and performance metrics within your organization and the sector as a whole:

- **FHI 360**—A nonprofit human development organization (with Tessie San Martin as CEO) working in over sixty countries. How to get involved: Explore job opportunities or partner on projects.
- **Modernizing Foreign Assistance Network (MFAN)**—A coalition promoting more effective US foreign assistance. How to get involved: Join their mailing list, attend events, or support their policy recommendations.
- **InterAction**—An alliance of international NGOs and partners in the US that provides a platform for improving sector-wide governance and effectiveness. How to get involved: Attend their annual forum, join as a member organization, or participate in their working groups.
- **Friends of Publish What You Fund**—Supports greater aid transparency. How to get involved: Use their Aid Transparency Index, advocate for transparency in aid, or support their research efforts.
- **BoardSource**—Supports nonprofit board leadership. How to get involved: Attend their training sessions, use their board assessment tools, or become a member.
- **Independent Sector**—A national membership organization that brings together nonprofits, foundations, and corporations to promote effective practices and

ethical standards. How to get involved: Join as a member, attend their conferences, or use their resources on nonprofit governance.

- **Charity Governance Code**—Promotes good governance practices in the UK charity sector. How to get involved: Adopt their governance code in your organization, participate in their consultations, or use their resources for board improvement.
- **The Center for Effective Philanthropy**—Provides data and insight for philanthropic funders to improve their effectiveness. How to get involved: Use their assessment tools, attend their conferences, or participate in their research studies.

These simple daily actions can help you improve your profession (whatever it may be):

- Stay informed about best practices in your field.
- Advocate for transparency and accountability in your organization.
- Participate in professional development opportunities.
- Mentor younger professionals in your field.
- Join professional associations and actively contribute.
- Share knowledge and experiences with colleagues.
- Critically evaluate your organization's performance metrics.
- Encourage diverse perspectives in decision-making processes.
- Promote ethical practices in your daily work.
- Seek feedback from beneficiaries or clients of your organization.

- Contribute to discussions about improving sector-wide standards.
- Volunteer for leadership roles in professional committees.
- Read and share research on governance and effectiveness in your field.
- Encourage your organization to adopt clear performance metrics.
- Foster a culture of continuous improvement in your workplace.

PART III

ACT

CHAPTER 22

BUILD BRIDGES: BILL CLINTON

The Person

William Jefferson Clinton, known to the world simply as "Bill" Clinton, served as the forty-second president of the United States from January 1993 to January 2001.

The Lesson

It's easy to believe that doing more good requires doing *more* of something. But sometimes, it actually requires doing less. This is true when it comes to imparting judgement on others. To really be of service, we sometimes have to turn toward ourselves first and put our personal opinions aside. Bill Clinton has always been a master at this—listening carefully to opposing viewpoints to find common ground. Following his lead, we make the world a better place when we shake hands and build bridges with *everyone*—even though (and especially when) it's hard. Because this, as evidenced by the impact he's had on so many lives, is exactly what creates a world in which we all get more of the important work done.

Our Connection

The author with Bill Clinton

In 2007, I left my corporate job to join a Dutch nonprofit (SNV) whose mission was—and still is—to eliminate poverty and raise the standard of living in Africa, Latin America, and Asia. This mission, part of a global effort known as international development, gave me a new perspective. I was convinced that the government and corporate lessons I had learned in the course of my career could be applicable to nonprofit organizations such as SNV. What if aspects of private industry (knowledge of how to make a profit) could combine with aspects of government (knowledge of how to make policy) to improve the efficiency and effectiveness of nonprofits engaged in helping impoverished nations and communities? A change of approach was certainly needed. After decades of attempts to assist those in need, a significant part of the world's population was still living in abject poverty. The time was ripe for a new paradigm, and the Clinton Global Initiative (CGI)—founded by Bill and Hillary Clinton—provided just that.

I had seen the huge divide between the haves and have-nots firsthand in India, and I saw my role as the chief executive officer of SNV USA as an opportunity to help the world's less fortunate. After speaking with Clinton Global Initiative leaders, I was convinced that SNV could be a great partner in their work. We had boots on the ground in more than thirty-five countries and a forty-year tradition of value chain development, local empowerment, and cross-sector collaboration. Our model of inclusive growth and impact investing resonated with CGI. After reaching out to the Initiative, I received a letter of invitation from President Clinton to join in its efforts to make international development more effective.

I was an active participant in CGI for many years, including an engagement with the planning committee in which I attended a retreat to brainstorm ideas for bringing people and resources together. This involvement gave me the opportunity to observe Bill Clinton in action and to absorb the essence of his "superpower"—the ability to build bridges and get things done. In a conversation with M. Sanjayan, then the lead scientist for the Nature Conservancy, Clinton's impressive knowledge of climate change was evident to me as the discussion moved from a green building in the Netherlands to a village in West Africa. Yet, consistent with the theme of the retreat—"Turning Ideas into Action"—his knowledge was more than just talk. During his tenure as president, the Clinton administration reduced the federal government's carbon emissions by 24 percent relative to 1990 levels, spearheaded major initiatives to improve energy efficiency, and forged partnerships with industry to reduce greenhouse gas emissions.[102]

My most memorable conversation with President Clinton was about the Global Youth Initiative, an organization I founded (described in more detail in the chapter on Hillary Clinton) to engage and empower young people to find community-based solutions to some of the most urgent issues of our time: poverty, racial and religious discrimination, and violence. I had limited time to get Clinton's attention, and it was not an easy pitch—in fact, almost everyone I had spoken with prior to this had needed several explanations of our model before they fully grasped it, and the fault was not theirs. I explained that stimulating youth participation could have a long-term impact in addressing systemic problems surrounding youth, such as unemployment and criminality. President Clinton listened intently. "I get the concept," he said. "How would you reach these youths in so many different communities?" He had distilled, almost instantly, our fundamental challenge: scale. I was reminded that beneath his easygoing demeanor, he was a Rhodes Scholar. Not only did his question show me the way to better focus our efforts, but it also validated my thinking. I was grateful that he had been so attentive and seriously considered what I proposed. It was impossible not to like this man.

Bill Clinton in conversation with the author and another CGI conference participant

On another occasion—one of the annual CGI America meetings in Denver, which brought together a broad array of leaders interested in improving conditions for struggling communities in the US—I approached him to say hello. I had recently purchased the book *Hard Choices*, written by Hillary Clinton, and happened to be holding it as we talked. When he saw it in my hand, he immediately offered—out of genuine kindness—to get it signed by the author. I politely declined, as I did not want to ask a favor of either him or Hillary in the middle of a busy conference schedule, but I was touched nonetheless.

I am thrilled to see the revival of the Clinton Global Initiative. In April 2023, I had an opportunity to speak with President Clinton at an event in Washington, DC, and we briefly discussed the content of my book. He reminded all of us at the event that every day presents a choice, and it is in our power to make a commitment to act.

How Bill Clinton Bettered the World

When Clinton's term in the White House ended, he was still a relatively young man of fifty-four—full of energy, brimming with ideas, and no longer constrained by immediate political considerations. In 2001 he founded the William J. Clinton Presidential Foundation (now the Clinton Foundation). He located the headquarters in New York City—not in the banking district of Wall Street or in the diplomatic enclave surrounding the United Nations, but in Harlem, home to the cultural life and aspirations of people of color. It was a statement of purpose. "Harlem symbolized the economic efforts I had made to include Americans that were left out when I became president," he later explained.[103] In 2005, the Foundation launched the

Clinton Global Initiative (CGI)—which, as I've described in the previous section, I became intimately involved with a few years later.

CGI brought together business executives, heads of nonprofit organizations, investors, politicians, college presidents, professors, ambassadors, and others—each with a proven track record of leadership and impact in their respective fields—to work on global challenges and develop innovative solutions. The events were by invitation only, and attendees were expected to make a specific commitment to action in the form of a concrete plan to address a global challenge. The commitments needed to be measurable and achievable, and they had to have a significant impact. Over the years, CGI made notable progress in areas including global health, sustainable development, women's and girls' empowerment, disaster relief, and cross-sector collaboration.

Of course, Clinton's knack for building bridges predated CGI. During his time in the White House, he worked to foster relationships with other world leaders, including those in the Middle East and Europe, and history will remember him for the peace deals he brokered in the Middle East, the former Yugoslavia, Northern Ireland, and between North and South Korea. His willingness to listen to opposing viewpoints, and his dedication to finding common ground and solutions to complex problems, is something to learn from.

Like all politicians, Bill Clinton is not everyone's cup of tea. Over the years, outside the comfort zone of CGI, I was party to numerous conversations about him and his presidency and heard a wide range of opinions, but one moment in particular has stuck with me. Many years ago the late Barbara Walters asked

Bill O'Reilly, the archconservative pundit, what he thought of former President Clinton. "Brilliant," O'Reilly said. "I think he did a good job as president."[104] High praise for Clinton's performance, coming as it did from an ideological adversary. I have heard the same from Democrat and Republican friends alike. And I think it all goes back to Clinton's gift for putting the *issue* at the heart of the discussion—and understanding what might motivate another person, be they friend or foe, to join him in addressing it. Perfect unanimity does not exist, but you can always find common ground on some aspect of a given issue and move from there.

How Bill Clinton Made *Me* Better

While attending various CGI conferences, meetings, planning sessions, and fireside chats, I witnessed the power of successful collaborations and saw how a good partnership can turn great ideas into action. I also observed the role President Clinton was playing to build bridges between communities, sectors, countries, and policy makers. Great ideas are important and the world is flooded with them, but CGI helped to turn those ideas into reality. What was its secret? In a word: Bill. Over the span of five years, I spoke with many community, business, nonprofit, and local leaders from Africa, Asia, and Latin America, and they shared a common assessment of Clinton's recipe for success: his understanding of the issues, his conviction that we are all in this together, and his ability to connect people with diverse interests and backgrounds to get things done.

Watching Clinton was one of the most incredible learning experiences of my life. Regardless of the topic, he always had an informed point of view backed up with stats, specifics, and stories. I watched him connect with conference participants with respect, share story after story to boil a complex issue down to something everyone could relate to, and evoke a can-do spirit of optimism.

Everyone who has met President Clinton knows how personable and engaging he is. He has an incredible gift for connecting with people on an individual level. When he is speaking with you, you feel as if you are the only person he is interested in, as if your problem is also his problem. Over the years, I listened to his speeches and his interactions with global leaders and heads of state, CEOs and business executives, philanthropists, nonprofit leaders, celebrities, and media professionals. On multiple occasions during CGI annual meetings, I was in the same room during his interviews with Charlie Rose (formerly of PBS), Erin Burnett (CNN), and Fareed Zakaria (CNN). It may not surprise those who know him well, but for the rest of us it was rather extraordinary to watch these interviews up close. Speaking without notes, he moved effortlessly from a discussion on the price of electricity in Puerto Rico to the threat of ISIS in Iraq to green building practices in Amsterdam to a specific woman from China with a severe disability, all without missing a beat. It is no wonder that his fellow former president, Barack Obama, referred to Clinton as the "Explainer in Chief" at the 2012 Democratic National Convention.

That quality was on full display when Obama joined Clinton at CGI for a discussion of the Affordable Care Act, the national health plan commonly known as "Obamacare." At that meeting, which I also attended, Clinton explained in simple language the benefits of the Act. After the session, many in the audience expressed how much clarity Clinton had brought to this complicated and often confusing program.

During my time with CGI, observing President Clinton in action taught me how connecting with a wide range of people on an individual level—and facilitating their connections with one another—can help accomplish challenging goals. It might sometimes seem as if spending the time to build such bridges requires too much effort, but Bill Clinton's example taught me otherwise. If you want to get things done, make sure your actions include connecting with others in ways that show respect and demonstrate understanding. Their support will be yours when you need it.

How You Can Build More Bridges *Now*

A diversity of experiences, cultures, and attitudes can spark new ideas. Conversely, confirmation bias has taught us that it's human to inherently believe we're right and then go about proving it. Getting out of our own heads is an ongoing journey, and the most important element is being open to other ideas. Building bridges may start at home for many of us—committing ourselves to being more Bill-like in our encounters, focusing not on where we disagree, but where we can meet others in the middle.

Many organizations actively work to build bridges, and more are coming to the forefront every day to counter the increasing divisiveness in this country.

- **Clinton Global Initiative (CGI)**—Founded by Bill and Hillary Clinton to foster collaboration and turn ideas into action, CGI brings together global leaders to develop innovative solutions to world challenges. How to get involved: Attend events, make commitments, or support their initiatives.

- **The Morton Deutsch International Center for Cooperation and Conflict Resolution**—Provides resources for organizations working to bridge social divides. How to get involved: Identify bridge-building organizations that interest you, use their resources, attend events, or support their research.

To build bridges and find common ground with others, make these actions part of your daily life:

- In discussions and negotiations, focus on the issue rather than on conflicting views.
- Seek out news sources from various political perspectives.
- Engage in respectful dialogue with people who have different opinions.
- Look for points of agreement in disagreements before focusing on differences.
- Volunteer for community projects that bring diverse groups together.
- Attend local town halls or community meetings to hear diverse viewpoints.
- Practice empathy by trying to understand others' motivations and experiences.
- Share meals or social activities with people from different backgrounds.
- Participate in interfaith or intercultural events in your community.

- Use social media to promote positive, constructive dialogue rather than divisiveness.
- Learn about and practice conflict resolution techniques.
- Mentor or tutor someone from a different background.
- Organize or participate in community discussions on local issues.
- Practice finding compromise in your personal and professional relationships.
- Educate yourself about different cultures, religions, and political ideologies to broaden your perspective.

CHAPTER 23

STEP UP: ROSA PARKS

The Person

Rosa Parks was a civil rights activist who in 1955 famously refused to give up her seat on an Alabama bus to a white passenger—an act of civil disobedience that led to the Montgomery bus boycott and, the following year, to a federal ruling that declared bus segregation unconstitutional.

The Lesson

Who, as an individual in a world with more than eight billion people, hasn't felt insignificant? As of 2024, there were 337 million people in the United States alone. Yet despite those numbers, one person's actions can still make a difference. With a single act, Rosa Parks became a symbol of how ordinary individuals can stand up against injustice and inspire widespread change. Her lesson is as true today as it was then: If you act with conviction to call attention to an important issue, your action can become much larger than yourself.

Our Connection

One of my early memories of growing up in Kolkata, India, is a small piece of paper on which I had scribbled the words, "Tolerance is key." It seems surprising, coming from a child, but it stands to reason. I grew up in an environment where speaking out for justice, especially on behalf of vulnerable segments of the population, was encouraged. My father was an activist who spoke out frequently, and whose convictions eventually landed him in a political prison. Throughout my childhood, and later in my personal and professional life, I have been focused on promoting tolerance, respect, and understanding among people of different races, religions, and cultures.

Soon after moving to the United States, I developed a keen interest in the American civil rights movement and its leaders. I started to lend my voice, time and financial support to various organizations. One of these was the National Campaign for Tolerance, where Rosa Parks served as one of the co-chairs along with Morris Dees, a prominent civil rights lawyer and activist. In recognition of my involvement, in 2005 I received a certificate, signed by Parks and Dees, acknowledging my stand against hate, injustice, and intolerance. It was a great honor, made all the more poignant and precious for me by the passing of Parks in October of that same year.

How Rosa Parks Bettered the World

With a single act, Rosa Parks changed the course of history. On December 1, 1955, she refused to surrender her seat in the Black section of a Montgomery, Alabama, city bus to a white passenger, as she was legally obliged to do. She was removed from the bus and arrested. Yet her spontaneous defiance sparked the ensuing Montgomery bus boycott, a movement of Blacks and whites that took shape within hours of her arrest and catalyzed the civil rights movement across the United States. The boycott lasted for over a year—a year in which Black commuters walked, rode bikes, or accepted rides from sympathetic whites, causing financial distress for the city—until a district court ruling declared bus segregation unconstitutional. This ruling was upheld by the US Supreme Court, striking down the practice across the country. And this was just the beginning. The boycott galvanized a national network of support, and created a cadre of committed activists that would form the backbone of the civil rights movement for decades to come.

Rosa Parks's protest did not come out of nowhere. She had been an activist for over a decade. She had joined the National Association for the Advancement of Colored People (NAACP) in 1943, twelve years before that fateful commute. In her first years in the organization, she worked specifically on criminal justice and its application in Alabama communities. One part of this was protecting Black men from false accusations and lynchings. The other was ensuring that Black people who had been sexually assaulted by white people could get their day in court. This particular issue was particularly close to Parks's heart. In 1931 a white male neighbor had attempted to assault her. Parks resisted and later said of the incident, "I was ready to die, but give my consent, never. Never. Never."[105]

Interestingly for me, as a son of India, Parks's defiance was a self-conscious and deliberate act inspired in part by her study of Mahatma Gandhi's civil disobedience movement. Parks credited Gandhi's philosophy of nonviolence and his tactics of civil disobedience in shaping her own activism.

Parks continued her journey, becoming a tireless activist for civil rights and social justice and eventually working alongside Dr. Martin Luther King, Jr.—who had come to prominence during the boycott—and other leaders. Together they were instrumental in organizing the 1963 March on Washington, at which Dr. King delivered his "I Have A Dream" speech. The vast support for civil rights engendered by the march led to the passage of the Voting Rights Act of 1965.

Rosa Parks continued to make significant contributions to promoting tolerance, justice, and equality, and her legacy continues to inspire and influence social justice movements today. Along with her involvement in the NAACP and the National Campaign for Tolerance (mentioned previously), she was involved in the Southern Christian Leadership Conference (SCLC) and the Rosa and Raymond Parks Institute for Self-Development. Through this broad and visible presence, she touched countless citizens and fellow civil rights supporters.

In 1999, Parks was awarded the Congressional Gold Medal, the highest honor the United States bestows on a civilian. When she died at age ninety-two, she became the first woman in the nation's history to lie in honor in the Rotunda of the US Capitol building.

How Rosa Parks Made *Me* Better

In her autobiography, *Rosa Parks: My Story*, written by in collaboration with Jim Haskins, Parks vividly recounts her childhood in Tuskegee, Alabama, the joy of education, the pain of leaving school to support her dying grandmother and ailing mother as a seamstress, as well as her work as a civil rights activist, her role in the Montgomery bus boycott, and more.[106] The book is filled with lessons drawn from a life lived with conviction:

- The importance of standing up for what is right.
- The need to persevere, since change takes time and effort.
- The power of nonviolence.
- The importance of intersectionality. Parks's activism was not limited to the issue of racial segregation, but it also encompassed related issues such as economic justice and women's rights.

While all of these are compelling for me, there is one that encompasses and animates all the rest, and it is a simple one: The power of individuals to effect social change.

As Rosa Parks said of her decision to stay seated on that December day in 1955, "I knew someone had to take the first step."[107]

How has this lesson impacted my life and work? Strongly, deeply, constantly.

It was her lesson that led me to meet another civil rights hero, Representative Elijah Cummings, a Democrat from my adopted home state of Maryland. This happened in 2014 during a reception at the Smithsonian National Museum of African

Art, which I co-hosted—along with the museum's director, Dr. Johnnetta Betsch Cole—on behalf of SNV USA. The event honored SNV's fifty years of commitment to alleviating poverty through sustainable and locally led development, while also showcasing the art and culture of Africa, where SNV's efforts were helping people change their lives for the better. During his long tenure in Congress (1996–2019), Rep. Cummings truly personified the lessons of Rosa Parks. He was a champion of grassroots activism and community organizing; he believed in the power of ordinary citizens to effect change; and he encouraged his constituents to get involved in the political process.

Throughout his career, Cummings was a vocal advocate for civil rights and social justice, working tirelessly to promote policies that addressed issues such as poverty, voter suppression, and police brutality. In this small social encounter, I could feel the expansion of the network that Rosa Parks had set in motion.

Another interesting aspect of Rosa Parks's impact is the way it has deepened my own understanding of my calling. Remember my boyhood declaration of intent, "Tolerance is key"?

Thanks to Rosa Parks, that's not good enough anymore.

I understand that while tolerance is an important first step toward promoting equality and justice, the ultimate goal should be to move beyond tolerance and toward acceptance. Tolerance implies that there is something about someone that we may not like or agree with, but that we will put up with it. It is generally understood as a necessary component of a functioning democracy and stable world order. But there is a hint of segregation about it. It's like that Montgomery bus, with whites up front tolerating the presence of Blacks in the back. Acceptance, on the other hand, means embracing and celebrating diversity and recognizing the inherent value and dignity of every individual.

Today we must advocate for policies that support equal access to education, employment, and healthcare and challenge systemic barriers that prevent marginalized communities from achieving full equality. It will require all of us to recognize our own biases and limitations along with a willingness to challenge them and change ourselves. It will require continuous outreach to create a more inclusive and equitable society.

How You Can Step Up *Now*

In my leadership roles at various NGOs, one key point I stressed repeatedly to team members, donors and stakeholders was that each individual can make a difference. There is an urgent need to change the mindset that "my voice or my contribution will not make any difference." Barack Obama said, "Change will not come if we wait for some other person or some other time. We are the ones we've been waiting for. We are the change that we seek."[108]

Just because you understand your power as an individual doesn't mean you shouldn't join a community of other activists. Even Rosa Parks was a member of the NAACP before making her statement on the bus. The following are among the organizations working to promote civil rights in the United States:

- **Rosa and Raymond Parks Institute for Self-Development**—Founded by Rosa Parks herself, this organization educates youth about civil rights history and develops their leadership skills. How to get involved: Volunteer as a mentor for their youth programs, donate to support their educational initiatives, participate in their annual Rosa Parks birthday celebrations, or attend their workshops and seminars on civil rights and social justice.

- **National Association for the Advancement of Colored People (NAACP)**—The NAACP, with which Parks was actively involved, addresses issues like voter suppression, police brutality, and economic inequality through legal action, advocacy, and community organizing. How to get involved: Join a local chapter and participate in their initiatives, volunteer for their voter registration drives, attend their national convention to network and learn, support their legal defense fund through donations, or use their resources to advocate for policy changes in your community.
- **Southern Poverty Law Center (SPLC)**—The SPLC fights hate and bigotry, seeking justice for the most vulnerable members of society. How to get involved: Report hate incidents through their website, use their "Teaching Tolerance" curriculum in schools, attend their webinars on combating hate and extremism, support their legal cases through donations, or share their intelligence reports on hate groups to raise awareness.
- **Equal Justice Initiative (EJI)**—EJI challenges excessive punishment and advocates for equal treatment under the law. How to get involved: Visit their Legacy Museum and National Memorial for Peace and Justice, organize community screenings of their documentaries, use their educational resources in schools and community groups, support their legal work through

donations, or participate in their annual Peace and Justice Summit.

- **American Civil Liberties Union (ACLU)**—The ACLU's work in defending civil liberties aligns with Parks's stand for individual rights and against discriminatory laws. How to get involved: Become a card-carrying member, volunteer for their election protection efforts, use their online tools to contact legislators about key issues, attend their local chapter meetings and events, or support their legal cases through donations.
- **National Urban League**—This organization focuses on economic empowerment, education, and civil rights, addressing systemic inequalities. How to get involved: Participate in their job training and placement programs, volunteer for their education initiatives like Project Ready, attend their annual conference on civil rights and urban issues, support their policy advocacy efforts, or donate to their programs for underserved communities.

Along with looking into any of the above groups, you can also take individual action for social change:

- Speak up against discrimination or injustice when you witness it.
- Educate yourself about civil rights history and current social issues.
- Use your social media platforms to raise awareness about important causes.
- Register to vote and participate in local elections.

- Support businesses owned by people from marginalized communities.
- Engage in respectful conversations with people who have different views.
- Volunteer for local community organizations.
- Attend town hall meetings or community forums.
- Write letters to your representatives about issues you care about.
- Practice and promote inclusivity in your workplace or school.
- Challenge your own biases and assumptions regularly.
- Mentor someone from an underrepresented group in your field.
- Participate in peaceful protests or demonstrations for causes you believe in.
- Share stories of everyday heroes who have made a difference in their communities.
- Encourage others to take action, no matter how small, for positive change.

CHAPTER 24

STAY TRUE TO YOUR PURPOSE: JIMMY CARTER

The Person

After serving as a state senator and then governor of Georgia, Jimmy Carter became the thirty-ninth president of the United States in 1977. He continued to work to protect democracy and human rights long after leaving office and was awarded the Nobel Peace Prize in 2002 for his efforts.

The Lesson

It has been said that there are two occasions of prime importance in each of our lives. The first is our birth—the fact that we are here. The second is when we realize *why* we are here. Another word for that "why" is *purpose.* For Jimmy Carter, his purpose centered on advancing democratic ideals, upholding human rights, and promoting peace throughout the world—monumental tasks to be sure, but ones to which he remained dedicated for more than half a century. Most of us don't take on such global challenges, but each of us has the ability to identify our purpose and pursue it, to figure out how we can make the most difference, and to persevere in making it.

Our Connection

My knowledge of, interest in, and respect for Carter's work grew exponentially when I left the corporate world and joined the nonprofit and international development sector in 2007. It was then that I learned about the Carter Center, a nonprofit organization founded by Carter and his wife Rosalynn in 1982, dedicated to advancing democracy—and with it peace, health, and human rights—around the world. The Carter Center has built a reputation for fairness and compassion in monitoring elections, promoting human rights, eradicating diseases like Guinea worm and river blindness, and supporting conflict resolution in countries like Sudan, South Sudan, and Liberia. I visited a few of these countries and saw firsthand the desperate need for conflict resolution work. In addition, President Carter has been directly involved in Habitat

US National Archives and Records Administration

Jimmy Carter

for Humanity, an organization I greatly admire and where my son once volunteered. When I say "directly involved," I mean he has actually hammered nails to build homes for the poor.

As I was planning to write this book, I thought about meeting President Carter and sent a letter to him directly in early 2021. President Carter and Mrs. Carter were not able to meet with me but asked their scheduling secretary, Beth Davis, to respond. I appreciated the gesture, which demonstrated that Carter's commitment to democratic principles extended, through the Carter Center, even to such mundane details as taking the time to respond to an inquiry from a regular citizen.

How Jimmy Carter Bettered the World

The television personality Geraldo Rivera once introduced Jimmy Carter as "a breath of fresh air."[109] That was in 1975, at a benefit concert for Carter's long-shot presidential campaign featuring one of the hottest musical acts of the year, the Allman Brothers Band. The event raised enough money for the largely unknown governor of Georgia to buy his first TV ads, which helped him win the Iowa caucuses and set him on a course to the White House.

After a decade of conflict that had seen the assassinations of Robert Kennedy and Martin Luther King, Jr., the agony of Vietnam, and the disillusionment of Watergate, "fresh air" meant simplicity, integrity, authenticity. And after the two "imperial" presidencies of Lyndon Johnson and Richard Nixon, who had consolidated so much power in the executive branch, it meant a return to the grassroots of American democracy.

Carter embodied this moment. He was a plain-speaking man from the tiny town of Plains, Georgia. And he was a man with a clear sense of purpose: to expand democracy. It was this purpose that fed his advocacy for civil rights, environmental protection, and world peace, and for a time he brought a renewed sense of idealism and hope to the nation's political scene.

Years later, this is how Carter described himself: "In my lifetime, I have been a farmer, a naval officer, a Sunday school teacher, an outdoorsman, a democracy activist, a builder, governor of Georgia and recipient of the Nobel Peace Prize. And from 1977 to 1981, I had the privilege of serving as the 39th president of the United States."[110]

I find it interesting that his presidency is the last thing on the list. This is not false modesty, it's perspective. For he has accomplished so much more in the forty-odd years since his administration than he did during his time in office, a feat not achieved—or even aspired to—by many presidents. I'm tempted to think he'd like us to concentrate on his other roles first.

That is why, for me, he is still a "breath of fresh air."

In 1979, then-president Carter addressed the erosion of national consensus, which he defined as a "crisis of confidence." For him, the crisis was about something deeper than politics; it was about the spiritual values that animate society and hold it together. And to counteract this erosion, he believed something more than politics would be needed: "We simply must have faith in each other, faith in our ability to govern ourselves, and faith in the future of this Nation. Restoring that faith and that confidence to America is now the most important task we face. It is a true challenge of this generation of Americans."[111]

The challenge remains, two generations later, with even greater urgency—both here and abroad. And so the Carter Center's work to promote democracy and prevent conflict around the world has never run out of things to do and places to go.

It has monitored 125 elections in 40 countries, helping to ensure democratic elections that reflect the will of the people.[112] The Center has worked to further the avenues to peace in Ethiopia, Eritrea, Liberia, Sudan, South Sudan, Uganda, the Korean Peninsula, Haiti, Bosnia and Herzegovina, and the Middle East.

In the 1990s, Carter became known and revered as the ultimate honest broker, a trustworthy mediator above political partisanship. For this reason, Carter peace initiatives led to the resumption of dialogue between North Korea and the United States, helped Haiti avert a US-led invasion, and produced a four-month cease-fire between Bosnian Muslims and Serbs in the former Yugoslavia in 1994. Facilitated by President Carter, a summit of presidents from the Great Lakes region of Africa examined how to begin the safe return of Rwandan refugees; stop the cycle of violence in Burundi; and promote peace, reconciliation, and justice in the region.

I think that his experience as a farmer may have taught Carter the virtue of patience and the importance of persistence over time. Witness Sudan: According to the Carter Center Annual Report, in 2011, the Carter Center deployed more than one hundred observers to monitor a referendum that led to the establishment of the Republic of South Sudan as an independent nation.[113] I visited South Sudan in August 2014 and was pleased to see what peace can bring to common citizens even in dire poverty. Seven years later, in the wake of the 2019 coup, the Center trained Sudanese youth surveyors to identify and interview members of the resistance and youth-led organizations, laying the foundation for the Sudan Youth Citizen Observer Network—a key component in the political transition process.[114] Despite those accomplishments, today Sudan is once more the scene of conflict and humanitarian disaster. It is a stark reminder that the work to build and maintain peace is a complex long-term process, often littered with setbacks, not all of which are foreseeable.

For this reason, it is necessary to understand the totality of the forces at work, and this is where the Carter Center has excelled, in my opinion.

Just as Carter personally hammered nails, the Center gets deep into the nuts and bolts of addressing structural issues. One example is the Rule of Law Program, which works to advance accountability, transparency, information, and justice to build trust in government and improve lives, particularly of women and other marginalized groups. In an effort to reestablish the rule of law in Liberia, for example, the Carter Center—in response to a request by the Liberian government—implemented the Access to Justice project to inform citizens of their legal rights and help train and equip those who administer the law.[115] In 2021, the Inform Women, Transform Lives campaign launched in twelve major cities to provide services to women and increase awareness of women's right to information. In Bangladesh, Guatemala, and Liberia, the program helped thousands of women access information to improve their lives, leading to Guatemalan women receiving seeds to grow food, Bangladeshi women benefiting from government allowances, and Liberian women receiving college scholarships.[116]

How Jimmy Carter Made *Me* Better

To be honest, I was not deeply aware of Carter during his presidency. I was barely twenty when he was elected, didn't even arrive in the US until 1984, and by then—amid the "Rambo" mentality of the Reagan years—Carter had become a byword for America's loss of influence. History has, of course, vindicated both the man and his work.

My admiration for Carter has to do with his approach to philanthropy, as reflected in the work of the Carter Center. He believes that people can improve their own lives when provided with the necessary skills, knowledge, and access to resources. Helping people to help themselves is at the core of all the nonprofits I have had the honor to serve. Each one provided capacity building, technology, tools, and resources to vulnerable populations so they could build lives of their own choosing.

This relates directly to my strongest motivation to write this book: my unwavering belief in a "democratic society" where we all—including the most marginalized—have a voice. For the past several years, I have been very concerned that after significant progress over a period of decades, democracy is in danger in many parts of the world. Authoritarian regimes are gaining power. Even established bastions of democracy, such as Europe and the United States, are not immune to the appeal and influence of anti-democratic forces. Freedom of the press is threatened even in countries with democratically elected governments, combining with new technological capacities like AI and deepfakes to make it hard for citizens to even agree on what constitutes reality. Media algorithms have successfully divided the electorate into "info-bubbles" of like-minded people, making it easier for mis- and disinformation to supplant facts, and for one-sided opinion to crowd out constructive discussion.

Against this background, Carter's vision appears extremely prescient. In various speeches, he was clear about his belief that democracy is not only a political system but also a way of life that is fundamental to protecting human rights and fostering diversity and inclusivity. Carter also emphasized the importance of peaceful transitions of power and the need for people to work together, regardless of their differences, to strengthen democratic institutions and values.

The mighty Carter legacy of peace, justice, and all the rest has grown from one seed: a commitment to democracy. The work of the Carter Center reflects the incredible complexity of today's world. But for me, the lesson of Jimmy Carter is as simple and straightforward as the man himself: Maintain a clear sense of purpose throughout your life. Throughout *his* long life, that sense of purpose led Carter to pursue democratic ideals. For any of us, it can provide a lifelong compass to work for what we value.

How You Can Stay True to Your Purpose *Now*

You'll know your particular purpose when you find it. Meanwhile, if you're like me, the example of Jimmy Carter's life provides inspiration with which to move forward—and plenty of areas where our paths intersect. Perhaps some of the following organizations will resonate with you as well.

- **The Carter Center**—Founded by Jimmy and Rosalynn Carter, dedicated to advancing democracy and human rights, and alleviating suffering worldwide. How to get involved: Volunteer, donate, or apply for internships and job opportunities. Participate in their public health programs or election observation missions.

- **The Elders**—An independent group of global leaders working to promote peace and human rights, of which Carter was a founding member. How to get involved: Support their campaigns, share their content on social media, or donate to support their work.
- **National Democratic Institute (NDI)**—Works to support and strengthen democratic institutions worldwide. How to get involved: Volunteer as an election monitor, contribute to their research, or support their programs through donations.
- **Peace Corps**—Immerses volunteers in community change in more than sixty countries around the world. How to get involved: Apply to become a Peace Corps volunteer, or support their work through donations or partnerships.
- **United Nations Volunteers (UNV)**—Promotes volunteerism to support peace and development worldwide. How to get involved: Apply for volunteer assignments, both in-person and online, or promote volunteerism in your community.
- **The International Foundation for Electoral Systems (IFES)**—This organization works to advance good governance and democratic rights by providing technical assistance to election officials, empowering the underrepresented to participate in the political process, and applying field-based research to improve

the electoral cycle. How to get involved: Support their programs through donations, participate in their democracy-building initiatives, attend their events, or apply for internships and job opportunities. They also offer resources for civic education that you can use in your community.

Consistent with the work carried out by the organizations listed above, you can do your own work to find, pursue, and adhere to your purpose:

- Reflect regularly on your personal purpose and how you can contribute to society.
- Stay informed about global issues and share accurate information with others.
- Participate in local democratic processes, including voting and attending town halls.
- Volunteer for community service projects.
- Practice and promote conflict resolution in your daily life.
- Support organizations working for peace and human rights.
- Engage in respectful dialogue with those who hold different views.
- Advocate for fair and transparent elections in your community and beyond.
- Mentor young people in civic engagement and leadership.
- Support initiatives that promote public health and disease prevention.
- Practice empathy and compassion in your interactions with others.

- Educate yourself about ongoing conflicts and peace processes worldwide.
- Promote environmental conservation efforts in your community.
- Encourage and participate in interfaith dialogue and understanding.
- Support free press and responsible journalism.

CHAPTER 25

MAKE HARD CHOICES: HILLARY CLINTON

The Person

Hillary Clinton served as First Lady during the Clinton administration, as a senator from the state of New York in the early 2000s, and as Secretary of State during the Obama administration—in addition to being the first woman ever to win a US presidential primary and run for the nation's highest office.

The Lesson

Decisions are a part of life, but often we base them on what we feel will win us the approval of others, rather than on what we consider to be right. Many rewards reinforce this behavior, which makes it especially difficult to act in keeping with our inner moral compass. You might say it's what makes hard decisions hard. Time and again in her career, Hillary Clinton has acted based on her convictions rather than on political popularity or expedience. It hasn't always made her or her decisions popular, but if your objective is to act on behalf of others—rather than for yourself—it has made her very much worth emulating.

Our Connection

When I first met Hillary Clinton in 2014 at the Clinton Global Initiative (CGI) meeting in New York City, I had a goal in mind. I had just formulated the concept for a new organization, Global Youth Initiative (GYI), and I was reaching out to a variety of leaders—including Clinton—for their response, hoping to stimulate word-of-mouth buzz that would lead to participation and funding.

The author with Hillary Clinton at the 2014 CGI meeting in New York City

GYI's aim was to engage and empower young people globally to identify and apply innovative community-based solutions to the most urgent issues of our time: poverty, racial and religious discrimination, and violence.

Too many large-scale development projects waste resources because they attempt to solve problems without addressing root causes, or because they are implemented without much input from the people they are trying to help. This is particularly counterproductive in developing nations, especially in Africa and the Middle East, where the median age is under twenty-five. In Niger, for example, nearly 60 percent of the population is under twenty years old. Yet development decisions are being made by seniors in Europe and North America. At GYI, we wanted to break this cycle by giving youth a seat at the table, encouraging youth to look at their own surroundings and apply their personal ethics to finding everyday opportunities for immediate and positive change.

And so I came to New York hoping to deliver my pitch to, among others, Secretary Clinton. I already admired her, not only for her responsibilities as former First Lady, junior senator from New York, and secretary of state in the Obama administration, but for her compassionate and sincere efforts to change the lives of vulnerable people around the world. Her contributions to poverty reduction, women's economic empowerment, children's legal rights, and environmental protection were already significant.

When the opportunity arose to speak with Secretary Clinton, I briefly explained the basic idea and goals of GYI. She listened carefully, then promised to get back to me. And get back she did, with a brief but encouraging response to my concept. In this and subsequent interactions with Secretary Clinton, I found her to be extremely sincere, knowledgeable, and resilient, with a great sense of humor—quite at odds with the picture painted by her critics.

How Hillary Clinton Bettered the World

To understand Clinton better, I read her 2003 memoir, *Living History*. Looking at her upbringing and her life journey, it seemed to me that her resiliency was the product of the choices she had made throughout her life. Her mother, Dorothy, had a hard childhood, and that helped shape Clinton's political and human perspective. Dorothy's parents had a bad marriage, and neither of them wanted to take care of Dorothy, then eight years old, or her little sister. Both girls were sent to live with their grandparents, who were strict even in those times. When she turned fourteen, Dorothy left her grandparents' home and began working as a maid for three dollars per week.

"Learning about my mother's childhood sparked my strong conviction that every child deserves a chance to live up to her God-given potential,"[117] Clinton wrote. This no doubt contributed to her decision to begin her own career as an attorney for the Children's Defense Fund, where she was later board chair, and she has remained committed to child advocacy throughout her life.

In terms of party affiliation, her mother was a Democrat, while her father was a staunch Republican. Their differing political perspectives led to some lively debates at the dinner table, which young Hillary Rodham avidly absorbed. "I grew up between the push and tug of my parents' values, and my own political beliefs reflect both,"[118] she wrote. As a teen, she canvassed for Republican presidential nominees Richard Nixon and Barry Goldwater. However, her views gradually shifted while she was a student at Wellesley College. Taking a big step in a new direction, she supported the Democratic senator Eugene McCarthy—unofficial leader of the peace movement against the Vietnam War—during the 1968 presidential primaries.

This was one of many difficult choices that have defined her personal and professional life, making the title of her 2014 book, *Hard Choices*, unusually accurate and, like Hillary Clinton herself, courageously honest.

In *Hard Choices*, Clinton articulates the pivotal, defining decisions that most of us face in our lifetimes. Common personal choices can include what opportunities to provide for our children, how to care for aging parents, what job to apply for (and what to do if we lose it), whether to get married, and whether to stay married. *Hard Choices* deals mainly with the choices Clinton made as secretary of state in the Obama administration. Rather than seeing hard choices as things to be avoided, she emphasized how important it is to embrace them and the opportunity they provide for learning, adapting, and doing better. In the book, she also wrote at length about listening to one's heart and one's head—sometimes just one or the other and sometimes both.

One of the hardest choices she faced was whether to accept the Cabinet position offered to her by newly elected President Obama. She had campaigned hard against this charismatic newcomer during the Democratic primaries. She was disappointed and exhausted in defeat and was looking forward to returning to the Senate to focus on the issues she cared about. So when Obama initially invited Clinton to join the Cabinet as secretary of state, she politely declined. Obama refused to accept a "no," however, so Clinton promised to think about his offer. It was a very difficult choice to make. This was not just any Cabinet job offered to keep a rival close. It was a job with real potential to change the world for the better. Clinton cared deeply about foreign policy and believed it was essential to restore our country's damaged standing due to the ongoing wars in Iraq and Afghanistan. But she also felt passionate about her role representing New York state in the Senate, where she concentrated on reversing job losses, addressing the nation's healthcare deficits, and many other issues. After much deliberation, Clinton made a hard choice and accepted Obama's offer. As secretary of state, she visited 112 countries to strengthen relations, made women's rights a priority, and worked to promote women's political participation, economic empowerment, and access to healthcare around the world. Among Clinton's many accomplishments was the New START treaty with Russia, which represented a significant step toward global nuclear disarmament. During her tenure, Clinton advocated for an expanded role in global economic policy for the State Department and cited the need for an increased US diplomatic presence around the world. Her legacy was not lost on her former colleagues in Congress. In an interview for *Politico*, Senate Majority Leader Harry Reid, a Democrat from Nevada, said, "American foreign policy was stronger when Hillary Clinton left the State Department than when she arrived." At the time Clinton came to the office, America's reputation was deeply damaged for a variety of reasons. "From the agreement to prevent Iran from obtaining a nuclear weapon, to the landmark normalization of relations with Cuba, nearly every foreign policy victory of President Obama's second term has Secretary Clinton's fingerprints on it."[119]

Clinton also articulated a larger approach to foreign policy, known as "Smart Power" or "3D" (diplomacy, defense and development). She believed in the importance of diplomacy in order to resolve conflicts and advance US interests. She also believed in using military force when necessary, but emphasized the importance of using it judiciously and in conjunction with other foreign policy tools. Clinton also wholeheartedly considered development assistance to be a key component of foreign policy. She maintained that supporting education, healthcare, and infrastructure in developing countries was crucial to promote economic growth, stability and democracy. Clinton's 3D approach resonated with me. My career path coincidentally has taken me through positions with the Australian Government, in US defense contracting, the private sector, and, for more than a decade, in international development and the NGO sector, where I traveled extensively in Africa, Asia, and Latin America and have seen the value of this approach.

I was born in India but always felt a connection with the Middle East and Africa. I have always believed that the US should openly acknowledge some of the policy mistakes it made in these regions over the years and do more to help them achieve democracy, stability, and growth. I also realize that this is not easy for a superpower, especially one that tries to combine its superpower ambitions with claims to a moral high ground. Idealism and pragmatism are forever pulling policymakers in different directions. For Secretary of State Clinton, this tension led to numerous hard choices, especially in the Middle East, which she acknowledged in her book with some frustration: "It's easy to give speeches and write books about standing up for democratic values, even when it may conflict with our security interests, but when confronted with the actual, real-world trade-offs, choices get a lot harder."[120]

Still, avoiding choices doesn't make them easier. So Clinton waded in, time and again, accepting that the outcomes were unlikely to be black-and-white success stories.

She made several attempts to restart negotiations between Israel and the Palestinian Authority during her tenure, but these efforts ultimately failed to produce a lasting peace agreement. Clinton's decision to support the Iran nuclear deal was a difficult one for her because it was a complex issue with many political and strategic implications. She knew that many of her constituents and allies, particularly supporters of Israel, were deeply skeptical of the deal. However, Clinton recognized that the deal offered a real opportunity to prevent Iran from obtaining nuclear weapons through peaceful means, and ended up voting to ratify it.

Clinton was a strong supporter of the pro-democracy movements that swept across the Middle East in 2011—movements collectively known as the Arab Spring. During a conversation with young people in Tunisia in 2012, a young lawyer took the microphone and expressed the general feeling of mistrust toward the west and toward the United States in particular. Clinton responded, "I will be the first to say we, like any country in the world, have made mistakes. I will be the first to say that. We've made a lot of mistakes. But I think if you look at the entire historical record, the entire historical record shows we've been on the side of freedom, we've been on the side of human rights, we've been on the side of the free markets and economic empowerment."[121] The young lawyer nodded and sat down. Based on my conversations with friends and colleagues in the Middle East, Clinton is still respected for her efforts to promote democracy, human rights, and women's empowerment in the region.

Is Hillary Clinton an idealist or realist? At the end of the day, the answer lies in what she has accomplished. She was the first woman to win a major political party's nomination for president of the United States, and her nomination in 2016 broke a major barrier in our country's political history. As First Lady, she also led the enormous battle for a national healthcare plan. That initiative met fierce resistance from those who profit from a private system, but it planted the seeds of the Affordable Care Act adopted under President Obama.

Clinton is seen by many as a polarizing figure, with people either strongly supporting or strongly opposing her. Some will argue that this polarization is in part due to her long history in politics, as well as being the first woman to win a major party's presidential nomination, or to a remark she made about the role of First Lady during her husband's 1992 Presidential campaign, that a woman is capable of more than "baking cookies." She is criticized for being a poor campaigner, which translates as being unwilling to say what the audience wants to hear in order to get votes. Making hard choices means that someone is going to be unhappy. Secretary Clinton is both wise enough to know that this is the nature of the world and strong enough to live with the consequences.

How Hillary Clinton Made *Me* Better

All of us face difficult decisions during our lives. Some are personal, and some are professional. For my part, there are certainly many choices that, with hindsight, I should not have made. What keeps me going is my desire to acknowledge them and my drive to improve. While reviewing Clinton's life story, I found a similar characteristic. She emphasized the need for leaders to make tough choices and take calculated risks, even when the outcomes are uncertain. This willingness to accept the consequences of one's choices is something that, with her example, I've tried to incorporate into my own life.

Hillary Clinton has always been open to new ideas and perspectives. And her ability to evolve and grow as a leader has enabled her to remain relevant and influential over many decades.

Of all the pages I have read about Secretary Clinton and her accomplishments, one quote in particular stands out for me: "If you believe you can make a difference, not just in politics, in public service, in advocacy around all these important issues, then you have to be prepared to accept that you are not going to get 100 percent approval."[122]

How You Can Make Hard Choices *Now*

Knowing what you believe is right and consistently acting on that knowledge are two different things. If we want to have the greatest positive impact in the world, we all need help making hard choices—whether through the advice of close friends or the counsel of trusted colleagues. You can supplement such guidance with help from the following resources:

- **Clinton Global Initiative (CGI)**—Founded by Bill and Hillary Clinton to foster collaboration and turn ideas into action, CGI brings together global leaders to develop innovative solutions to world challenges. <u>How to get involved</u>: Attend events, make commitments, or support their initiatives.
- **The Aspen Institute**—An educational and policy studies organization, the Institute hosts the Aspen Ideas Festival, a gathering of global leaders, thinkers, and entrepreneurs to discuss pressing global issues. <u>How to get involved</u>: Use this platform to engage deeply with complex topics and make informed decisions.

- **Global Citizen**—A platform that unites people around the world in a commitment to "defeat poverty, demand equity, and defend the planet"[123] worldwide, Global Citizen attracts people who have chosen to make a difference. How to get involved: Donate, sign a petition, apply for employment as part of the movement, or take actions to end extreme poverty (and earn free tickets to attend the annual Global Citizen Festival!).

Here are a few tips to make it easier to make hard choices:

- Seek out different perspectives. Talk to people who may have a different view than you. Their insights can help you see the full picture.
- Listen to your moral compass. What does your gut say is the right thing to do?
- Check your emotions. Hard choices often stir up fear, anger, or sadness. Pause and let the feelings pass before deciding.
- Write out the pros and cons. Getting it all down can clarify your thoughts.
- Be willing to be unpopular. The best choice is not always the popular one. Have courage in your convictions.
- Start small. Practice with low-stakes decisions to build your "hard choice" muscles. Making tough calls gets easier with practice.

CHAPTER 26

ENGAGE IN PUBLIC SERVICE: ROSS PEROT

The Person

Ross Perot was an entrepreneur and philanthropist who campaigned for the US presidency in 1992 and 1996 as an independent, bringing together a coalition of nearly 20 million voters as one of the most successful third-party candidates in American history.

The Lesson

For some people, patriotism expresses itself as nationalism: fiercely defensive, isolationist, even xenophobic. Sometimes it can take the form of a political stance—a cynical and calculated appeal to voters. For Ross Perot, patriotism was a genuine love of country that expressed itself through selfless public service. If you share that love, as I do, and want to show it, then engaging in public service will come naturally.

Our Connection

Along with being drawn to Perot by his love of America, I remember being impressed by the strength of his loyalty—something I learned more about when I met him in 2017. At the time, I was part of the leadership team of Global Fund for Children (GFC), an organization that invests in community-based organizations around the world to help children and youth reach their full potential and advance their rights. The Perot Foundation was a donor of GFC, and Margot Perot, Ross's wife, kindly hosted a tea gathering in Texas to raise awareness and funds—something she had been doing for many years. It was an honor for me to speak at this gathering, which gave me the opportunity to meet many of Mrs. Perot's friends, also supporters of GFC. Later that day, Mrs. Perot introduced us to her husband. He suggested we visit Legacy Hall—a private museum that showcases memorabilia from Perot's life. We immediately accepted the invitation, and one of his staff gave us a tour. This was the experience of a lifetime, and it gave me a much better understanding of Perot the patriot and loyalist. Many of us knew him primarily from his numerous appearances on prime-time TV advertorials and the presidential debates during his two presidential runs, but the museum went much deeper. I got to know Perot as a man who, during the Vietnam War, made numerous trips to North Vietnam, negotiating with a hostile government in an attempt to free American prisoners of war (POWs). His quest to support the POWs became daily front-page news in papers across the country during the 1969 holiday season, including the *New York Times*, which covered his every stop and every announcement. I got to know Perot as a man who planned a real-life covert mission to free two of his Electronic Data

Systems (EDS) employees from an Iranian prison. One entire hallway was dedicated to the rescue. Perot assembled a crack team of military veterans to break them out. As it happened, the Iranian Revolution broke out, and when a crowd stormed the prison to liberate political opponents of the Shah of Iran's regime, the EDS men were swept along, eventually linking up with Perot's "commandos," who sneaked them into neighboring Turkey and from there to Europe. The incident is recounted in Ken Follett's purportedly nonfiction thriller, *On Wings of Eagles*. The book underscores the loyalty Perot felt toward his country and his employees. During the Iran episode, Perot risked his own reputation, resources, and personal safety (he himself visited Iran during that time) to rescue his imprisoned employees, showcasing his bravery and dedication to their well-being.

How Ross Perot Bettered the World

Born in 1930 in Texarkana, Texas, to a cotton broker and a lumber company secretary, Henry Ross Perot learned early to turn his humble beginnings to his advantage. The country was mired in the Great Depression, and while the Perot family was better off than many others, times still were not easy. Yet young Perot had no basis of comparison. He simply knew what he wanted and set about getting it. When he was six, he wanted a bike, so he sold flower seeds and Christmas cards to earn the five dollars needed to purchase one, secondhand. He worked throughout his childhood, breaking horses, delivering newspapers, and selling magazines. He was curious, energetic, and motivated to get ahead, and he wasn't about to let his age stand in his way.[124] For this child of a free America, that motivation paid off. In 1984,

Perot sold the company he founded, Electronic Data Systems (EDS), to General Motors for $2.5 billion.[125]

If Perot had only been interested in money, that would have been the end of his rags-to-riches story. But he had a big heart, and that is the key to the other aspect of his patriotism: his deep belief that "America is great because her people are good."[126]

In his autobiography, *Ross Perot: My Life & the Principles for Success*, he cited numerous examples to prove his point. As a boy working for the newspaper, he was often sent to collect delinquent advertising fees, sometimes riding his secondhand bicycle eight to ten miles to knock on a customer's door. He explained that in most cases these people weren't criminals, but they hadn't sold the product and so couldn't afford to pay for the ad. However, when they saw him covered with sweat from the long, hot bike ride, they always paid. Perot referred to them as "good people, with deep consciences."[127] Accounts like this resonated with me. I have had similar experiences of American decency and compassion, even as a nonwhite immigrant in regions notorious for bigotry. I deeply cherish those values of average Americans. In fact, I was motivated to write this book as much by those encounters with "ordinary" Americans as by my contacts with illustrious figures.

This love for America, its promise and its people, was the source of Perot's public service and his connection with voters. As a citizen, Perot served on various committees and task forces at the state and national level. In 1979, he was appointed to lead Texas's effort to toughen drug laws and increase public awareness. In 1984, he led a Texas education reform initiative that recommended pay increases for teachers, funding for preschool programs, and increased state aid for property-poor school districts. As a philanthropist he supported education, veterans affairs, and other causes. As a businessman, he lobbied to protect American jobs and industries from unfair trade practices, outsourcing, and globalization. As a candidate, he opposed the North American Free Trade Agreement (NAFTA) because he feared the collapse of American manufacturing—and the middle-class prosperity it supported—if employers were enabled to seek the lowest possible labor and environmental standards. He campaigned for gun control and a balanced budget, supported LGBTQ rights and a woman's right to choose, and pushed for electronic voting, among other reforms. This broad platform reflected his sincere, pragmatic, and commonsense desire to preserve the American way of life. Voters responded. And it's interesting to note that half of those who voted for Perot were moderates, with the other half evenly divided from among more liberal Democrats and conservative Republicans.

Perot passed away in 2019, but his work is carried on by his surviving family: his wife, Margot Perot (whom I met); his son Ross Perot, Jr., and daughter-in-law Sarah; and his four daughters, Nancy, Suzanne, Carolyn, and Katherine. While the Perot family members have led largely private lives, they have made notable contributions to various charitable causes, reflecting their commitment to making a positive impact on society. In his book, Follett quotes Perot as having sometimes told interviewers that he would measure his success in life by how his children turned out. If they grew into good citizens with a deep concern for other people, he would consider his life worthwhile.

How Ross Perot Made *Me* Better

One of the themes running through this book is the underlying unity of the human condition, despite the diversity of our biographies, ethnicities, nationalities, faiths, and political viewpoints. By writing it, I have hoped to turn up the volume on several aspects of this unity in response to the deafening roar of division that currently fills the air. In many ways, the individuals I have profiled are avatars of unity. Nearly all of them have embarked on a journey during which they overcame forces of division and arrived at a place of openness and inclusion. They have thought for themselves, blazed their own trails, and lived their convictions with courage and integrity. This gathering would be incomplete without Ross Perot.

Perot has recounted his unusual journey in several books, including the autobiography *Ross Perot: My Life & the Principles for Success* and *United We Stand.* In them I found the qualities that made him a hero to many and an inspiration to me: patriotism and loyalty.

Perot's love for America—both the idea and the reality—was fundamental. It was not blind flag-waving, but a deeper appreciation for the ways in which the country's principle of freedom can enable individuals of any background to succeed. In Perot's view, if a person has a good upbringing and works very hard—and enjoys a bit of luck—the potential for success is unlimited.

This might sound simplistic in our age of increasing inequality of wealth and opportunity, not to mention the multigenerational trauma surrounding the nation's deep legacy of racism. But it was Perot's story. And in his political campaigns, he set out to make that principle work for those who had been left behind, regardless of their background, ethnicity, or gender.

Looking back, I can't help but hear echoes of Perot's presidential campaigns in many of today's conversations around our political future. Many of his viewpoints have proven prescient, especially those relating to his concerns about our national debt, the dangers of guns, and globalization. Many voters feel disconnected from traditional "establishment" parties and respond positively to outsiders with bold visions that cross traditional ideological divides. But Perot was, as they say, "the real deal," a genuine leader who wanted to get things done for the benefit of all—not a demagogue. He stands apart, as much for his courage to speak his mind as for his selflessness in the service of America.

Quite recently I was again made aware of Perot's lasting impact. It was a hot Sunday afternoon in June 2023. My son, Ryan, and I had been hiking at Rocky Gap State Park in the mountains of western Maryland. We spent the night in the small city of Cumberland, Maryland. I remembered reading somewhere that Cumberland had not recovered the manufacturing jobs that it lost many years ago and still had a higher-than-average poverty rate. I thought about Ross Perot and the loss of American jobs that he talked about throughout his campaigns. That afternoon we visited the Charis Winery & Distillery (Allegany County's first winery) and fell to chatting with the owner, Chuck Park. During our conversation, I decided to ask Chuck about Ross Perot and if he remembered him. His face lit up. He fondly remembered Perot as a presidential candidate who brought fresh perspectives. Chuck reminded me of the everyday man Perot talked about—and with whom Perot's ideas resonated. That's exactly why I wanted to write about Perot.

How You Can Engage in Public Service *Now*

If you're ready to show your love for your country, here are some groups through which you can actively engage in civic life, address societal challenges, and work to improve the lives of fellow citizens, regardless of their background:

- **The Perot Foundation**—Supports various charitable causes including education and healthcare. How to get involved: Research their initiatives and support the organizations they fund.
- **National Coalition for Homeless Veterans**—Addresses the needs of homeless veterans. How to get involved: Volunteer, donate, or advocate for policy changes.
- **Alliance for American Manufacturing**—Works to strengthen American manufacturing. How to get involved: Sign up for their action alerts, share their content, or use their resources.

There are plenty of ways you can engage in selfless public service as an individual. Here are some that will help you begin:

- Stay informed about local and national issues.
- Participate in local government meetings.
- Volunteer for community organizations.
- Support veteran-focused initiatives.
- Engage in civil discourse with those holding different views.
- Practice fiscal responsibility in personal and professional life.
- Support American-made products when possible.
- Mentor young people in civic engagement.

- Participate in neighborhood cleanup or improvement projects.
- Register to vote and encourage others to do the same.
- Write to elected officials about important issues.
- Donate to causes that address national challenges.
- Organize or participate in community forums on local issues.
- Support small businesses in your community.
- Share knowledge and skills to help others in your community.

CHAPTER 27

PROTECT DEMOCRACY: JOHN KUFUOR

The Person

A member of the Ghanian Parliament for two decades, John Kufuor helped found the New Patriotic Party (NPP) in 1992 and served as president of the Republic of Ghana from 2001 to 2009.

The Lesson

Those of us in democratic societies can easily take democracy's benefits for granted. Of course each of us has a voice. Of course we can participate in the political process to elect our leaders. Of course we can influence and improve our communities, our states, and our nation. Yet that "of course" is neither a birthright nor a given. Because it can erode or be taken away entirely, democracy needs to be protected. John Kufuor understood the power of democratic principles to achieve social progress in Ghana, and he acted to protect and preserve—as well as to apply—those principles while in office. The lives of his country's people improved as a result.

Our Connection

I am indebted to SNV Netherlands Development Organization for many of the experiences that enhanced my knowledge about international development in Africa, Latin America, and Asia. Working for SNV was my first foray into international development and ultimately shaped the course of my life. And without SNV, I would not have met John Kufuor.

SNV opened my mind to Africa. People outside Africa often hold stereotypes and generalizations about the continent and its people. Some of the more common stereotypes involve poverty, disease, conflict, or exoticism. Besides being rooted in racial prejudice and the colonial mentality, these stereotypes overlook the diversity, progress, and contributions of African societies. This limited narrative can hinder a more nuanced and accurate understanding of the continent and its people. SNV had an extensive local presence in Africa, working on various projects in the agriculture value chain and food security, water sanitation and hygiene, and energy. I had the opportunity to visit SNV programs in Kenya, Ethiopia, Mozambique, Uganda, Zimbabwe, South Sudan, and Ghana. And it was during these visits off the beaten path that my horizons were truly redefined. I fell in love with Africa because of its unmatched natural beauty, crowned by stunning wildlife and breathtaking views; its diversity, food, and culture; and most importantly, its people.

In 2008, I was part of an SNV leadership team that wanted to form an international advisory board (IAB) with leaders who were at the forefront of poverty reduction and good governance in Africa, Asia, and Latin America. It was vitally important that these leaders embody democratic values and that their work advance democracy in their countries. In discussions about possible African leaders, John Kufuor's name was mentioned repeatedly. Kufuor had just completed his second term in office, during which he had established himself as a role model for democracy and the peaceful transition of power. SNV invited Kufuor to join the board, and he kindly accepted our invitation. It was a great partnership. SNV brought its reputation as a mission-driven global development organization rooted in the contexts and societies where it works, which was key for Kufuor. For his part, Kufuor brought expertise gained from experience in his government's five priority program areas in Ghana: good governance, modernization of agriculture for rural development, private sector participation, enhanced social services, and infrastructure development.

Renée Jones-Bos (Dutch ambassador), John Kufuor, and the author

How John Kufuor Bettered the World

Kufuor's is not a household name in the global North. This is unfortunate, because this man is a giant whose life has been dedicated to service in the name of democracy. Especially in our time, with growing authoritarian parties and influence in Europe and North America, democracy needs heroes, and Kufuor was certainly that.

When John Kufuor was sworn in as president on January 9, 2001, Ghana had not seen a peaceful transfer of power between democratically elected administrations since 1957, when the country gained independence. Kufuor's 30-year public service career exemplifies his unwavering commitment to democracy. He played a key role in drafting Ghana's constitutions in 1979 and 1982. He was a founding member of multiple democratic parties and served twice as a member of Parliament. Despite facing political detention during military coups, he consistently fought for democratic governance. As Secretary for Local Government under the Provisional National Defense Council (PNDC), he authored policies for Ghana's decentralized governance but resigned within seven months in protest of the regime's intolerance and corruption. Kufuor's leadership culminated in his election as Ghana's president in 2000, marking a historic democratic transition that has continued through multiple elections to this day.[128] Yet in many ways, that success has not reflected the trend elsewhere in the world.

According to a report on democracy from the Varieties of Democracy (V-Dem) Institute at the University of Gothenburg in March 2022, "70 per cent of the world's population now live in dictatorships"—bleak news for the state of democracy worldwide. "For the average world citizen in 2021, the level of democracy is back at 1989 levels, which means that the last 30 years of democratic progress are now a thing of the past."[129]

What strikes me about Kufuor's trajectory is the connection between democracy and development. For Kufuor, the two went hand in hand and made Ghana a model for peaceful, sustained material and social progress, while some countries in Africa remained mired in postcolonial cycles of chaos and dictatorship, or spiraled into failed states. As a result, under Kufuor's leadership based on good governance, transparency, and cooperation, Ghana became the first sub-Saharan African country to cut the number of people suffering from hunger in half.

Kufuor's administration implemented electoral reforms aimed at enhancing the transparency and integrity of the electoral process. These reforms included the introduction of biometric voter registration and verification systems, which helped to improve the accuracy and efficiency of elections. Kufuor focused on strengthening democratic institutions and promoting good governance. He supported the establishment of independent bodies such as the Electoral Commission, the National Commission for Civic Education, and the Commission on Human Rights and Administrative Justice. These institutions played crucial roles in ensuring the transparency, fairness, and accountability of Ghana's democratic processes. Kufuor's administration fostered an environment that allowed for freedom of speech and press freedom, enabling Ghana to consistently rank high in indexes on freedom of the press, and permitted media outlets to operate with relative independence and without significant government interference. Kufuor emphasized the importance of upholding the rule of law and promoting a strong, independent, and effective judiciary, contributing to the overall stability and accountability of Ghana's democratic system. Kufuor's government also undertook initiatives to improve Ghana's human rights situation, addressing issues such as torture, arbitrary arrest, and unlawful detention.

In the course of his tenure, Kufuor implemented significant economic reforms that helped stabilize Ghana's economy and promote growth. His administration pursued policies aimed at reducing inflation, improving fiscal discipline, attracting foreign investment, and promoting private sector development. Kufuor also made significant progress in addressing poverty while president. Under his leadership, Ghana's poverty rate decreased from 51.7 percent in 1991 to 26.5 percent in 2008, and the proportion of citizens suffering from hunger went from 34 percent in 1990 to 9 percent in 2004.[130]

During Kufuor's presidency, education was also a priority. His administration implemented a program that aimed to provide free basic education for all Ghanaian children. He also instituted the free School Feeding program to provide one nutritious locally produced meal a day for school children in kindergarten (age four) to junior high school (age fourteen). Thanks to Kufuor's influence and knowledge, SNV implemented several school feeding programs in Ghana with the support of the Bill & Melinda Gates Foundation.

Kufuor initiated several infrastructure projects to enhance Ghana's development. Notable projects include the expansion and improvement of the country's road network, the expansion of the Takoradi Harbour, and the construction of the Bui Dam to increase hydroelectric power generation.

Kufuor was not content to build democracy and prosperity only in Ghana, but he also played an active role in regional and international affairs. He served as the chairperson of the African Union (AU) from 2007 to 2008 and was involved in conflict resolution efforts in countries like Côte d'Ivoire, Togo, and Sierra Leone. These involvements allowed him to promote good governance, democracy, and economic cooperation—not only in Africa, but around the world. For example, he was invited to be key speaker at Jawaharlal Nehru Commemorative International Conference at Vigyan Bhawan, India, in 2014. India's first Prime Minister, Jawaharlal Nehru was a strong believer in democracy. While remembering Nehru in his speech, Kufuor observed that many citizens of African nations look to India as a role model of democracy, given India's history of democracy after gaining independence from British rule in 1947. Kufuor emphasized the importance of peace and development for all as the key pillar of a democratic government.

In the fifteen years since leaving office, Kufuor has remained committed to the principles of democracy, rule of law, justice, and accountability in government. He has continued to speak up against corruption and the commoditization of politics. In a recent interview with TV3 Ghana, Kufuor emphasized the importance of rule of law, along with government by the people and for the people. His belief in the mission of public service is inspiring, giving hope to a new generation of Ghanaians.

How John Kufuor Made *Me* Better

Part of Kufuor's stature can be attributed to his personal presence, which projects sincerity, trustworthiness, and character. I vividly remember my first meeting with Kufuor at his residence in 2009 along with Dirk Elsen, SNV Global CEO, and Larry Attipoe, SNV Country Director in Ghana. Kufuor was gracious and keen to learn more about the work we were doing in Africa. We discussed SNV's experience and perspective on development and our approach in Africa. It was heartening to discover how many areas of overlap existed between Kufuor's vision and that of SNV. Kufuor made a commitment to stay in touch and stay engaged with SNV. He followed through the very next day by visiting the SNV office in Accra, Ghana, where he met with my colleagues and discussed at length our programs in his country.

I stayed in touch with him via his special assistant, Ivor Agyeman-Duah. My goal was to find a way to bring Kufuor to Washington, DC, so the international development community could hear from him directly about his experience. An opportunity finally presented itself through the Society for International Development (SID), of which my friend Dan Runde (senior vice president, CSIS, and author of *The American Imperative: Reclaiming Global Leadership through Soft Power*) was president at that time. As a result of this connection, the SID World Congress invited Kufuor to appear as a keynote speaker in 2011.

Prior to the start of the SID conference, I co-hosted a dinner with the Dutch Ambassador Renée Jones-Bos at the ambassador's Washington, DC, residence. During their pre-dinner remarks to the leaders of the international organizations in attendance, both President Kufuor and the ambassador acknowledged SNV's work in agriculture and highlighted our successes. Kufuor in particular emphasized the importance of public-private sector initiatives for agricultural and international development, citing USAID (United States Agency for International Development) and MCC (Millennium Challenge Corporation) as examples of organizations that have taken deliberate steps to engage the private sector. Kufuor articulated both the accomplishments of Ghana and how the development community can work with Ghana.

With each encounter I had with Kufuor, my respect for him grew. His devotion to democratic principles and their effectiveness in development has confirmed and strengthened my own belief in the power of democracy to get things done.

How You Can Act on Your Convictions *Now*

President Kufuor has shown that democracy, even with its flaws, is key to prosperity. I strongly believe that each of us should do what we can to protect it, not only in the United States but throughout the world. And if you, too, are convinced that the rule of law and a government based on the will of the people can create better living conditions than existing alternatives—if you understand the potential fragility of any system of government—then you might want to take protective action as well. Here are some organizations you can work through:

- **The John A. Kufuor Foundation**—Promotes and sustains development in Africa. How to get involved: Support their programs, attend their events, or apply for their leadership programs.
- **Transparency International**—Combats global corruption and promotes transparency. How to get involved: Join a local chapter, report corruption, or support their campaigns.

Don't underestimate your own ability to strengthen democracy. Any of these actions can help:

- Participate in local elections and encourage others to vote.

- Stay informed about local and national political issues.
- Engage in respectful political discussions with people of differing views.
- Support independent journalism and fact-checking initiatives.
- Report any instances of corruption or abuse of power.
- Support organizations that promote civic education.
- Volunteer for local government committees or advisory boards.
- Advocate for transparency in government operations.
- Respect and uphold laws in your daily life.
- Engage with your elected representatives on important issues.
- Participate in peaceful demonstrations for causes you believe in.
- Support initiatives that promote fair and free elections.
- Mentor young people in civic engagement and democratic values.

CHAPTER 28

CHOOSE PRAGMATISM: SOMNATH CHATTERJEE

The Person

One of the longest-serving members of the Indian Parliament—including a term as its speaker—Somnath Chatterjee was known for his nonpartisan, pragmatic approach to government.

The Lesson

Idealism—aiming to attain preconceived visions—is often opposed to pragmatism, the search for workable, realistic solutions. In my observation of political life, while idealists project a bolder image that makes them attractive candidates, they tend to be far worse than pragmatists when it comes to actually governing. Meanwhile, pragmatists are willing to compromise on their stated intentions, and even on their ideals, to achieve a greater good for a greater number. In his political career,

Somnath Chatterjee was a prime example of a pragmatist who prioritized results over party politics, and his record of accomplishment has something to say to all of us.

Our Connection

I first met Chatterjee shortly after moving back to India from the United States in 1993. My plan was to start a manufacturing plant in Kolkata for fire safety and security products. At that time, along with his role as a member of the Indian Parliament, Chatterjee was serving as the chairman of the West Bengal Industrial Development Corporation (WBIDC). The WBIDC is a statutory body and the premier agency of the Government of West Bengal responsible for promoting industrial development in the state and providing support to industries and investors. It might seem strange to see a communist leading what amounted to a chamber of commerce, but it was a characteristically pragmatic move by Chatterjee on behalf of his people.

Chitta Ranjan Ghosh, Somnath Chatterjee, Sadhan Dutt, Shanta Ghosh, Nilima Ghosh, and the author

West Bengal had once been the industrial heartland of India, accounting for nearly a quarter of manufacturing output. By the early 1990s, that had dwindled significantly. Freight equalization of some industries from 1951 to 1993 was the main cause of the economic downturn in West Bengal.[131] Then in 1991, the Indian government launched the New Economic

Policy (NEP). In 1994, NEP got rid of the License Raj, a rule by which the Centre—the government of India—could withhold any and all licenses to states that were not in favor of the ruling party at the center. This had been hugely detrimental to West Bengal. Now, many sectors of the economy that had been paralyzed by bureaucracy were privatized. In particular, several key regulations that had disadvantaged West Bengal in comparison with southern and western states were done away with. The states were suddenly competing with one another for domestic and foreign investment. And who better to tout West Bengal's strengths than its most celebrated and respected political leader? My first discussion with Chatterjee was about our proposed factory in Kolkata. We formed an immediate bond once he learned about my father's role as a social justice activist and association with the left movement in West Bengal.

Returning to Kolkata was not easy. Starting a new venture in a city that I had left ten years before had its advantages and disadvantages. On the one hand, I was close to my parents and childhood friends and in the city I loved. On the other hand, Kolkata can be a challenging environment in which to start a venture at any time, but it was especially tough in 1993. Despite the optimism generated by the NEP, West Bengal was like a car that wouldn't start right away, despite getting a new battery. Our industries were old, and our workforce was increasingly agricultural. The leftist government tried its hand at liberalization, but local investors flocked to other states initially, amid negative perceptions of West Bengal as a communist stronghold.

I had an opportunity to listen to and interact with Jyoti Basu (Chief Minister of West Bengal), and I had a feeling that he was also trying to be more pragmatic. I vividly remember one such conversation, in which he acknowledged that consistent labor disputes in West Bengal were impacting productivity and hurting the state. However, I felt that this realization of the need for pragmatism by Jyoti Basu came too late in his political career.

The author with Jyoti Basu

But while our manufacturing venture did not succeed, I stayed in India, and opportunity soon came knocking. As a result of the new economic climate, foreign investors were officially welcome, and some of the first to show interest were Australian. I was offered a position with the Australian Government to open the Kolkata office of the Australian Trade Commission (Austrade), which was seeking to strengthen trade and investment between Australia and the eastern and northeastern states of India. During the next five years, I worked closely with Colin Hook, Jennie Lloyd, and other Austrade colleagues. I became a member of the Consular Corps of Kolkata and made some lifelong friends. And most importantly, my friendship with Chatterjee matured. We interacted much more frequently. On many occasions, I reached out to him for guidance and always received his most helpful support. In turn, my respect for him deepened. He had a vision for a more industrialized West Bengal. He wanted foreign investment, and at the same time he supported programs to lift people out of poverty. One such project was Haldia Petrochemicals. Haldia Petrochemicals Ltd., often referred to as HPL, is one of the largest petrochemical companies in India. Initially conceived in the early '80s, it was eventually formed through a joint venture between the Government of West Bengal, The Chatterjee Group, Soros Fund Management, and Tata Group in 1994. Commercial production started in 2001. The facility is located 125 km from Kolkata, at Haldia, in the Purba Medinipur district of West Bengal. With Chatterjee's support, I worked with the renowned industrialist Sadhan Dutta of DCL to bring the catamaran M V Rishi Aurobindo (Silverjet) from Australia to Kolkata. The goal of this project was to create a new mode of transportation from Kolkata to Haldia.

How Somnath Chatterjee Bettered the World

Somnath Chatterjee was the son of Nirmal Chandra Chatterjee, a renowned intellectual and lawyer. He was a prominent member of the Hindu nationalist establishment represented by the Akhil Bharatiya Hindu Mahasabha party. Somnath Chatterjee also completed his law degree, but in a show of independence, he joined the Communist Party of India (Marxist), or CPI(M), in 1968 and soon emerged as one of its prominent leaders. Chatterjee gave significant credit to Jyoti Basu for his involvement with CPI(M). Basu was one of the most prominent leaders of the Communist movement in India. From 1977 to 2000, he was Chief Minister of West Bengal, serving in that role longer than any of the five chief ministers before him. Chatterjee dedicated his 2010 memoir, *Keeping the Faith—Memoirs of a Parliamentarian*, to his parents, Nirmal Chandra and Binapani Debi, and to Jyoti Basu, his political leader. Chatterjee's dedication reads, "To my leader, Jyoti Basu, who persuaded me to join politics and taught me that politics provided the best opportunity to serve the people. . . ."[132] I remember my father had a similar respect for Jyoti Basu.

Chatterjee was elected to the Lok Sabha (the lower house of the Indian Parliament) a record ten times from Burdwan, Jadavpur, and Bolpur constituencies in West Bengal, serving from 1971 to 2009 with a break of one year from 1984 to 1985. Chatterjee held various important positions in Parliament, including Speaker of the Lok Sabha (House of the People)—roughly equivalent to the role and stature of Speaker of the US House of Representatives—from 2004 to 2009.

As speaker, he maintained a reputation for upholding the dignity and impartiality of the office, and he played a crucial role in managing the functioning of the Parliament during his tenure. Chatterjee was known for his deep knowledge of parliamentary procedures, eloquence, and adherence to democratic principles. He actively participated in debates on various national issues, including economic policies, social justice, and minority rights. He was also known for his statesmanlike conduct and fairness. As the Speaker of the Lok Sabha, he ensured that all members had an opportunity to voice their opinions and maintained order and decorum during debates. His impartial approach in presiding over parliamentary proceedings—even when these became unruly—earned him respect across party lines. Chatterjee advocated for social justice and emphasized the need for inclusive policies. One of his more significant accomplishments in this regard was the creation of Lok Sabha TV, the public cable network begun in 2006, with the aim of making the work of the political and legislative bodies of India accessible and transparent to all, in Hindi and English, twenty-four hours a day.

Chatterjee's career was as complex as Indian politics. It was inevitable that his pragmatism would eventually be challenged by many events. One such event happened in July 2008, when the left parties led by the CPI(M) voted to withdraw their support from the government of Manmohan Singh over their opposition to the Indo-US nuclear deal. Among other things, this agreement brought India's nuclear program into the community of nuclear powers whose programs were overseen by the International Atomic Energy Agency. The CPI(M) and its allies took the position that the deal would weaken Indian sovereignty and accused the government of hiding details about the deal's impact on India's nuclear program. As he was a member of the CPI(M), Chatterjee was called upon by his party to resign his position as speaker. Chatterjee gave the matter a great deal of thought, ultimately—and controversially—concluding that this would amount to a betrayal of his mandate as Speaker of the Lok Sabha. He argued that the speaker was expected to be nonpartisan and should not toe a party line. Chatterjee paid a heavy price for his decision. He was removed from the CPI(M), the party that had been his political home for over forty years, on what he described as "one of the saddest days"[133] of his life. In the wake of his expulsion, Chatterjee suggested that future speakers should resign from their parties while serving as speaker, to help ensure the nonpartisan standing of the position.

In *Keeping the Faith—Memoirs of a Parliamentarian*, Chatterjee tackled the controversy surrounding his unceremonious sacking from the party that he served so long and so passionately. The book is an in-depth study of some of the darkest phases of the history of modern India, including the Emergency (1975–77), when the ruling Congress Party led by Indira Gandhi assumed dictatorial powers, suspending civil liberties and jailing opposition figures, including my own father. Chatterjee recalled that what made the despair of those days bearable were numerous messages of support from all over the world, including from within India. For example, Tarun Gogoi, who was to become Chief Minister of Assam in July 2008, sent a message to Chatterjee stating, "I salute you for upholding and maintaining the dignity of the high office of Speaker of the Lok Sabha above party politics … the whole county is proud of you for enhancing the prestige of this high office in the most dignified manner."[134]

That is the Somnath Chatterjee I had the privilege to know. His action during that time in Indian politics demonstrated not only his courageous character and love for the Indian constitution, but above all his decision to favor pragmatism over idealism. While a great many idealists simply disappeared from public life, he worked within the confines of the Emergency to protect and nurture what he could of the parliamentary principles and rule of law he loved so dearly.

How Somnath Chatterjee Made *Me* Better

Whenever I met with Chatterjee, I was amazed at his calm and composed demeanor, which was astounding considering the conflicts raging in the CPI(M) around economic development in West Bengal. The party was having its own internal struggle between idealists and pragmatists. Chatterjee was known for his integrity, deep knowledge of parliamentary procedures, and unwavering commitment to democratic values. He had extensive knowledge of national and international issues and a quick wit and humor. But most important, the man I saw continuously worked to embrace change and fight idealists in his own political party. I saw him not as someone who was compromising his values but as a leader who deeply cared about improving the lives of common people.

I learned a lot about Chatterjee—as well as from him—through these direct interactions. However, his autobiography gave me new insights and an even deeper appreciation for his thoughtful approach to political life. Chatterjee learned much about good governance from his friend Abdul Halim, the longest-serving Speaker of the West Bengal Assembly. The book is full of vivid portraits of his political adversaries—stalwarts of Indian politics including Indira Gandhi, Manmohan Singh, Biju Patnaik, L.K. Advani, Pranab Mukherjee, Lalu Prasad Yadav, and many others. Chatterjee and many of these figures were poles apart ideologically, yet true to his character, Chatterjee highlighted the accomplishments of many of his political rivals, rather than their shortcomings. For this pragmatist, getting things done was more important than party affiliation.

I saw him as a role model not only for other politicians or parliamentarians but for all of us. When my son, Ryan Sohan, was born in 1996, I asked Chatterjee to be Ryan's godparent. The word "godparent" is an ever-evolving and open-ended term in Indian life. For many, the term has its roots in holy traditions, and there are others who see it as having nothing to do with religion at all. As a Hindu by birth, I found this term endearing and felt this was an opportunity to provide Ryan with another adult role model who I knew would want the best for him throughout his life. Although this is not a common practice in Indian society, Chatterjee eagerly accepted that role and attended Ryan's rice ceremony[135] in Kolkata. Ryan and I visited him in Delhi while he was Speaker of the Indian Parliament and again much later at his residence in Santiniketan. Over the years, Chatterjee and I remained in touch, and he always responded with great kindness and sincerity to all my questions. When Chatterjee led a delegation of West Bengal business leaders to the US, I hosted a dinner for him at our residence in Silver Spring. It was an incredible honor and pleasure to be able to finally introduce him to my American friends and colleagues, who had already heard so much about him from me.

The author with his son, Ryan, and Somnath Chatterjee

Chatterjee passed away on August 13, 2018, in Kolkata, at the age of eighty-nine. His death was mourned by politicians from various parties, highlighting his reputation as a respected and principled parliamentarian. Chatterjee left a lasting legacy as an eminence who dedicated his life to democratic values and parliamentary democracy. He is remembered for his contribution to Indian politics and his unwavering commitment to upholding the principles of justice and fairness. His passing was a great personal loss for me, but his life imparted a lesson I will not forget.

How You Can Choose Pragmatism *Now*

Idealism has its own merits, enabling us to visualize and pursue higher values, moral principles, and a more just and equitable society. However, time and again I have seen that we must remain flexible and find common ground to find solutions to complex problems. The following organizations—in India, the US, and elsewhere—all take a pragmatic approach to accomplishing positive change:

- **PRS Legislative Research**—Provides objective research on legislative and governance issues in India. How to get involved: Use their resources, attend their events, or support their work.
- **Observer Research Foundation**—Aims to lead and aid policy thinking toward building a strong and prosperous India. How to get involved: Participate in their programs, use their resources, or contribute to their research.
- **National Foundation for India**—Works toward a just, equitable, and sustainable society in India. How to get involved: Support their programs, apply for their fellowships, or donate.
- **India Development Foundation**—Focuses on research-based policy advocacy. How to get involved: Engage with their research, attend their events, or support their initiatives.
- **Common Cause**—Works toward good governance, democratic rights, and livelihood issues in India. How to get involved: Join their campaigns, use their resources, or support their legal initiatives.

- **Brookings Institution**—Conducts in-depth research that leads to new ideas for solving problems facing society. How to get involved: Engage with their research, attend their events, or support their work.

Ironically, though they have opposing approaches, idealists and pragmatists need one another. Without the dreamers, the doers would have nothing to do. Without the doers, the dreamers' dreams would never come true. This also applies to our own inner conversation: A big part of who we are in the world comes down to finding the balance that feels true to ourselves.

Whatever your ultimate balance may be, here are some tips for developing your pragmatic side:

- Seek to understand different perspectives before making decisions.
- Focus on finding practical solutions rather than adhering to rigid ideologies.
- Practice active listening in discussions, especially with those who hold different views.
- Regularly challenge your own assumptions and beliefs.
- Look for common ground in disagreements.
- Prioritize outcomes over ideological purity in problem solving.
- Stay informed about current events from diverse sources.
- Engage in respectful dialogue with people of different ideological backgrounds.
- Consider the long-term consequences of decisions, not just short-term ideological wins.
- Be willing to compromise for the greater good.

- Practice empathy and try to understand the motivations behind others' views.
- Evaluate policies and ideas based on their practical effects rather than their ideological origins.
- Encourage nuanced thinking in discussions about complex issues.
- Support leaders and initiatives that prioritize pragmatic problem solving.
- Reflect on your own experiences and how they shape your worldview.

CHAPTER 29

LEAVE A LEGACY: MY SON, RYAN SOHAN GHOSH

The Person

When I look at my son Ryan, I see the most important person in my life—the biracial child of divorced but devoted parents working together amicably (and successfully, I hope) to provide a grounding sense of family.

I see a child who has overcome obstacles, including coming to terms with his identity, on the way to maturity, and I see the obstacles yet to come, and I know these, too, cannot slow him. But the training wheels are off, and I am largely a spectator now—and a proud one at that—happy to help him move his belongings but willing to let him use the wings we gave him, trusting in his judgment and moral compass.

When the world looks at Ryan, it sees a twenty-eight-year-old chemical engineer who graduated with a Banneker/Key

Scholarship from the University of Maryland, College Park, as well as a restlessly curious spirit who worked for several multinational companies before deciding to pursue an MBA at Northwestern University's Kellogg School of Management in the Hawryluk Biopharmaceutical Scholars program. It sees—as I do—a young man with a great deal of promise, one with much of his life still ahead of him.

The Lesson

In the twenty-eight years I have known him, Ryan has taught me many valuable things.

I've learned a lot about him, his generation, the world, and myself. I have learned a lot about love, emotional investment, communication, support, trust—things that only he, and the experience of being his father, could have taught me.

But the lesson I'd like to share here goes beyond what a parent can learn from a child. It is a lesson that applies to all of us, and it is this: Leaving a legacy—while it leaves the world better for the future—is also something that changes you in the present.

Whether you're raising a child, writing a book, pursuing a career that fills a need, or actively finding ways to make a difference in the world, you're creating a feedback loop that alters you. And leaving a positive legacy alters you for the better.

Our Connection

When Ryan was young, I told him, "Please know I am not your only role model." He was puzzled and asked, "You aren't my only role model?" I had to deliver the bad news that I was an imperfect person; he should only adopt the good qualities from me and not my shortcomings. I urged him to follow the example set by several of my friends whom I respect, and that they could be role models, too. Initially, he was very uncomfortable with the idea that his dad could be imperfect, but slowly, he came to understand the need to think critically and independently, to see life as a learning experience, and to accept lessons from wherever they may come.

Language was a massive barrier between Ryan and his Dida (my mother) and Dadai (my father). My parents spoke broken and limited English, and long-distance phone conversations made it even more complicated. Ryan made numerous visits to India—some with me, some with Michele (his mother), and some alone. Even during those limited and scattered visits, Ryan learned many valuable lessons from his grandparents in India.

"These visits to India taught me about myself," he said. "From my grandparents, I learned empathy and courage. Despite living in conditions below the American poverty line—a small, open-air flat with no running water and no car—they insisted on sending money to others who had even less. Growing up, I felt their warmth and love and witnessed how they treated everyone with respect and dignity, no matter their caste or background."

Throughout his childhood, I had many talks with Ryan in which I tried to instill values of helping others. I often made the point that there are good and not-so-good qualities in every person and that we must learn the good qualities from every person while being self-aware and not mimicking the negative attributes, including those of his father. Our learning journey never ends, but I am pleased to see that he has not only incorporated some of the lessons this book highlights into his own life, but he is still working on learning and growing. He has a continuous desire to better himself and an openness to new experiences. He, too, appreciates that there is no better feeling than the one you get from helping others.

How Ryan Bettered the World

As a young man still pursuing his formal education, Ryan has not yet made his mark on the world—nor would I expect him to. He is in the midst of assembling his worldview, solidifying his values, and finding his path. But like the rest of his generation, he has inherited a catastrophically warming planet, widening income disparity, a resurgence of ethnic and religious violence and war, a breakdown of democratic institutions and a rise of authoritarianism, and a lack of many economic opportunities that previous generations enjoyed, to mention only a few of the headwinds he must face. And like his peers, the pressures of those realities will both shape him and test him.

His generation is nothing if not clear-eyed and resilient. Many of today's most potent social and political movements around the world are being led by youth, for example in the arenas of gun violence, peace, climate change, and race relations. While they might be quick to dismiss the entitlement of my generation ("OK, boomer. . . .") and despise hypocrisy, they are respectful of those elders who are credible and "walk the walk." They are intellectually fearless, willing to challenge their own assumptions. They know time is of the essence, so they are impatient for positive change and willing to make it happen.

How Ryan Made *Me* Better

Adventure into Understanding—My son has always had an adventurous spirit. From a young age, Ryan's curiosity knew no bounds. He was constantly asking, "Why?" in response to almost every instruction, which, although sometimes exhausting, revealed his relentless quest for knowledge. On our walks, he would often dash off to follow the trail of a deer, trace the path of insects, or explore the woods next to our home in Maryland. His energy and inquisitive nature were constant reminders of the joy of discovery.

By the time Ryan was a sophomore in high school, I was excited to combine my interest in engaging with people with his sense of adventure. He had become a catalyst for me, an incentive to push my own boundaries in encountering the world. That year, we planned a trip to Jackson Hole, Wyoming, from which we visited Grand Teton National Park. I have always been fascinated by the history and struggles of Native Americans, so after a few days of hiking in the park, I inquired about visiting the Wind River Indian Reservation—the current home of the Eastern Shoshone and Northern Arapaho tribes.

Concerned for our safety, our hotel manager and the local chamber of commerce urged us not to go. We understood the concerns. Poverty on the reservation is extreme and the crime rate is more than five times the national average. Still, we were determined to visit to gain some firsthand knowledge of the life of the people living there. On the reservation, we had memorable interactions with residents, including Sarah Aoah, an elderly Shoshone woman; Rocky, a Shoshone tribe member working at a local school; and Kesley Lasost (Alfred), an Arapaho artist. Despite our initial challenges in connecting with their community, our persistence led to profound conversations and a deeper understanding of their lives, challenges, and histories. This awareness was important for both of us.

Our experience highlighted the importance of engaging with local communities to uncover stories of resilience and connection beyond the typical tourist path. It also cemented my conviction that there are good people everywhere, and that the key to finding them is to abandon your preconceptions—and embrace the adventure.

Unity in Diversity—Ryan is a child of mixed ancestry. His mother is Anglo-American, and I am Indian American. He was raised amidst an ethos of love, kindness, and acceptance, yet he has always been conscious of his complex "otherness." In him, the diversity that merged through his mother and me is expressed as both a symbolic and an actual unity.

If not for Ryan—and my wanting him to appreciate the religious diversity of the India I had known as a child—I might not have made the pilgrimage that he and I embarked on in early 2024. This was an opportunity to connect Ryan to his Indian roots while deepening our own spiritual relationship.

Our journey was a vibrant tapestry of experiences, leading us to explore various historic sites and religious establishments across the country. The awe-inspiring Ajanta and Ellora caves in Maharashtra left us spellbound, while the spiritual aura of Varanasi and Sarnath in Uttar Pradesh filled us with a profound sense of humility. Sarnath, the site of the Buddha's first sermon, and Varanasi, the heart of Hinduism, are both revered by Buddhists, Muslims, Christians, Sikhs, and Jains. As we continued our journey, we embraced the serene ambiance of the Haji Ali Dargah mosque in Mumbai and Jama Masjid in Varanasi. We also experienced the solemn dignity of a synagogue at Knesset Eliyahoo in Mumbai, dating back to 1884, and the peaceful aura of a Sikh Gurdwara—"Gurdwara Sri Guru Ka Bagh" in Varanasi—which commemorates the visit of Guru Nanak, the founder of the Sikh religion, in the sixteenth century.

Along with touring these landmarks, we visited Kolkata, the "city of joy" where both Ryan and I were born. It was a special homecoming. Among my reasons for making this trip was a deep concern about the increasing religious polarization in India in recent years. Growing up, we were taught that the fundamental principle of Hinduism is that God is in everyone, that everyone is divine, and that all human beings are fundamentally equal. Throughout our journey, I spoke with citizens from all walks of life—friends, fellow airline passengers, Uber drivers, hotel staff, tour guides, and many others. It was clear to me that most citizens are more interested in a prosperous India than a divided nation.

As a father, I am even more committed to ensuring that Ryan's generation will inherit a world that celebrates rather than persecutes religious differences. As he and I shared our impressions, energized with wonder, we were struck anew by the beauty and strength that reside in our diversity. And we returned home to Maryland convinced that we could build a more harmonious and prosperous future together, regardless of our beliefs.

Resolve out of Tragedy—On August 12, 2017, a white nationalist drove his car into a crowd opposing his views, killing thirty-two-year-old Heather Heyer. When I heard the news, I was instantly overwhelmed by grief, sadness, anger, and confusion. Unable to come to rest, I resolved, on the spot, to drive to Charlottesville, Virginia—where the tragedy had taken place—to calm my nerves, gain some clarity, and, honestly, to respond to the powerful urge to *do* something.

There were a couple of big questions on my mind: What must we do as a nation to come together? How does this horrific incident align with my view of America and with the article I had recently written on the empathy and kindness of everyday Americans ("What Is The Secret of America's Success?," *Huffington Post*, July 5, 2016)?

I decided to interview residents of Charlottesville and neighboring Scottsville, partly to gain some understanding of the events, but also to find solace in communion. If they were feeling the same things I was, I wouldn't feel so alone and powerless. I approached residents of all ages and ethnicities, including a ten-year-old girl walking with her mother. During these conversations, I found out that some hold diverse political views and differing opinions of what we must do as a nation. However, some common themes emerged from those conversations: "learn from our history," "build bridges," and "teach our kids to reject hate because wherever people are joined in love, there is strength."

Nearly seven years later (in June, 2024), I wanted to revisit those themes by returning to Charlottesville with my son, who I see as part of Heather's generation. I know that it will be up to him—and others like him—to find ways to dispel the hatred that creates such tragedies, and I wanted to see the situation through his eyes.

We discussed at length the incident in 2017 and walked the street—now Heather Heyer Way—where it took place, talking with more residents. As I observed Ryan's response, I could feel his generation's thirst for justice, inclusivity, peace, and love. I could feel the pain of Heather's family and friends at the loss of one so hopeful, loving, and courageous in the face of racist hatred and violence.

Ryan and I reflected together and left Charlottesville in a solemn mood, heavy hearted, but determined that we must do whatever we can to share the lessons we learned, to learn from our history, and to build more bridges.

During each of these travels with my son, he and I became closer. On the Wyoming reservation, I perceived the strength of his genuine regard for the intrinsic worth of other people and ways of life. As we toured India, I witnessed his acceptance of all spiritual paths as sharing a fundamental validity. And in Charlottesville, I saw the urgency of his conviction that people must do better—must work harder to connect with and respect one another.

Noticing these attributes and beliefs in Ryan reaffirmed for me the worth of what my parents taught. It reassured me that these core values are being passed to the next generation. It gave me hope.

How You Can Leave a Legacy *Now*

You might not have realized it, but by reading this book, you are taking the first step in leaving a legacy for future generations. Any time you take action to positively impact the lives of others, you are reaching beyond yourself to touch lives yet to be lived. The following organizations are among the many that can help you directly influence the future:

- **StoryCorps**—Records and preserves stories of everyday Americans, promoting understanding between generations. How to get involved: Record your story or listen to others' stories.

- **The Intergenerational Foundation**—Works toward fairness between generations by addressing issues of intergenerational equity. How to get involved: Support their research, use their resources, or participate in campaigns.
- **The Nature Conservancy**—Works to conserve lands and waters for future generations. How to get involved: Volunteer, donate, or participate in conservation projects.
- **The Future Project**—Works to unlock the potential of young people in high schools across America. How to get involved: Become a Dream Director or support their programs.
- **Ashoka Youth Venture**—Supports young people in launching their own social ventures to create lasting change in their communities. How to get involved: Apply to become a Youth Venturer or mentor young social entrepreneurs.
- **Generation Citizen**—Promotes youth civic engagement through action civics education. How to get involved: Volunteer as a Democracy Coach or support their programs.
- **Rock the Vote**—Engages and builds the political power of young people. How to get involved: Register to vote, volunteer, or join their campaigns.

It has often been said that change begins at home. When looking for ways to leave a legacy, there's no better place to start than within your own family or community. My parents certainly did—and nearly everything I have done in my life is the result.

I'd like to leave you with this final set of simple actions—any one of which could start a chain reaction for good:

- Share your life experiences and lessons learned with younger family members or colleagues.
- Ask young people for their perspectives on current issues and truly listen to their responses.
- Start a journal or blog to document your thoughts and experiences for future generations.
- Participate in mentoring programs at work or in your community.
- Engage in activities that reduce your carbon footprint to preserve the environment for future generations.
- Have regular family discussions about values, history, and aspirations.
- Volunteer for causes that will have a long-term positive impact on your community.
- Learn a new skill or technology from a younger person.
- Share family recipes, traditions, or cultural practices with younger generations.
- Participate in local government or community planning to shape the future of your area.
- Create a time capsule with your family to be opened in the future.
- Support and encourage young people's initiatives and ideas.
- Practice active listening when engaging with people from different generations.
- Share your professional expertise through teaching or writing.
- Regularly reflect on your personal growth and the impact you want to have on the world.

ACKNOWLEDGMENTS

I have been blessed with amazing friends and mentors throughout the world. While working on *Do More Good*, I have benefited from the wisdom and compassion of countless people. I am grateful for the immense encouragement and support I have received.

I first met **Matt Westbrook** in 1985, a year after arriving in the United States, while working at a gift shop in New Orleans. I came to know this incredible person upon moving to the DC area, and we have been friends ever since. As a copyeditor of this book, he reviewed the manuscript with love, sincerity, and passion. Matt not only came up with the book's working title and suggested the format but also brought his poetic sensibility to the project, enriching it immeasurably.

I began working with **Steven Krolak** in 2008. As this book's substantive editor, Steven guided me throughout the writing process with his research and deep understanding of the subject matter. Steven thoroughly understands the development/philanthropic sector, and his insights were invaluable in shaping the narrative.

My literary agent, **Michele Martin** of MDM Management, contributed her extensive understanding of the publishing business to help me enhance the book's content. Michele also navigated the proposal process and secured a book deal for me. As a first-time author, I learned much from her and am forever grateful.

Amy Scher, a bestselling and award-winning author of four books, provided critical input on the book's structure and offered insightful suggestions to make it more effective and reader friendly.

Walter Heiser, an undergraduate student at New York University, engaged in research that has been instrumental in making this book even more valuable to readers.

Together, they nurtured this project from concept to reality.

I met many of the remarkable individuals profiled in this book during my tenure with the Australian Trade Commission, SNV Netherlands Development Organisation/SNV USA, Global Fund for Children, SOS Children's Villages, Veterans Engineering, and MGR Professional Services. I am grateful to my colleagues in these organizations for their support. Their impact has been significant, though their names are too numerous to mention.

I would like to sincerely thank my friends Dr. Ashim Roy, Kristin Lobron, Dirk Elsen, A LeMaitre, Piyali Callahan, Asok Motayed, Saumyendra Basu, and Raj Kumar who read the manuscript provided valuable comments and guidance. Many thanks also to Bill Reese for his encouragement.

I am grateful to the staff at the Tollygunge Club in Kolkata, India, who always make me feel at home during my yearly visit and provide an environment conducive to positive thinking.

And I want to extend my gratitude to Alan Crandall of Patheos, the Office of His Holiness the Dalai Lama, and the Office of President Bill Clinton for their support.

Many thanks to my publisher, Post Hill Press, and distributor, Simon & Schuster, for believing in this book. Thanks also to my publicist, Smith Publicity, and my marketing firm, Woodworks Communications, for their efforts in promoting it.

For encouraging me to write this book, I am forever grateful to Sharmistha Ganguly.

Lastly, I would like to thank the extraordinary individuals whose stories I share in these pages. This book would not exist without the opportunities I had to interact with and be inspired by them.

NOTES

1 Jarad A. Denton, "Life's most persistent question," Joint Base Langley-Eustis, December 17, 2012, https://www.jble.af.mil/News/Commentaries/Display/Article/260233/lifes-most-persistent-question/.

2 "Live as if you were dying tomorrow," CUInsight, February 6, 2014, https://www.cuinsight.com/live-as-if-you-were-dying-tomorrow/.

3 Harold Kushner, foreword to Viktor E. Frankl, *Man's Search for Meaning* (Beacon Press, 2006).

4 Nathan Christensen, "Is There ROI In Empathy?" *Forbes*, July 28, 2021. https://www.forbes.com/councils/forbesbusinesscouncil/2021/07/28/is-there-roi-in-empathy/.

5 Dalai Lama and Victor Chan, *The Wisdom of Compassion* (Riverhead Books, 2012), 116-17.

6 Maykel Verkuyten et al., "Maintaining a Tolerant National Identity: Divergent Implications for the Acceptance of Minority Groups," *Journal of Applied Social Psychology* 53 (2023): 1027–1039, https://doi.org/10.1111/jasp.12993.

7 Christopher Oveis, E. J. Horberg, and Dacher Keltner, "Compassion, Pride, and Social Intuitions of Self-Other Similarity," *Journal of Personality and Social Psychology* 98, no. 4 (2010): 618–630, https://doi.org/10.1037/a0017628.

8 An agriculture value chain is the series of interconnected activities involved in producing, processing, distributing, and consuming agricultural goods, aimed at adding value at each stage to enhance efficiency and profitability. For more information, see "Markets and Value Chains," International Fund for Agricultural Development (IFAD), https://www.ifad.org/en/markets-and-value-chains.

9 My column can be found at https://www.patheos.com/blogs/buildingbridges/.

10 In South Indian culture, the word *da* is often placed after a person's name as a term of endearment.

11 Clayton M. Christensen, et al., *How Will You Measure Your Life?* (HarperCollins, 2012).

12 John Wooden and Don Yaeger, *A Game Plan for Life: The Power of Mentoring* (Bloomsbury USA, 2009).

13 "About Us," All India Imam Organization, https://www.allindiaimamorganization.org/about.html.

14 Renee Garfinkel, "What Works? Evaluating Interfaith Dialogue Programs," United States Institute of Peace, July 1, 2004. https://www.jstor.org/stable/resrep12246

15 Ari Gordon, "Indian Muslim Peace Delegation Arrives in Israel on Project Interchange," *Worldwide Faith News*, August 15, 2007, https://archive.wfn.org/2007/08/msg00183.html.

16 Bala Chauhan, "Insaniyat is foremost, religion comes next: Dr. Imam Umer Ahmed Ilyasi," Deccan *Chronicle*, June 22, 2017, https://www.deccanchronicle.com/nation/in-other-news/230617/insaniyat-is-foremost-religion-comes-next.html.

17 "Insaniyat," Deccan *Chronicle.*

18 Omid Safi, ed., *Progressive Muslims: On Justice, Gender, and Pluralism* (Oneworld Publications, 2003).

19 "Insaniyat," Deccan *Chronicle.*

20 "What Works?," United States Institute of Peace.

21 “Julia M. Chan, “How to honor RBG by supporting her favorite causes,” *CNN*, September 19, 2020, https://www.cnn.com/2020/09/19/us/ruth-bader-ginsburg-rbg-favorite-causes-charity-iyw/index.html.

22 Ibid.

23 Scott Dodson, ed., *The Legacy of Ruth Bader Ginsburg* (Cambridge University Press, 2015).

24 Daniel Politi, “Read Justice Ruth Bader Ginsburg’s Touching Statement on Scalia,” *Slate*, February 14, 2016, https://slate.com/news-and-politics/2016/02/read-justice-ruth-bader-ginsburgs-touching-statement-on-scalia.html.

25 “Ruth Bader Ginsburg in pictures and her own words,” *BBC News*, September 19, 2020, https://www.bbc.com/news/world-us-canada-54218139.

26 Liz Mineo, “The life and legacy of RBG,” *Harvard Gazette*, September 20, 2020. https://news.harvard.edu/gazette/story/2020/09/harvard-community-reflects-on-the-life-achievements-of-ruth-bader-ginsburg/.

27 Ibid.

28 Sarah B. Boxer, “Ruth Bader Ginsburg on Trump, Kaepernick and her lifelong love of the law,” *Yahoo News*, October 10, 2016, https://www.yahoo.com/news/ruth-bader-ginsburg-on-trump-kaepernick-and-her-lifelong-love-of-the-law-132236633.html.

29 “Challenging Inequality,” Ford Foundation, https://www.fordfoundation.org/work/challenging-inequality/.

30 Darren Walker, *From Generosity to Justice: A New Gospel of Wealth* (Disruption Books, 2023), 6, https://institutomol.org.br/wp-content/uploads/2021/08/generositytojustice.pdf.

31 “Darren Walker,” Ford Foundation, updated September 28, 2024, https://www.fordfoundation.org/about/people/darren-walker/.

32 Jasmine Aguilera, “How Philanthropy Can Help Achieve Racial Justice,” *Time*, June 4, 2020. https://time.com/5846620/darren-walker-ford-foundation-time-100-talks/.

33 Sim Ying, "Let's talk facts, leadership, economics, foreigners and inspiration: Sim Ying," *The Online Citizen*, September 6, 2017, https://www.theonlinecitizen.com/2017/09/06/lets-talk-facts-leadership-economics-foreigners-and-inspiration-sim-ying/.

34 Father Mario Attard, "Mother Teresa and the Call of God," *Catholic Insight*, September 10, 2024, https://catholicinsight.com/mother-teresa-and-the-call-of-god/.

35 "Kolkata, India Population 2024," World Population Review,https://worldpopulationreview.com/cities/india/kolkata.

36 John McCain and Mark Salter, *Character Is Destiny: Inspiring Stories Every Young Person Should Know and Every Adult Should Remember* (Random House, New York, 2005), 297.

37 "Honorary citizen of the United States," Wikipedia, updated November 23, 2024, https://en.wikipedia.org/wiki/Honorary_citizenship_of_the_United_States.

38 "Missionaries of Charity," Wikipedia, updated November 26, 2024, https://en.wikipedia.org/wiki/Missionaries_of_Charity.

39 Elizabeth Dias, "How Pope Francis and Mother Teresa Are Linked," *Time*, August 29, 2016, https://time.com/4470920/how-pope-francis-and-mother-teresa-are-linked/.

40 "Catholic Church," Wikipedia, updated December 8, 2024, https://en.wikipedia.org/wiki/Catholic_Church#:~:text=The%20Catholic%20Church%2C%20also%20known,Catholics%20worldwide%20as%20of%202024.

41 Dias, "How Pope Francis."

42 "About Grameen Bank," Grameen Bank, https://grameenbank.org.bd/about/introduction.

43 Muhammad Yunus, *Banker to the Poor: Micro-Lending and the Battle Against World Poverty*, (PublicAffairs, 2008).

44 Muhammad Yunus, "Commencement address by Muhummad Yunus," *MIT News*, June 6, 2008, https://news.mit.edu/2008/yunus-0606.

45 Marc. J. Epstein and Kristi Yuthas, "The Critical Role of Trust in Microfinance Success: Identifying Problems and Solutions," *Journal of Developmental Entrepreneurship (JDE)*, 2011, https://ideas.repec.org/a/wsi/jdexxx/v16y2011i04ns1084946711001951.html.

46 Demetri Sevastopulo, "Amartya Sen: The Nobel Laureate Who Has Redefined Development Economics," *Financial Times*, March 25, 2021, https://www.ft.com/content/2a4096b4-4fef-4d6e-bd14-e30cff8426e1.

47 Christina Pazzanese, "Amartya Sen's nine-decade journey from colonial India to Nobel Prize and beyond," *The Harvard Gazette*, June 3, 2021, https://news.harvard.edu/gazette/story/2021/06/tracing-amartya-sens-path-from-childhood-during-the-raj-to-nobel-prize-and-beyond/.

48 Encyclopaedia Britannica, "Decency," *Britannica Dictionary*, https://www.britannica.com/dictionary/decency.

49 Walter Shapiro, "Opinion: Joe Biden—The Most Decent Man in Politics," *Roll Call*, November 15, 2017, https://rollcall.com/2017/11/15/opinion-joe-biden-the-most-decent-man-in-politics/

50 Jonathan Martin and Amie Parnes, "McCain: Obama not an Arab, crowd boos," *Politico*, October 10, 2008, https://www.politico.com/story/2008/10/mccain-obama-not-an-arab-crowd-boos-014479.

51 "McCain Says Ohio Steel Jobs Not Coming Back," *Reuters*, October 22, 2008. https://www.reuters.com/article/world/us-politics/mccain-says-ohio-steel-jobs-not-coming-back-idUSN22472705/.

52 John McCain and Mark Salter, *Character Is Destiny*, xi.

53 Jonathan Allen, "John McCain's legacy: A sense of honor that has become rare in a polarized Washington," *NBC News*, August 25, 2018, https://www.nbcnews.com/politics/politics-news/john-mccain-s-legacy-sense-honor-has-become-rare-polarized-n903911.

54 "Introduction," US Cyberspace Solarium Commission, https://www.solarium.gov.

55 "Remarks by President Biden Honoring the Legacy of Senator John McCain and the Work We Must Do Together to Strengthen Our Democracy," The White House, September 28, 2023, https://www.whitehouse.gov/briefing-room/speeches-remarks/2023/09/28/remarks-by-president-biden-honoring-the-legacy-of-senator-john-mccain-and-the-work-we-must-do-together-to-strengthen-our-democracy/.

56 "Bush accepts Sen. McCain's torture policy," *NBC News*, December 15, 2005, https://www.nbcnews.com/id/wbna10480690.

57 "Clean Cooking Alliance Releases 2023 Annual Report," Clean Cooking Alliance, March 6, 2024, https://cleancooking.org/.

58 "A Plate of Hope," *Leaders Online*, April 2, 2023, https://leadersmag.com/issues/2023.2_Apr/Resilience/LEADERS-Jose-Andres-World-Central-Kitchen.html.

59 "World Central Kitchen," Global Food Security Is a Human Right, updated 2024, https://gfshr.org/world-central-kitchen/#:~:text=We%20don't%20just%20deliver,rebuild%20our%20sense%20of%20community.

60 "400 million meals served: WCK named one of TIME's Most Influential Companies," World Central Kitchen, May 30, 2024, https://wck.org/news/time100#.

61 "A Plate of Hope," *Leaders Online*.

62 "John Glenn," Wikipedia, updated December 7, 2024, https://en.wikipedia.org/wiki/John_Glenn.

63 John Glenn with Nick Taylor, *John Glenn: A Memoir* (Bantam Books, New York, 1999), 359.

64 "NASA Honors a Legendary Astronaut," NASA, February 21, 2006, https://web.archive.org/web/20161220085954/https:/www.nasa.gov/vision/space/features/glenn_ambassador_of_exploration.html.

65 Ibid.

66 Howard Wilkinson, "John Glenn Had the Stuff U.S. Heroes Are Made Of," *The Cincinnati Enquirer*, February 20, 2002.

67 Brendan Doherty, "Icons of Impact: Kevin Bacon Backs Social Enterprise Delivering Hope After CA Wildfires," *Forbes*, January 20, 2019, https://www.forbes.com/sites/bdoherty/2019/01/20/icons-of-impact-kevin-bacon-backs-social-enterprise-delivering-hope-after-ca-wildfires/?sh=3180aaaf1741.

68 "Kevin Bacon's Guide to Empathy: Unveiling the Infinite Power of Connection," *Virgin Pulse*, December 4, 2023, https://www.virginpulse.com/blog-post/kevin-bacons-guide-to-empathy-unveiling-the-infinite-power-of-connection/.

69 "How Empathy Drives Action with Kyra Sedgwick and SixDegrees.org," Apple Podcasts, November 28, 2023, https://podcasts.apple.com/us/podcast/how-empathy-drives-action-with-kyra-sedgwick/id1704724572?i=1000636753180.

70 Mishal Husain, "Malala, the girl who was shot for going to school," BBC, October 7, 2013, https://www.bbc.com/news/magazine-24379018.

71 Ibid.

72 "Girls' Education," UNICEF, https://www.unicef.org/education/girls-education.

73 Ahmad Mukhtar, "The Taliban Banned Afghan Girls from School 1,000 Days Ago, but Some Brave Young Women Refuse to Accept It," *CBS News*, June 7, 2024, https://www.cbsnews.com/news/taliban-girls-school-ban-afghanistan-1000-days-underground-schools/.

74 "10 reasons to educate girls," UNICEF, September 2, 2022, https://www.unicefusa.org/stories/10-reasons-educate-girls#:~:text=Girls%20who%20complete%20a%20secondary,invest%20more%20in%20their%20communities.

75 In mastery-based learning, students progress through a curriculum at their own pace, advancing only when they demonstrate a

thorough understanding of a topic or skill. This educational method focuses on competency rather than time spent in class.

76 *2013 Global Philanthropy Forum Conference Transcript*, Global Philanthropy Forum, San Francisco, 2013, https://philanthropyforum.secure.nonprofitsoapbox.com/storage/documents/2013-gpf-conference-transcript.pdf.

77 Adam Cheise, "82 Khan Academy Statistics for 2024 (Data & Facts)," ProsperityForAll, September 2, 2024, https://www.prosperityforamerica.org/khan-academy-statistics/.

78 *Learning Gets Personal: How Idaho Students and Teachers Are Embracing Personalized Learning through Khan Academy,* FSG, Spring 2015, https://www.fsg.org/wp-content/uploads/2021/08/Learning-Gets-Personal_How-Idaho-Students-and-Teachers-Are-Embracing-Personalized-Learning-through-Khan-Academy.pdf.

79 Julie Phillips Randles, "Sal Khan Describes the Passion Behind Khan Academy," ISTE Blog, June 25, 2014, https://iste.org/blog/sal-khan-describes-the-passion-behind-khan-academy.

80 Salman Khan, *The One World Schoolhouse: Education Reimagined* (Twelve, 2012), 4.

81 "Stories," Khan Academy, https://www.khanacademy.org/stories#.

82 Khan, *One World*, 15.

83 Khan, *One World*, 37.

84 Megan Kuhfeld, et al., "The pandemic has had devastating impacts on learning. What will it take to help students catch up?" The Brookings Institute, March 3, 2022, https://www.brookings.edu/blog/brown-center-chalkboard/2022/03/03/the-pandemic-has-had-devastating-impacts-on-learning-what-will-it-take-to-help-students-catch-up/.

85 Ibid.

86 Peter Laugharn, "Philanthropy for global education comes of age," *Alliance*, April 29, 2013, https://www.alliancemagazine.org/blog/philanthropy-for-global-education-comes-of-age/.

87 "Caught Caring: The Jolie-Pitts, Asprey and Education Partnership for Children of Conflict," People, November 26, 2009, https://people.com/parents/caught-caring-the-jolie-pitts-asprey-and-education-partnership-for-children-of-conflict/.

88 Susan Devaney, "The Urgent Social Causes Angelina Jolie Truly Cares About," *British Vogue*, February 1, 2021. https://www.vogue.co.uk/arts-and-lifestyle/article/angelina-jolie-charity-work

89 "Camp Skyhook," Skyhook Foundation, https://skyhookfoundation.org.

90 "The Skyhook Foundation" Skyhook Foundation, https://skyhookfoundation.org.

91 Kareem Abdul-Jabbar and Alan Steinberg, *Black Profiles in Courage: A Legacy of African-American Achievement* (William Morrow, 1996).

92 Alison Beard, "Life's Work: An Interview with Kareem Abdul-Jabbar," *Harvard Business Review*, January-February 2012, https://hbr.org/2012/01/kareem-abdul-jabbar.

93 Ibid.

94 "Shimon Peres reflects on working toward peace," The Markkula Center for Applied Ethics, Santa Clara University, 2014, https://www.scu.edu/mcae/architects-of-peace/Peres/essay.html (site discontinued).

95 "About Us," The Peres Center for Peace and Innovation, https://www.peres-center.org/en/the-organization/about-us/.

96 The Associated Press, "Israel's 'biggest dreamer': Bill Clinton praises Shimon at former president's funeral," *Salon*, September 30, 2016, https://www.salon.com/2016/09/30/the-latest-clinton-peres-was-israels-biggest-dreamer/.

97 "Giving USA: Total U.S. Charitable Giving Remained Strong in 2021, Reaching $484.85 Billion," Philanthropy Network Greater Philadelphia, June 21, 2022, https://philanthropynetwork.org/news/giving-usa-total-us-charitable-giving-remained-strong-2021-reaching-48485-billion.

98 "NPOs Added $1.4 Trillion To U.S. Economy," *The NonProfit Times*, July 5, 2022, https://thenonprofittimes.com/report/npos-added-1-4-trillion-to-u-s-economy/.

99 Muhammad Yunus, *Banker to the Poor: Micro-Lending and the Battle Against World Poverty* (PublicAffairs, 2007), 13.

100 Anand Giridharadas, *Winners Take All: The Elite Charade of Changing the World* (Knopf, New York, 2018).

101 "Upton Sinclair 1878–1968," Oxford Reference, https://www.oxfordreference.com/display/10.1093/acref/9780191826719.001.0001/q-oro-ed4-00010168?rskey=IIMhWd&result=3364.

102 "The Clinton Presidency: Protecting Our Environment and Public Health," The White House, https://clintonwhitehouse5.archives.gov/WH/Accomplishments/eightyears-08.html#:~:text=President%20Clinton%20has%20made%20the%20Federal%20government,its%20annual%20energy%20bill%20by%20$800%20million.

103 "NY1 –: Bill Clinton Reflects on 20 Years in Harlem," Clinton Foundation, August 2, 2021, https://www.clintonfoundation.org/press-and-news/general/ny1-bill-clinton-reflects-on-20-years-in-harlem/.

104 "Bill O'Reilly Transforms Into His 'Culture Warrior' Persona for Barbara Walters Interview," *News Hounds*, September 22, 2006, https://www.newshounds.us/2006/09/22/bill_oreilly_transforms_into_his_culture_warrior_persona_for_barbara_walters_interview.php (site discontinued).

105 Madison Gray, "Rosa Parks' Archived Writing Reveals Attempted Rape," *Time*, July 29, 2011, https://newsfeed.time.com/2011/07/29/rosa-parks-archived-writing-reveals-attempted-rape/.

106 Rosa Parks and James Haskins, *Rosa Parks: My Story* (Dial Books, 1992).

107 Rosa Parks and Gregory J. Reed, *Quiet Strength: The Faith, the Hope, and the Heart of a Woman Who Changed a Nation* (Zondervan, 1994).

108 "Barack H. Obama," Columbia Celebrates Black History and Culture, https://blackhistory.news.columbia.edu/people/barack-h-obama.

109 Matt Ozug and Courtney Dorning, "Jimmy Carter's Relationship with the Allman Brothers Band Helped Him Become President," NPR, March 29, 2023, https://www.npr.org/2023/03/29/1166891522/jimmy-carters-relationship-with-the-allman-brothers-band-helped-him-become-presi.

110 "Jimmy Carter, the president who tried to save the planet," *Washington Post*, February 21, 2023, https://www.washingtonpost.com/climate-environment/2023/02/21/jimmy-carter-environment-energy-alaska/.

111 Jimmy Carter, "Crisis of Confidence Speech," American Rhetoric, updated August 28, 2024, https://www.americanrhetoric.com/speeches/jimmycartercrisisofconfidence.htm.

112 "Waging Peace Through Elections," The Carter Center, updated August 5, 2024, https://www.cartercenter.org/peace/democracy/observed.html.

113 The Carter Center, *Celebrating 30: Annual Report 2010-2011* (The Carter Center, 2011), 14, https://www.cartercenter.org/resources/pdfs/news/annual_reports/annual-report-11.pdf.

114 "U.N. Peacebuilding Fund Highlight," The Carter Center, August 2022, https://www.cartercenter.org/donate/corporate-government-foundation-partners/archives/united-nations-peacebuilding-fund.html.

115 "Access to Justice in Liberia," The Carter Center, https://www.cartercenter.org/peace/ati/access-to-justice/index.html.

116 "Inform Women, Transform Lives," The Carter Center, https://www.cartercenter.org/peace/info4women/index.html.

117 Hillary Rodham Clinton, *It Takes a Village* (Simon & Schuster, 2006), xii–xiii.

118 Hillary Rodham Clinton, *Living History* (Simon & Schuster, 2003).

119 "What Is Hillary's Greatest Accomplishment?," *Politico Magazine*, September 17, 2015, https://www.politico.com/magazine/story/2015/09/carly-fiorina-debate-hillary-clintons-greatest-accomplishment-213157/.

120 Hillary Rodham Clinton, *Hard Choices* (Simon & Schuster, New York, 2014).

121 "Town Hall with Tunisian Youth," U.S. Department of State, February 25, 2012, https://2009-2017.state.gov/secretary/20092013clinton/rm/2012/02/184656.htm.

122 "Clinton Resigns as US Secretary of State," *Al Jazeera*, February 2, 2013, https://www.aljazeera.com/news/2013/2/2/clinton-resigns-as-us-secretary-of-state.

123 "Who We Are," Global Citizen, https://www.globalcitizen.org/en/about/who-we-are/.

124 "Early Life," The Life and Legacy of Ross Perot, https://www.rossperot.com/life-story/early-life.

125 "Entrepreneur Extraordinaire," The Life and Legacy of Ross Perot, https://www.rossperot.com/life-story/entrepreneur-extraordinaire.

126 "Perot, the Unpolitician," *Chicago Tribune*, May 24, 1992, https://www.chicagotribune.com/1992/05/24/perot-the-unpolitician/.

127 Ross Perot, *Ross Perot: My Life & the Principles for Success* (Tapestry Press, 2002), 39.

128 "John Agyekum Kufuor," Columbia University World Leaders Forum, September 2003, https://worldleaders.columbia.edu/directory/john-agyekum-kufuor.

129 "Dictatorships advancing globally," University of Gothenburg, March 3, 2022, https://www.gu.se/en/news/dictatorships-advancing-globally.

130 "2011: Kufuor and Lula," World Food Prize Foundation, https://www.worldfoodprize.org/en/laureates/20102019_laureates/2011_kufuor_and_lula/#:~:text=Continuing%20Ghana's%20tradition%20of%20stability,to%209%20percent%20in%202004.

131 Subhash C. Ray, "The Political Economy of Decline of Industry in West Bengal: Experiences of a Marxist State Within a Mixed Economy," University of Connecticut Department of Economics Working Paper Series, May 2011, https://media.economics.uconn.edu/working/2011-10.pdf.

132 Somnath Chatterjee, *Keeping the Faith: Memoirs of a Parliamentarian* (HarperCollins India, 2010).

133 "Veteran Political Leader Somnath Chatterjee Passes Away at 89. All You Need to Know About Him," *India TV News*, August 13, 2018, https://www.indiatvnews.com/news/india-somnath-chatterjee-death-former-lok-sabha-speaker-profile-all-you-need-to-know-457880.

134 Chatterjee, *Keeping the Faith*.

135 In India, the rice ceremony celebrates a baby's first solid meal—a tradition comparable to the Christian christening or baptism rituals.

SELECTED BIBLIOGRAPHY

This book is a work of love and respect for some of the people who have touched my life and from whom I have learned a great deal. In general, those I write about are people I have encountered in person, with a few exceptions where I have been inspired from afar. I have done my best to describe the circumstances surrounding those meetings. For these descriptions as well as background information, I have relied on my powers of recollection, both visual and emotional, along with personal stories, personal letters, notes kept over the years, many books, and—where necessary—the internet. In instances where I relied on books and autobiographies, I have cited them directly in the text to keep the narrative going, and since this is how my mind works. The sources I have listed below represent some of the books, articles, and websites that stood out for me as I prepared these chapters. I've included a few of my own articles where they might be of interest. I hope that readers interested in learning more about the lives profiled here will find these links helpful for further exploration.

Introduction / My Inspiration—and Now Yours

Frankl, Viktor E. *Man's Search for Meaning* Beacon Press, 2006.

Chapter 1 / Live with Empathy: My Parents

Christensen, Nathan. "Is There ROI In Empathy?" *Forbes*, July 28, 2021. https://www.forbes.com/councils/forbesbusinesscouncil/2021/07/28/is-there-roi-in-empathy/.

Sinclair, Shane, et al. "Sympathy, empathy, and compassion: A grounded theory study of palliative care patients' understandings, experiences, and preferences." National Library of Medicine, August, 2017. https://www.ncbi.nlm.nih.gov/pmc/articles/PMC5405806/.

Chapter 2 / Practice Compassion: The Dalai Lama

His Holiness the Dalai Lama and Victor Chan. *The Wisdom of Compassion* Riverhead Books, 2012.

Lopez, Donald S. "Who Is the Dalai Lama?," *New York Times*, February 25, 2020. https://www.nytimes.com/2020/02/25/books/review/the-dalai-lama-by-alexander-norman.html.

Oveis, Christopher, E. J. Horberg, and Dacher Keltner. "Compassion, Pride, and Social Intuitions of Self-Other Similarity." *Journal of Personality and Social Psychology* 98, no. 4 (2010): 618–630, https://doi.org/10.1037/a0017628.

Sherwood, Harriet. "Religious intolerance is 'bigger cause of prejudice than race,' says report." *The Guardian*,

November 15, 2020. https://www.theguardian.com/world/2020/nov/15/religious-intolerance-is-bigger-cause-of-prejudice-than-race-says-report.

Verkuyten, Maykel, et al. "Maintaining a Tolerant National Identity: Divergent Implications for the Acceptance of Minority Groups." *Journal of Applied Social Psychology* 53 (2023): 1027–1039, https://doi.org/10.1111/jasp.12993.

Chapter 3 / Mentor Others: Asok Motayed

Christensen, Clayton M., et al. *How Will You Measure Your Life?* HarperCollins, 2012.

Decaro, Monica W. "The Many Benefits of Mentorship." *Strategic Finance*, March 1, 2017. https://www.sfmagazine.com/articles/2017/march/the-many-benefits-of-mentorship/?psso=true.

"How mentoring contributes to economic growth?" *Mentoring Complete*, December 9, 2022. https://www.mentoringcomplete.com/how-mentoring-contributes-to-economic-growth/.

"The Mentoring Effect." Mentor. https://www.mentoring.org/resource/the-mentoring-effect/.

Timpe, Zach C., and Erika Lunkenheimer. "The Long-Term Economic Benefits of Natural Mentoring Relationships for Youth." National Library of Medicine, September 2015. https://www.ncbi.nlm.nih.gov/pmc/articles/PMC4643259/#:~:text=We%20also%20estimated%20the%20lifetime,those%20without%20a%20male%20mentor.

Wooden, John, and Don Yaeger. *A Game Plan for Life: The Power of Mentoring* (Bloomsbury USA, 2009).

Chapter 4 / Embrace Religious Diversity: Imam Ilyasi

All India Imam Organization. "About Us." https://www.allindiaimamorganization.org/about.html.

Bagir, Zainal Abidin. "Interfaith Dialogue and Religious Education." United Nations Alliance of Civilizations. http://erb.unaoc.org/images/JournalArticles/bagir.pdf.

Chauhan, Bala. "Insaniyat is foremost, religion comes next: Dr. Imam Umer Ahmed Ilyasi." Deccan *Chronicle*, June 22, 2017. https://www.deccanchronicle.com/nation/in-other-news/230617/insaniyat-is-foremost-religion-comes-next.html.

Garfinkel, Renee. "What Works? Evaluating Interfaith Dialogue Programs." United States Institute of Peace, July 1, 2004. https://www.jstor.org/stable/resrep12246.

Gordon, Ari. "Indian Muslim Peace Delegation Arrives in Israel on Project Interchange." *Worldwide Faith News*, August 15, 2007, https://archive.wfn.org/2007/08/msg00183.html.

Gur, Haviv Rettig. "India's leading imam to visit Israel." Jerusalem Post, August 14, 2007. https://www.jpost.com/israel/indias-leading-imam-to-visit-israel.

Ingber, Sasha. "70 Muslim Clerics Issue Fatwa Against Violence And Terrorism." NPR, May 11, 2018. https://www.npr.org/sections/thetwo-way/2018/05/11/610420149/70-muslim-clerics-issue-fatwa-against-violence-and-terrorism.

Safi, Omid, ed. *Progressive Muslims: On Justice, Gender, and Pluralism*. Oneworld Publications, 2003.

Sammya. "Who is Umer Ahmed Ilyasi, chief cleric of All India Imam Organization?" Opoyi.22 November 2022. https://opoyi.com/india/who-is-umer-ahmed-ilyasi-chief-cleric-of-all-india-imam-organization-757427/ (site discontinued).

Chapter 5 / Learn from Everyone: Ruth Bader Ginsburg

BBC. "Ruth Bader Ginsburg in pictures and her own words." *BBC News*, September 19, 2020. https://www.bbc.com/news/world-us-canada-54218139.

Boxer, Sarah B. "Ruth Bader Ginsburg on Trump, Kaepernick and her lifelong love of the law," *Yahoo News*, October 10, 2016, https://www.yahoo.com/news/ruth-bader-ginsburg-on-trump-kaepernick-and-her-lifelong-love-of-the-law-132236633.html.

Chan, Julia M. "How to honor RBG by supporting her favorite causes." *CNN*, September 19, 2020. https://www.cnn.com/2020/09/19/us/ruth-bader-ginsburg-rbg-favorite-causes-charity-iyw/index.html.

Dodson, Scott. *The Legacy of Ruth Bader Ginsburg* (Cambridge University Press, 2015).

Editorial Board. "Ruth Bader Ginsburg's Legacy." *New York Times*, September 19, 2020. https://www.nytimes.com/2020/09/19/opinion/ruth-bader-ginsburg-legacy.html.

Mineo, Liz. "The life and legacy of RBG." *Harvard Gazette*, September 20, 2020. https://news.harvard.edu/gazette/story/2020/09/harvard-community-reflects-on-the-life-achievements-of-ruth-bader-ginsburg/.

Politi, Daniel. "Read Justice Ruth Bader Ginsburg's Touching Statement on Scalia." *Slate*, February 14, 2016. https://slate.com/news-and-politics/2016/02/read-justice-ruth-bader-ginsburgs-touching-statement-on-scalia.html.

Chapter 6 / Look Beyond: Darren Walker

Aguilera, Jasmine. "How Philanthropy Can Help Achieve Racial Justice." *Time*, June 4, 2020. https://time.com/5846620/darren-walker-ford-foundation-time-100-talks/.

Ford Foundation. "A path to peace through inclusion." October 2, 2019. https://www.fordfoundation.org/work/learning/research-reports/a-path-to-peace-through-inclusion/.

Ford Foundation. "Beyond Inclusion." September 25, 2020. https://www.fordfoundation.org/work/learning/research-reports/beyond-inclusion/.

Ford Foundation. "Challenging Inequality." https://www.fordfoundation.org/work/challenging-inequality/.

Ford Foundation. "People: Darren Walker, President." https://www.fordfoundation.org/about/people/darren-walker/.

Fox, Justin. "Piketty's 'Capital,' in a Lot Less than 696 Pages." *Harvard Business Review*, April 24, 2014. https://hbr.org/2014/04/pikettys-capital-in-a-lot-less-than-696-pages.

Ghosh, Neil. "Building Bridges." *Stanford Social Innovation Review*, Spring 2021. https://ssir.org/articles/entry/building_bridges.

Partnership for Public Service. "2022 Samuel J. Heyman Spirit of Service Award Winner: Darren Walker." https://servicetoamericamedals.org/honorees/darren-walker/.

Seltzer, Michael. "Darren Walker, President, Ford Foundation: Philanthropy and Social Justice." *Philanthropy News Digest*, January 2, 2014. https://philanthropynewsdigest.org/features/newsmakers/darren-walker-president-ford-foundation-philanthropy-and-social-justice.

Walker, Darren. *From Generosity to Justice: A New Gospel of Wealth* Disruption Books, 2023.

Walker, Darren. "We must be 'firefighters' for justice." *Houston Chronicle*, July 16, 2016. https://www.houstonchronicle.com/opinion/outlook/article/Walker-We-must-be-firefighters-for-justice-8382339.php.

Ying, Sim. "Let's talk facts, leadership, economics, foreigners and inspiration: Sim Ying." *The Online Citizen*, September 6, 2017. https://www.theonlinecitizen.com/2017/09/06/lets-talk-facts-leadership-economics-foreigners-and-inspiration-sim-ying/.

Chapter 7 / Listen for Your Calling: Mother Teresa

"66 years of Mother Teresa's Missionaries of Charity: Facts you should definitely know on the charity." India Today, October 7, 2016. https://www.indiatoday.in/education-today/gk-current-affairs/story/missionaries-of-charity-345373-2016-10-07.

Attard, Father Mario. "Mother Teresa and the Call of God." *Catholic Insight*, September 10, 2024. https://catholicinsight.com/mother-teresa-and-the-call-of-god/.

Dias, Elizabeth. "How Pope Francis and Mother Teresa Are Linked." *Time*, August 29, 2016. https://time.

com/4470920/how-pope-francis-and-mother-teresa-are-linked/.

Macrotrends. "Calcutta, India Metro Area Population 1950-2024." https://www.macrotrends.net/cities/21211/calcutta/population#:~:text=The%20current%20metro%20area%20population,a%201.07%25%20increase%20from%202021.

Mathew, Meghna. "Power, Poverty & People: Kolkata's History From 1880 to 1971 In Pictures." *Homegrown*, January 25, 2022. https://homegrown.co.in/homegrown-explore/power-poverty-people-kolkatas-history-from-1880-to-1971-in-pictures.

McCain, John and Mark Salter. *Character Is Destiny: Inspiring Stories Every Young Person Should Know and Every Adult Should Remember* Random House, 2005.

Spink, Kathryn. *Mother Teresa: A Complete Authorized Biography* HarperCollins, 1997.

Wikipedia. "Catholic Church." Updated December 8, 2024. https://en.wikipedia.org/wiki/Catholic_Church#:~:text=The%20Catholic%20Church%2C%20also%20known,Catholics%20worldwide%20as%20of%202024.

Wikipedia. "Honorary citizen of the United States." Updated November 23, 2024. https://en.wikipedia.org/wiki/Honorary_citizenship_of_the_United_States.

Wikipedia. "Missionaries of Charity." Updated November 26, 2024. https://en.wikipedia.org/wiki/Missionaries_of_Charity.

World Population Review. "Kolkata, India Population 2024." https://worldpopulationreview.com/cities/india/kolkata.

Chapter 8 / Offer Trust: Muhammad Yunus

Epstein, Marc J. and Kristi Yuthas. "The Critical Role of Trust in Microfinance Success: Identifying Problems and Solutions." *Journal of Developmental Entrepreneurship* 16, no. 4 (2011). https://www.worldscientific.com/doi/10.1142/S1084946711001951).

Grameen Bank. "About Grameen Bank." https://grameenbank.org.bd/about/introduction.

Justice, Glen. "Weaving Trust Into Progress." Aspen Institute, November 22, 2022. https://www.aspeninstitute.org/blog-posts/weaving-trust-into-progress/.

Lewis, Abbey. "Good Leadership? It All Starts With Trust." *Harvard Business Publishing*, October 26, 2022. https://www.harvardbusiness.org/good-leadership-it-all-starts-with-trust/.

Vallier, Kevin. "The connection between trust and human dignity." Charles Koch Foundation, October 26, 2022. https://charleskochfoundation.org/stories/the-connection-between-trust-and-human-dignity/#:~:text=Researchers%20have%20found%20that%20social,even%20improve%20our%20psychological%20health.

Wikipedia contributors. "Muhammad Yunus." Wikipedia. https://en.wikipedia.org/wiki/Muhammad_Yunus.

Yunus, Muhammad. *Banker to the Poor: Micro-Lending and the Battle Against World Poverty* PublicAffairs, 2008.

Yunus, Muhammad. "Commencement address by Muhummad Yunus." *MIT News*, June 6, 2008. https://news.mit.edu/2008/yunus-0606.

Yunus, Muhammad. *Creating a World Without Poverty: Social Business and the Future of Capitalism* PublicAffairs, 2007.

Yunus, Muhammad. "'Each of you has the power to change the world'—Muhammad Yunus at MIT." *MIT Press*, June 6, 2008. https://studyunus.wordpress.com/2008/09/05/each-of-you-has-the-power-to-change-the-world-muhammad-yunus-at-mit/.

Zak, Paul J. "The Neuroscience of Trust." *Harvard Business Review*, January–February 2017. https://hbr.org/2017/01/the-neuroscience-of-trust.

Chapter 9 / Think Deeply: Amartya Sen

The Nobel Foundation. "Amartya Sen." October 14, 1998. https://www.nobelprize.org/prizes/economic-sciences/1998/press-release/.

Pazzanese, Christina. "Amartya Sen's nine-decade journey from colonial India to Nobel Prize and beyond." *The Harvard Gazette*, June 3, 2021. https://news.harvard.edu/gazette/story/2021/06/tracing-amartya-sens-path-from-childhood-during-the-raj-to-nobel-prize-and-beyond/.

Sen, Amartya. *Home in the World: A Memoir* Liveright Publishing Corporation, 2022.

Sevastopulo, Demetri. "Amartya Sen: The Nobel Laureate Who Has Redefined Development Economics." *Financial Times*, March 25, 2021. https://www.ft.com/content/2a4096b4-4fef-4d6e-bd14-e30cff8426e1.

Wells, Thomas. "Sen's Capability Approach." Internet Encyclopedia of Philosophy. https://iep.utm.edu/sen-cap/.

Chapter 10 / Respect Your "Opponents": Joe Biden

Biden, Joe, *Promise Me, Dad: A Year of Hope, Hardship and Purpose* (Flatiron Books, 2017).

Shapiro, Walter. "Opinion: Joe Biden—The Most Decent Man in Politics." *Roll Call*, November 15, 2017. https://rollcall.com/2017/11/15/opinion-joe-biden-the-most-decent-man-in-politics/.

Chapter 11 / Honor Your Principles: John McCain

Allen, Jonathan. "John McCain's legacy: A sense of honor that has become rare in a polarized Washington." *NBC News*, August 25, 2018. https://www.nbcnews.com/politics/politics-news/john-mccain-s-legacy-sense-honor-has-become-rare-polarized-n903911.

Biden, Joe. *Promise Me, Dad: A Year of Hope, Hardship and Purpose* Flatiron Books, 2017.

Martin, Jonathan, and Amie Parnes. "McCain: Obama not an Arab, crowd boos." *Politico*, October 10, 2008. https://www.politico.com/story/2008/10/mccain-obama-not-an-arab-crowd-boos-014479.

The McCain Institute. "Who We Are." https://www.mccaininstitute.org/about/.

McCain, John, and Mark Salter. *Character Is Destiny: Inspiring Stories Every Young Person Should Know and Every Adult Should Remember* Random House, 2005.

NBC News. "Bush accepts Sen. McCain's torture policy." *NBC News*, December 15, 2005. https://www.nbcnews.com/id/wbna10480690.

Shapiro, Walter. "Opinion: Joe Biden–The Most Decent Man in Politics." *Roll Call*, November 15, 2017. https://rollcall.com/2017/11/15/opinion-joe-biden-the-most-decent-man-in-politics/.

US Cyberspace Solarium Commission. "Introduction." https://www.solarium.gov.

The White House. "Remarks by President Biden Honoring the Legacy of Senator John McCain and the Work We Must Do Together to Strengthen Our Democracy." September 28, 2023. https://www.whitehouse.gov/briefing-room/speeches-remarks/2023/09/28/remarks-by-president-biden-honoring-the-legacy-of-senator-john-mccain-and-the-work-we-must-do-together-to-strengthen-our-democracy/.

Chapter 12 / Make Your Gift Matter: José Andrés

Clean Cooking Alliance. "Award-Winning Chef José Andrés Joins Global Alliance for Clean Cookstoves." September 13, 2011. https://cleancooking.org/news/09-13-2011-award-winning-chef-jos-andr-s-joins-global-alliance-for-clean-cookstoves/.

Clean Cooking Alliance. "Clean Cooking Alliance Releases 2023 Annual Report." March 6, 2024. https://cleancooking.org/.

Global Food Security Is a Human Right. "World Central Kitchen." Updated 2024. https://gfshr.org/world-central-kitchen/#:~:text=We%20don't%20just%20deliver, rebuild%20our%20sense%20of%20community.

Johns Hopkins Bloomberg School of Public Health. "Chef José Andrés and His World Central Kitchen to Receive

Goodermote Humanitarian Award." June 17, 2021. https://publichealth.jhu.edu/2021/chef-jose-andres-and-his-world-central-kitchen-to-receive-goodermote-humanitarian-award.

Leaders Online. "A Plate of Hope." April 2, 2023. https://leadersmag.com/issues/2023.2_Apr/Resilience/LEADERS-Jose-Andres-World-Central-Kitchen.html.

World Central Kitchen. "400 million meals served: WCK named one of TIME's Most Influential Companies." May 30, 2024. https://wck.org/news/time100#.

Chapter 13 / Serve with Humility: John Glenn

Glenn, John, with Nick Taylor. *John Glenn: A Memoir* Bantam Books, 1999.

NASA. "John H. Glenn." https://www.nasa.gov/content/profile-of-john-glenn.

NASA. "NASA Honors a Legendary Astronaut." February 21, 2006. https://web.archive.org/web/20161220085954/https:/www.nasa.gov/vision/space/features/glenn_ambassador_of_exploration.html.

O'Shea, Claire A. "NASA Names Astronauts to Next Moon Mission, First Crew Under Artemis," NASA, April 3, 2023. https://www.nasa.gov/press-release/nasa-names-astronauts-to-next-moon-mission-first-crew-under-artemis/.

Pearlman, Robert Z. "President Obama Awards John Glenn With Medal of Freedom," Space.com, May 29, 2012. https://www.space.com/15908-john-glenn-medal-freedom-award.html.

Wall, Joan Slattery. "Launching a Legacy: John Glenn's Astronaut Career," John Glenn College of Public Affairs, The Ohio State University, March 15, 2022. https://glenn.osu.edu/news/launching-legacy-john-glenns-astronaut-career.

Wikipedia. "John Glenn." Updated December 7, 2024. https://en.wikipedia.org/wiki/John_Glenn.

Wilkinson, Howard. "John Glenn Had the Stuff U.S. Heroes Are Made Of." *The Cincinnati Enquirer*, February 20, 2002.

Chapter 14 / Challenge Friends: Kevin Bacon

Apple Podcasts. "How Empathy Drives Action with Kyra Sedgwick and SixDegrees.org." November 28, 2023. https://podcasts.apple.com/us/podcast/how-empathy-drives-action-with-kyra-sedgwick/id1704724572?i=1000636753180.

Doherty, Brendan. "Icons of Impact: Kevin Bacon Backs Social Enterprise Delivering Hope After CA Wildfires." *Forbes*, January 20, 2019. https://www.forbes.com/sites/bdoherty/2019/01/20/icons-of-impact-kevin-bacon-backs-social-enterprise-delivering-hope-after-ca-wildfires/?sh=3180aaaf1741.

The Harry Walker Agency. "Kevin Bacon." https://www.harrywalker.com/speakers/kevin-bacon.

SixDegrees.Org. "Kevin Bacon's SixDegrees.org is Partnering with SOS Children's Villages USA to Support Vulnerable Children and Youth in the United States through the #HomecomingChallenge." December 26, 2018. https://www.prnewswire.com/news-releases/

kevin-bacons-sixdegreesorg-is-partnering-with-sos-childrens-villages-usa-to-support-vulnerable-children-and-youth-in-the-united-states-through-th-e-homecomingchallenge-300770755.html.

SixDegrees.Org. "Meet the Team." https://www.sixdegrees.org/team.

Virgin Pulse. "Kevin Bacon's Guide to Empathy: Unveiling the Infinite Power of Connection." *Virgin Pulse*, December 4, 2023. https://www.virginpulse.com/blog-post/kevin-bacons-guide-to-empathy-unveiling-the-infinite-power-of-connection/.

Chapter 15 / Speak Out: Malala Yousafzai

Bill & Melinda Gates Foundation. "Education." 2019. https://www.gatesfoundation.org/equal-is-greater/element/education/ (site discontinued).

Husain, Mishal. "Malala, the girl who was shot for going to school." BBC, October 7, 2013. https://www.bbc.com/news/magazine-24379018.

Jones, Brian. "16-year-old Malala Yousafzai Leaves Jon Stewart Speechless With Comment About Pacifism." *Business Insider*, October 9, 2013. https://www.businessinsider.com/malala-yousafzai-left-jon-stewart-speechless-2013-10 fbclid=IwAR10c567YiYVkeenbq7qYNI5eM5mRrLnSN_CDoQyPDLSvn_RSNfsW51RN8E.

Mukhtar, Ahmad. "The Taliban Banned Afghan Girls from School 1,000 Days Ago, but Some Brave Young Women Refuse to Accept It." *CBS News*, June 7, 2024. https://www.cbsnews.com/news/taliban-girls-school-ban-afghanistan-1000-days-underground-schools/.

UNICEF. "10 reasons to educate girls." September 2, 2022. https://www.unicefusa.org/stories/10-reasons-educate-girls#:~:text=Girls%20who%20complete%20a%20secondary,invest%20more%20in%20their%20communities.

UNICEF. "Girls' Education." https://www.unicef.org/education/girls-education.

Chapter 16 / Rethink What You Know: Sal Khan

Cheise, Adam. "82 Khan Academy Statistics for 2024 (Data & Facts)." ProsperityForAll, September 2, 2024. https://www.prosperityforamerica.org/khan-academy-statistics/.

FSG. *Learning Gets Personal: How Idaho Students and Teachers Are Embracing Personalized Learning through Khan Academy*. Spring 2015. https://www.fsg.org/wp-content/uploads/2021/08/Learning-Gets-Personal_How-Idaho-Students-and-Teachers-Are-Embracing-Personalized-Learning-through-Khan-Academy.pdf.

Ghosh, Neil. "Support Children and Youth to Prevent the Next Pandemic." *Philanthropy News Digest*, May 28, 2020. https://philanthropynewsdigest.org/features/commentary-and-opinion/support-children-and-youth-to-prevent-the-next-pandemic.

Global Philanthropy Forum. *2013 Global Philanthropy Forum Conference Transcript*. San Francisco, 2013. https://philanthropyforum.secure.nonprofitsoapbox.com/storage/documents/2013-gpf-conference-transcript.pdf.

Khan, Salman. *The One World School House: Education Reimagined* Twelve, 2012.

Khan Academy. https://www.khanacademy.org/stories.

Kuhfeld, Megan, et al. "The pandemic has had devastating impacts on learning. What will it take to help students catch up?" The Brookings Institute, March 3, 2022. https://www.brookings.edu/blog/brown-center-chalkboard/2022/03/03/the-pandemic-has-had-devastating-impacts-on-learning-what-will-it-take-to-help-students-catch-up/.

Laugharn, Peter. "Philanthropy for global education comes of age." *Alliance*, April 29, 2013. https://www.alliancemagazine.org/blog/philanthropy-for-global-education-comes-of-age/.

The Lavin Agency. "Global Philanthropy Forum: Sal Khan's 'game changing' education speech." April 22, 2013. https://thelavinagency.com/global-philanthropy-forum-sal-khans-game-changing-education-speech/ (site discontinued).

Randles, Julie Phillips. "Sal Khan Describes the Passion Behind Khan Academy." ISTE Blog, June 25, 2014. https://iste.org/blog/sal-khan-describes-the-passion-behind-khan-academy.

Chapter 17 / Use Your Privilege: Angelina Jolie

Croneberger, Lynn. "Reflections on Angelina Jolie's First They Killed My Father." SOS Children's Villages USA, October 12, 2017. https://www.sos-usa.org/news/topics/ptsd-in-children/reflections-on-angelina-jolie's-first-they-killed.

Devaney, Susan. "The Urgent Social Causes Angelina Jolie Truly Cares About." *British Vogue*, February 1, 2021. https://www.vogue.co.uk/arts-and-lifestyle/article/angelina-jolie-charity-work

Morton, Andrew. *Angelina: An Unauthorized Biography* (St. Martin's Press, 2010).

SOS Children's Villages. "Angelina Jolie visits SOS Children's Village in Haiti." February 9, 2010. https://www.sos-childrensvillages.org/news/angelina-jolie-visits-sos-childrens-village-in-hai#:~:text=UNHCR%20Goodwill%20Ambassador%20Angelina%20Jolie%20visited%20the%20SOS%20Children's%20Village,devastating%20earthquake%20that%20hit%20Haiti.

People Magazine staff. "Caught Caring: The Jolie-Pitts, Asprey and Education Partnership for Children of Conflict." *People*, November 26, 2009. https://people.com/parents/caught-caring-the-jolie-pitts-asprey-and-education-partnership-for-children-of-conflict/.

Chapter 18 / Focus on Your Goal: Kareem Abdul-Jabbar

Abdul-Jabbar, Kareem, and Alan Steinberg. *Black Profiles in Courage: A Legacy of African-American Achievement* William Morrow, 1996.

Beard, Alison. "Life's Work: An Interview with Kareem Abdul-Jabbar." *Harvard Business Review*, January-February 2012. https://hbr.org/2012/01/kareem-abdul-jabbar.

Official Website of Kareem Abdul-Jabbar. "The writings of Kareem Abdul-Jabbar." https://kareemabduljabbar.com/articles/.

Skyhook Foundation. "Camp Skyhook." https://skyhookfoundation.org.

Skyhook Foundation. "The Skyhook Foundation." https://skyhookfoundation.org.

Chapter 19 / Invite Transformation: Shimon Peres

Adaret, Ofer. "Shimon Peres, 1923–2016: From Nuclear Pioneer to Champion of Peace." *Haaretz*, September 28, 2016. https://www.haaretz.com/israel-news/2016-09-28/ty-article-magazine/shimon-peres-from-nuclear-pioneer-to-champion-of-peace/0000017f-f6d3-d460-afff-fff7c73f0000.

American Academy of Achievement. "Shimon Peres." Updated March 1, 2022. https://achievement.org/achiever/shimon-peres/.

The Associated Press. "Israel's 'biggest dreamer': Bill Clinton praises Shimon at former president's funeral." *Salon*, September 30, 2016. https://www.salon.com/2016/09/30/the-latest-clinton-peres-was-israels-biggest-dreamer/.

Bahar, Dany. "How Shimon Peres saved the Israeli economy." Brookings Institute, September 30, 2016. https://www.brookings.edu/blog/markaz/2016/09/30/how-shimon-peres-saved-the-israeli-economy/.

Beilin, Yossi. "The transformation of Shimon Peres." *Foreign Policy*, July 24, 2014. https://foreignpolicy.com/2014/07/24/the-transformation-of-shimon-peres/.

Gradstein, Linda. "A visit to the Shimon Peres Center: You might learn something!" *Jerusalem Post*, August 10, 2022. https://www.jpost.com/jerusalem-report/article-714387.

Koltai, Steven R. "Shimon Peres: Godfather of Israeli entrepreneurship." Brookings Institute, October 14, 2016.

https://www.brookings.edu/blog/techtank/2016/10/14/shimon-peres-godfather-of-israeli-entrepreneurship/.
The Peres Center for Peace and Innovation. "About Us." https://www.peres-center.org/en/the-organization/about-us/.
The Peres Center for Peace and Innovation. "Shimon Peres: Leader, Poet, Dreamer." https://www.peres-center.org/en/shimon-peres/about/.
Peres, Shimon. "Shimon Peres reflects on working toward peace." 2014. The Markkula Center for Applied Ethics. Santa Clara University. https://www.scu.edu/mcae/architects-of-peace/Peres/essay.html (site discontinued).
Schwartz, Yardena. "Shimon Peres: 'Israel Will Be Stronger When She Achieves Peace'." *Time*, February 15, 2016. https://time.com/4217865/israel-exclusive-interview-shimon-peres/.
World Jewish Congress. "India." https://www.worldjewishcongress.org/en/about/communities/IN.

Chapter 20 / Pave Your Own Path: Mohamed Ousri

Gerzon, Mark. *American Citizen, Global Citizen: How Expanding Our Identities Makes Us Safer, Stronger, Wiser—and Builds a Better World* Spirit Scope Publishing, 2010.
Philanthropy Network Greater Philadelphia. "Giving USA: Total U.S. Charitable Giving Remained Strong in 2021, Reaching $484.85 Billion." June 21, 2022, https://philanthropynetwork.org/news/giving-usa-total-us-charitable-giving-remained-strong-2021-reaching-48485-billion.

Chapter 21 / Improve Your Profession: Tessie San Martin

Beasley, Stephanie. "Why are foundations and nonprofits losing public trust?" *Devex*, June 17, 2022. https://www.devex.com/news/why-are-foundations-and-nonprofits-losing-public-trust-103475.

FHI360. "Tessie San Martin, PhD, MPA, Chief Executive Officer." https://www.fhi360.org/experts/tessie-san-martin-phd-mpa.

Ghosh, Neil. "Wanted: Integrators." *Devex*, October 6, 2014. https://www.devex.com/news/wanted-integrators-84438.

Giridharadas, Anand. *Winners Take All: The Elite Charade of Changing the World* Knopf, 2018.

Gunn, Christopher. *Third-Sector Development: Making Up for the Market* Cornell University Press, 2003.

John, Lysa and Mandeep Tiwana. "NGOs and the Future of Trust." Edelman Trust Institute, January, 2022. https://www.edelman.com/edelman-trust-institute/rebuilding-trust/lysa-john-mandeep-tiwana#:~:text=Despite%20a%20percentage%20point%20decline,in%20dealing%20with%20the%20crisis.

Lilly Family School of Philanthropy. "2023 Global Philanthropy Tracker finds $70 billion in cross-border philanthropic giving at the height of COVID-19 global health crisis." April 20, 2023. https://philanthropy.indianapolis.iu.edu/news-events/news/_news/2023/2023-global-philanthropy-tracker-finds-70-billion-in-cross-border-philanthropic-giving-at-the-height-of-covid-19-global-health-crisis.html.

Mitchell, George E., et al. *Between Power and Irrelevance: The Future of Transnational NGOs* Oxford University Press, 2020).

Nonprofit Times. "NPOs Added $1.4 Trillion To U.S. Economy." *The NonProfit Times*, July 5, 2022. https://thenonprofittimes.com/report/npos-added-1-4-trillion-to-u-s-economy/.

Chapter 22 / Build Bridges: Bill Clinton

ABC News. "Bill O'Reilly Calls Himself 'T-Warrior.'" September 19, 2006. https://abcnews.go.com/2020/story?id=2465303&page=1.

Charlie Rose. "Bill Clinton." September 12, 2016. https://charlierose.com/videos/29151.

Clinton Foundation. "NY1 –: Bill Clinton Reflects on 20 Years in Harlem." August 2, 2021. https://www.clintonfoundation.org/press-and-news/general/ny1-bill-clinton-reflects-on-20-years-in-harlem/.

Clinton Foundation. "President Bill Clinton." https://www.clintonfoundation.org/about-the-clinton-foundation/leadership#president-bill-clinton/.

The White House. "The Clinton Presidency: Protecting Our Environment and Public Health." https://clintonwhitehouse5.archives.gov/WH/Accomplishments/eightyears-08.html#:~:text=President%20Clinton%20has%20made%20the%20Federal%20government,its%20annual%20energy%20bill%20by%20$800%20million.

Chapter 23 / Step Up: Rosa Parks

Chugh, Dolly. "The Truth About Rosa Parks And Why It Matters To Your Diversity Initiative." *Forbes*, February 4, 2019. https://www.forbes.com/sites/dollychugh/2019/02/04/the-truth-about-rosa-parks-and-why-it-matters-to-your-diversity-initiative/.

Columbia Celebrates Black History and Culture. "Barack H. Obama." https://blackhistory.news.columbia.edu/people/barack-h-obama.

Gray, Madison. "Rosa Parks' Archived Writing Reveals Attempted Rape." *Time*, July 29, 2011. https://newsfeed.time.com/2011/07/29/rosa-parks-archived-writing-reveals-attempted-rape/.

Guardian staff. "Civil rights champion Rosa Parks dies," *The Guardian*, October 25, 2005. https://www.theguardian.com/world/2005/oct/25/usa.

History.com editors. "Rosa Parks." History, updated February 20, 2024. https://www.history.com/topics/black-history/rosa-parks#:~:text=Rosa%20Parks%20(1913%E2%80%942005),organize%20the%20Montgomery%20Bus%20Boycott.

Legacy staff. "Inspired by Rosa Parks." Legacy.com, January 27, 2017. https://www.legacy.com/news/culture-and-history/inspired-by-rosa-parks/

Nowlin, Norton R. "Tolerance and liberty." *Seattle Times*, January 11, 2006. https://www.seattletimes.com/opinion/tolerance-and-liberty/.

Parks, Rosa, and James Haskins. *Rosa Parks: My Story* Dial Books, 1992.

Rudolph, Lloyd I., and Susanne Hoeber Rudolph. Letter to the editor, *New York Times Book Review*, April 25, 2013. https://www.nytimes.com/2013/04/28/books/review/parks-and-gandhi.html.

Chapter 24 / Stay True to Your Purpose: Jimmy Carter

Baker, Peter. "A Four-Decade Secret: One Man's Story of Sabotaging Carter's Re-election." *New York Times*, March 18, 2023. https://www.nytimes.com/2023/03/18/us/politics/jimmy-carter-october-surprise-iran-hostages.html.

Bennett, Geoff, Cybele Mayes-Osterman, Ali Schmitz, and Ian Couzens. "New claim about Iran hostage crisis may change narrative of Carter presidency." PBS, March 20, 2023. https://www.pbs.org/newshour/show/new-claim-about-iran-hostage-crisis-sabotage-may-change-narrative-of-carter-presidency.

The Carter Center. "Access to Justice in Liberia." https://www.cartercenter.org/peace/ati/access-to-justice/index.html.

The Carter Center. *Celebrating 30: Annual Report 2010-2011* The Carter Center, 2011. https://www.cartercenter.org/resources/pdfs/news/annual_reports/annual-report-11.pdf.

The Carter Center. "Inform Women, Transform Lives." https://www.cartercenter.org/peace/info4women/index.html.

The Carter Center. "Our Mission," https://www.cartercenter.org/about/index.html.

The Carter Center. "U.N. Peacebuilding Fund Highlight." August 2022. https://www.cartercenter.org/donate/

corporate-government-foundation-partners/archives/united-nations-peacebuilding-fund.html.

The Carter Center. "Waging Peace Through Elections." updated August 5, 2024. https://www.cartercenter.org/peace/democracy/observed.html.

Carter, Jimmy. "Crisis of Confidence Speech." American Rhetoric, updated August 28, 2024. https://www.americanrhetoric.com/speeches/jimmycartercrisisofconfidence.htm.

Hochman, Steven H. "Biography of the 39th President of the United States," Jimmy Carter Presidential Library, July 25, 2018. https://www.jimmycarterlibrary.gov/about_us/biography_of_jimmy_carter.

Nannestad, Chloë. "10 surprising facts you didn't know about Jimmy Carter," *Reader's Digest*, updated September 26, 2024. https://www.rd.com/list/jimmy-carter-presidency/.

Ozug, Matt, and Courtney Dorning. "Jimmy Carter's Relationship with the Allman Brothers Band Helped Him Become President." NPR, March 29, 2023. https://www.npr.org/2023/03/29/1166891522/jimmy-carters-relationship-with-the-allman-brothers-band-helped-him-become-presi.

Paul, Alan. "How the Allman Brothers Band Helped Make Jimmy Carter President," *Wall Street Journal*, February 23, 2023. https://www.wsj.com/articles/how-the-allman-brothers-band-helped-make-jimmy-carter-president-e7a576c6.

Strong, Robert A. "Jimmy Carter: Impact and Legacy," The Miller Center, University of Virginia. https://millercenter.org/president/carter/impact-and-legacy.

Strong, Robert A. "Jimmy Carter: Life After the Presidency," The Miller Center, University of Virginia. https://millercenter.org/president/carter/life-after-the-presidency.

Strong, Robert A. "Jimmy Carter: Overview," The Miller Center, University of Virginia. https://millercenter.org/president/carter.

Wallenfeldt, Jeff. "5 Things You Don't Know About Jimmy Carter," Britannica. https://www.britannica.com/story/5-things-you-dont-know-about-jimmy-carter.

Washington Post staff. "Jimmy Carter, the president who tried to save the planet." *Washington Post*, February 21, 2023. https://www.washingtonpost.com/climate-environment/2023/02/21/jimmy-carter-environment-energy-alaska/.

Wikipedia contributors. "Presidency of Jimmy Carter," Wikipedia. https://en.wikipedia.org/wiki/Presidency_of_Jimmy_Carter#:~:text=Jimmy%20Carter's%20tenure%20as,Ford%20in%20the%201976%20election.

Chapter 25 / Make Hard Choices: Hillary Clinton

AFP contributors. "Hillary Clinton's childhood, and how it shaped her politics." WION, November 2, 2016. https://www.wionews.com/world/hillary-clintons-childhood-and-how-it-shaped-her-politics-8189.

Al Jazeera staff. "Clinton Resigns as US Secretary of State." *Al Jazeera*, February 2, 2013. https://www.aljazeera.com/news/2013/2/2/clinton-resigns-as-us-secretary-of-state.

BrainyQuote. "Hillary Clinton Quotes." https://www.brainyquote.com/authors/hillary-clinton-quotes.

Chozick, Amy. "Hillary Clinton Embraces Her Mother's Emotional Tale." *New York Times*, June 12, 2015. https://www.nytimes.com/2015/06/13/us/politics/story-of-hillary-clintons-mother-forms-emotional-core-of-campaign.html.

Clinton, Hillary Rodham. *Hard Choices* Simon & Schuster, 2014.

Clinton, Hillary Rodham. *It Takes a Village* Simon & Schuster, 2006. xii–xiii.

Clinton, Hillary Rodham. *Living History* Simon & Schuster, 2003.

Global Citizen. "Who We Are." https://www.globalcitizen.org/en/about/who-we-are/.

Heer, Jeet. "Hillary Clinton's Legacy Is Huge and Lasting." *The New Republic*, September 14, 2017. https://newrepublic.com/article/144796/hillary-clintons-legacy-huge-lasting.

Politico Magazine. "What Is Hillary's Greatest Accomplishment?" *Politico Magazine*, September 17, 2015. https://www.politico.com/magazine/story/2015/09/carly-fiorina-debate-hillary-clintons-greatest-accomplishment-213157/.

Roberts, Dan. "Clintons continue to tout legacy where others see era of mistakes and scandals." *The Guardian*, May 21, 2016. https://www.theguardian.com/us-news/2016/may/21/hillary-clinton-bill-90s-nostalgia-reform-scandal.

Time staff. "The Ol' Switcheroo: Hillary Clinton, 1960s." *Time*, 2019. https://content.time.com/time/specials/packages/article/0,28804,1894529_1894528_1894517,00.html.

U.S. Department of State. "Town Hall with Tunisian Youth." February 25, 2012. https://2009-2017.state.gov/secretary/20092013clinton/rm/2012/02/184656.htm.

Wikipedia contributors. "Hillary Clinton," Wikipedia. https://en.wikipedia.org/wiki/Hillary_Clinton.

Chapter 26 / Engage in Public Service: Ross Perot

Biography.com editors. "Ross Perot." Biography.com, May 19, 2021. https://www.biography.com/political-figures/ross-perot.

Chicago Tribune staff. "Perot, the Unpolitician." *Chicago Tribune*, May 24, 1992. https://www.chicagotribune.com/1992/05/24/perot-the-unpolitician/.

CNN Editorial Research. "Ross Perot Fast Facts." CNN, April 12, 2020. https://www.cnn.com/2013/06/10/us/ross-perot-fast-facts/index.html.

Follett, Ken. *On Wings of Eagles: The Inspiring True Story of One Man's Patriotic Spirit—and His Heroic Mission to Save His Countrymen* William Morrow & Co., 1983.

Helman, Christopher. "The Museum of Ross Perot." *Forbes*, September 4, 2013. https://www.forbes.com/sites/christopherhelman/2013/09/04/the-museum-of-ross-perot/?sh=604deac5307c.

Jackson, Harold. "Ross Perot obituary." *The Guardian*, July 9, 2019. https://www.theguardian.com/us-news/2019/jul/09/ross-perot-obituary.

The Life and Legacy of Ross Perot. "Early Life." https://www.rossperot.com/life-story/early-life.

The Life and Legacy of Ross Perot. "Entrepreneur Extraordinaire." https://www.rossperot.com/life-story/entrepreneur-extraordinaire.

Perot, Ross. *Ross Perot: My Life & the Principles for Success* Tapestry Press, 2002.

Chapter 27 / Protect Democracy: John Kufuor

Columbia University World Leaders Forum. "John Agyekum Kufuor." Columbia University, September, 2003. https://worldleaders.columbia.edu/directory/john-agyekum-kufuor.

The Editors of Encyclopaedia Britannica. "John Kufuor." Britannica. https://www.britannica.com/biography/John-Kufuor.

Indian National Congress. "John Kufuor's speech on Jawaharlal Nehru Commemorative International Conference 2014." November 17, 2014. https://www.youtube.com/watch?v=dw-rl02qqVk.

Ray, Subhash C. "The Political Economy of Decline of Industry in West Bengal: Experiences of a Marxist State Within a Mixed Economy." University of Connecticut Department of Economics Working Paper Series, May 2011, https://media.economics.uconn.edu/working/2011-10.pdf.

Taylor, Mildred Europa. "10 ex-African presidents and their lives after leaving office." Face2Face Africa, January 24, 2018. https://face2faceafrica.com/article/10-ex-african-presidents-lives-leaving-office/9.

TV3 Ghana. "Exclusive interview with former President John Agyekum Kufuor." July 15, 2022. https://www.youtube.com/watch?v=a4vYp8pJO7o.

University of Gothenburg Department of Political Science. "Dictatorships advancing globally." University of Gothenburg, March 3, 2022. https://www.gu.se/en/news/dictatorships-advancing-globally.

Wikipedia contributors. "John Kufuor." Wikipedia. https://en.wikipedia.org/wiki/John_Kufuor.

World Food Prize Foundation. "2011: Kufuor and Lula." https://www.worldfoodprize.org/en/laureates/20102019_laureates/2011_kufuor_and_lula/#:~:text=Continuing%20Ghana's%20tradition%20of%20stability,to%209%20percent%20in%202004.

Chapter 28 / Choose Pragmatism: Somnath Chatterjee

Blanusa, Mary, Stacey Chen, and Nathan Huttner. "Bridging the Divide Between Idealism and Pragmatism." *Stanford Social Innovation Review*, May 25, 2018. https://ssir.org/articles/entry/bridging_the_divide_between_idealism_and_pragmatism.

Cagle, Kurt. "Idealism, Pragmatism, and the Rise of Magical Thinking." *Medium*, July 15, 2016. https://medium.com/thoughts-from-cascadia/idealism-pragmatism-and-the-rise-of-magical-thinking-b430824a56f1.

Chatterjee, Somnath. *Keeping the Faith: Memoirs of a Parliamentarian* HarperCollins India, 2010.

India TV News staff. "Veteran Political Leader Somnath Chatterjee Passes Away at 89. All You Need to Know

About Him." *India TV News*, August 13, 2018. https://www.indiatvnews.com/news/india-somnath-chatterjee-death-former-lok-sabha-speaker-profile-all-you-need-to-know-457880.

News Desk. "Somnath Chatterjee: The CPI(M) Leader Who Held Speaker's Position Above Party Affiliation." India.com, August 13, 2018. https://www.india.com/news/india/somnath-chatterjee-the-cpim-leader-who-held-speakers-position-above-party-affiliation-3219973/.

Outlook Web Bureau. "Somnath Chatterjee—Country's First Communist To Don The Role Of A Speaker," *Outlook India*, August 13, 2018. https://www.outlookindia.com/website/story/somnath-chatterjee-a-distinguished-parliamentarian-who-wore-many-hats/314940.

Chapter 29 / My Son, Ryan Sohan Ghosh

Ghosh, Neil. "What Is The Secret Of America's Success?—The Good Americans." HuffPost, July 5, 2016, updated July 6, 2017. https://www.huffpost.com/entry/what-is-the-secret-of-ame_b_10812956.

ABOUT THE AUTHOR

Photo Credit: Tim Coburn Photography

Neil Ghosh is the president of MGR Professional Services, senior advisor to The Ousri Family Foundation, and former CEO of SOS Children's Villages USA and SNV Netherlands Development Organisation USA. He is passionate about advocating for vulnerable children and climate action. To learn more about Ghosh, visit www.neilghosh.org.